CONTENTS

Tawnyard Lough

ACKNOWLEDGMENTS

My gratitude is due to many for their assistance during the putting together of this book, but I would like particularly to thank Jonathan Williams, who continues to give good advice and good-humoured encouragement, and Stan Austen, Des McConville and Edmund Ashe, who were willing and entertaining walking companions. My son David and Patricia Evans deserve my thanks for providing logistical support, as does my daughter Fiona for looking after the graphics, while my wife, Teresa, was a great walking companion and gave invaluable assistance and support in every aspect of the project. Thank you all!

AUTHOR'S NOTE

This guide deals only with signposted routes that are set up with the aid of, and approved and monitored by, Cospóir (The National Sports Council). The author and publishers have taken every care to ensure that the information contained in this book is accurate at the time of writing. In the nature of the subject, however, changes can and do occur in the countryside, even on way-marked trails. The author and publishers shall have no liability in respect to any loss or damage, however caused, arising out of the use of this guide. This includes—but is not limited to—loss or damage resulting from missing signs, future changes in routes, accidents and lost or injured persons.

INTRODUCTION

The first official Way-marked trail in the Republic of Ireland, the Wicklow Way, was planned by the late J. B. Malone and inaugurated in 1982. Since then nearly 2,000 kilometres of signposted Ways have been established throughout the country, and there is a long-term plan to link all the Ways, providing a complete circuit of Ireland. This guide describes what I consider to be the best of these routes.

The Ways are not just for experienced trekkers. On the contrary, they have been planned so that in the right conditions there is no reason why anyone of any ability should not be capable of walking any of the routes, at their own pace. While there are a few rugged stretches over open mountain passes, the routes in the main follow old disused roads, grassy boreens, and forest tracks. None of the routes involves really significant climbs; the highest point of all the Ways is near Mount Brandon on the Dingle Way, at 640 m (2,080 feet).

While experienced walkers may want to walk the routes from beginning to end, there is no reason why people with less experience should not choose to walk only the sections of the routes that suit their ability. Similarly, while hardier trekkers may carry tents, sleeping-bags and their breakfast on their backs, this guide acknowledges that many walkers are 'softies'—like myself—and enjoy the comforts of a bath or shower, a good meal and a comfortable bed at the end of the day. As far as possible, each of the Ways has been broken down into manageable stages that end at or near places where overnight accommodation and evening meals are available.

Way-marks

All the routes covered in this guide are marked at frequent intervals with special signposts, the most common of which is a sturdy post bearing a yellow arrow, sometimes accompanied by the motif of a walking figure. In some areas the arrows are painted on convenient rocks or stone walls. Because the routes are way-marked, this guide does not mention every turn or change of direction on a route. Walkers should be aware, however, that in some places the signs may be hidden by summer foliage or forest machinery, or simply missing, so on occasions a little direction-finding and map-reading may be required to reach the intended destination.

Overnight accommodation

If you are walking without having transport available at the end of the day, or during the high season, it is advisable to book your overnight accommodation in advance. Guesthouses mentioned in this guide welcome tired walkers, are reasonably priced and, with a few exceptions,

1

are registered and approved by Bord Fáilte. Only in areas where there is a shortage of accommodation have I mentioned places that may be a little more expensive or not in Bord Fáilte's listings. If all else fails, a telephone call to the nearest pub or post office will often help you to find local accommodation.

Public transport
Where available along the routes, public transport is mentioned, the bus services being referred to by their 'table number', *which is not always an actual bus number*. You are recommended to check with local bus offices for up-to-date times.

Maps and publications
Although the routes are way-marked, it is always advisable to carry a good map that covers the route. **The maps included here are intended only as an outline guide**, and it is important to familiarise yourself thoroughly with the route, its surroundings and all its features. Guides, maps and other publications available at time of writing that specifically deal with the routes concerned are listed in the introduction to each Way.

Walk planning
Carrying your home in a knapsack for the duration of a walking holiday can have its drawbacks, but it makes walking long distances relatively uncomplicated. For those who want to carry as little as possible and want to have a choice of where they eat and spend the night, the only real answer is to have transport or accommodation available at the finishing point for each day. In some areas it is possible, with careful planning, to use public transport to get to starting-points or from finishing points.

Another method is to walk with a small group, having two cars available; while this involves some driving at the beginning and end of each day, it leaves the walkers completely free to choose where they spend the night. For those who do not want to walk the full distance between stages, there are many opportunities on most Ways to reduce overall distances by driving the less interesting road sections.

In some areas, it is possible to arrange pick-ups and drop-offs with proprietors of bed-and-breakfast establishments.

Distances, climbs and times
Distances referred to in this guide are approximate, and depend on your not losing your way too much and having to backtrack. Remember, long zigzags up a steep mountain may make climbing easier, but they may increase the distance walked by a substantial amount.

The figure given for 'aggregate climb' over a stage is the total altitude climbed during the stage; where you have to cross, say, three ridges, the figure given will be the height of the ascent of the three ridges added together.

The time it takes to cover a particular route can depend on many more factors than the distance. Wet, boggy terrain, slow ascents and descents and frequent stops to take refreshments and enjoy the view (not to mention getting lost) can have a significant bearing on the time taken. The 'walking time' figures given for each route or stage are based on covering 4 km (2.5 miles) an hour and an ascent rate of 400 m (1,312 feet) per hour, with some adjustments for terrain, and should be used as a rough guide only. Prolonged or frequent stops along the route are not allowed for in these time estimates.

When to walk

Walking is one of the few activities that can be enjoyed in Ireland all year round. While continual rain or continual sweltering heat can be uncomfortable, these conditions rarely last very long here. Winter walking often has the advantage of clear, frosty, refreshing air, and most landscapes take on a special beauty after a light fall of snow. The worst that Ireland's winter has to offer can usually be weathered by wearing suitable gear and by taking it for granted that there are few places off the tarred road that are not at least partly wet and boggy.

In summertime there is great life in the countryside, with an abundance of young animals and birds swelling the wildlife population, and the terrain is usually drier. Be warned, however, that forests and foothills seem to produce prodigious numbers of flies in July and August, which descend in swarms on perspiring walkers! The special offerings of delicate new growth in spring and the rich russet shades of autumn make these seasons also special. My own favourite times for walking are spring and early summer, when growth has not yet hidden birds from sight, and wildflowers are at their fragrant best.

Dos and don'ts

It is wise not to trust maps and guides implicitly. I have found that even the best of maps can be incorrect, or out of date, or have omissions, and if this kind of problem occurs at a critical point, you can be led a long way astray. Similarly, individual interpretations of a written direction in a guide can vary, and it is not feasible to describe in detail every section of a route. On some Ways, detours from the originally planned route have been introduced in recent years, to prevent erosion, or due to problems with Rights of Way. I have included in this guide all the detours to date that I am aware of, but changes of this type will continue, sometimes rendering even the most accurate directions completely misleading. An entire forest can disappear in a matter of months when it is harvested, leaving a radically changed landscape, and newly planted forestry in the

Irish climate can assert itself on the landscape within very few years.

Do not trust the way-markers implicitly either, or depend on them always to point the way. On a few occasions while walking these routes I came upon posts that had been altered by some local wit, and on many occasions came to junctions where the arrow sign had been spirited away, or was deeply hidden in long grass, leaving the choice of direction to guesswork. **It is wise, therefore, to study the route well enough beforehand to have a good idea of where you are going, and to stay vigilant for indications that confirm you are on the right track, or otherwise.** Remember, walking the Ways is not simply about commuting from one place to another: there are plenty of well-signposted tarred roads for that purpose. Part of the enjoyment of cross-country walking is 'finding your way' across unfamiliar territory, the element of exploration, and the feeling of pioneering achievement when you succeed.

It is not necessary to equip and clothe yourself expensively to walk Ireland's Ways. For comfort and safety, however, the following rules should be followed if any hill or mountain walking is being attempted.

1. Wear sturdy and comfortable shoes or boots that give some ankle support and will keep your feet dry for at least most of the day.
2. Carry a light rucksack that contains waterproofs and headgear in case of rain, an additional warm pullover in case of cold, and a tasty energy-giving snack and a drink in case of the need of a morale boost!
3. Learn how to read maps and to use a compass, and always carry a compass and the appropriate map with you.
4. Always let someone know where you are going and when you should be expected back.
5. Never walk alone in isolated areas.
6. Always show respect for the countryside and for the people who live and work in it.

Useful phone numbers and addresses

Bus Éireann, Information Bureau, Travel Centre, Store Street, Dublin 1; telephone 01 8366111.

Iarnrod Éireann (rail passenger information) Connolly Station, Dublin 1; telephone 01 8366222

Bord Fáilte Éireann (Irish Tourist Board), Baggot Street Bridge, Dublin 2; telephone 01 6765871, Fax 01 6764764

An Óige (Irish Youth Hostel Association), 61 Mountjoy Street, Dublin 1; telephone 01 8304555, Fax 01 8305808

Independent Holiday Hostels, 21 Store Street, Dublin 1; telephone 01 8364710, Fax 01 8364710

Cospóir (The National Sports Council), Hawkins House, Hawkins Street, Dublin 2; telephone 01 8734700, Fax 01 6715270

1
THE ARAN WAYS

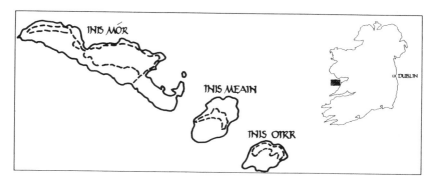

The Aran Islands are three high points of an otherwise submerged reef 16 km (10 miles) off the coast of Co. Clare, a continuation of the great limestone expanse of the Burren. Like the Burren, the islands have a landscape of bleak rock interspersed with wildflower-rich pastures, subdivided by thousands of kilometres of dry-stone walls. Much of the cultivated land was created through decades of back-breaking work, clearing loose stones, collecting sand and seaweed on the shore and spreading it over the bare bedrock.

Scattered across the islands are the remains of many prehistoric and Early Christian buildings, including astonishing cyclopean stone forts, of which Dún Aonghasa, perched on an 82 m (270 foot) clifftop, is probably the finest example in western Europe.

As you walk the islands you get a glimpse of the past: the fields, villages and people are still strongly redolent of old rural Ireland. You will hear the Irish language being spoken by young and old.

There are 437 varieties of wildflower on the Aran Islands, so for the enthusiast there is plenty to see and search for. Seals are common in all the coves and on the rocks, and dolphins, porpoises and the occasional basking-shark can be sighted offshore in summertime. The bird life is particularly rich, from waders of all kinds to choughs and auks; and if you are fortunate enough to be there in May, hardly an hour goes by in which you will not hear and see a cuckoo.

There are three Aran Ways: the Inis Mór Way, a circular walk of 33.75 km (21 miles); the Inis Meáin Way, a circular walk of 8 km (5 miles), and the Inis Oírr Way, a circular walk of 10.5 km (6.5 miles).

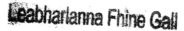

The Aran Ways

How to get there

Regular ferries run from Galway, Rossaveal (about 42 km—26 miles west of Galway), and Doolin (about 40 km from Ennis, Co. Clare).

A regular service to all three islands, using a comfortable nine-seater aircraft, is run by Aer Árann flying from Inverin, Co. Galway; this is a particularly enjoyable way to travel to all three islands.

Maps and guides

The route is covered by the Ordnance Survey Aran Islands 1:25,000 map, and a full-colour leaflet with maps in a handy plastic folder, called *Siúlóid Árann: a Guided Walking Tour of the Aran Islands*, can be purchased from bookshops, souvenir shops, and tourist offices.

The best map of the islands, however, is Tim Robinson's 1:29,000 (2.2 inch to 1 mile) map and guide, *The Aran Islands*, available from good bookshops, which describes the islands in considerable detail. In addition, I strongly recommend his marvellous book *Stones of Aran* for those who want to get a real feel for the place.

Enquiries

Comhar Chumann, Inis Meain, Co. Galway; telephone 099 73010

Wreck of the Plassy, *Inis Oírr*

THE INIS MÓR WAY

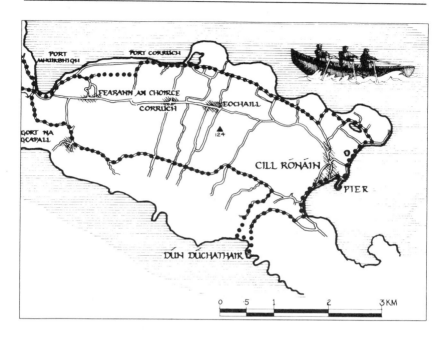

DISTANCE: 33.75 KM (21 MILES). WALKING TIME: 8.5 HOURS.

Inis Mór (more correctly called Árainn) is the biggest of the three Aran Islands, at nearly 13 km (8 miles) long, and has about 750 inhabitants. The Inis Mór Way introduces the walker to most of the main features of the island, from its rich flora and fauna to its fascinating prehistoric forts, and from its beaches and cliffs to its many relics of Early Christian occupation. The Way itself is 34 km (21 miles) long, with a number of short spurs to reach particular sites of interest. The village of Eoghanacht, where accommodation is available, marks roughly the half-way point.

The Way is mainly over quiet tarred roads and grassy boreens; and as the highest point of the island is only 139 m (456 feet) above sea level, there are no steep climbs involved. It is possible to cover the entire Way comfortably on a mountain bike, which can be hired at Cill Rónáin pier.

Bed-and-breakfast accommodation is available in most of the villages on the island, and there are independent hostels that provide very good value. While there is no bus service on the island, a number of minibuses take tourists to the sights, and there should be no difficulty arranging a pick-up with one of these if necessary. I found the islanders in general were very helpful and anxious to please.

The Inis Mór Way begins at Cill Rónáin pier and heads north along the road that backs the shingly Trá na bhFrancach (Beach of the French), so called from the drowned sailors who were washed ashore here when a French vessel sank off the island in the nineteenth century. A little further on, the beach becomes sandy, and the name changes to Trá an Charra (the Beach of the Ford), harking back to the time when there was a long sea inlet here. In the nineteenth century this inlet was filled by hand with mud, sand stones and seaweed to create the rich fields that you see behind the beach today. As the pressure for land receded in recent decades, however, the sluices that kept the sea out became choked up, and a lake established itself.

The Way follows the narrow boreen round Loch an Charra, out of which appear inundated field walls. The little lake is rich with waders and wildfowl most of the year; when I passed there shelducks, lapwings, turn-stones, whimbrel and sandpipers were active around the shore, and a solitary heron stood still at the water's edge, watching all.

The Way crosses the sandy beach of Trá na mBuailte before rising to join a tarred road. Although it is not much above sea level, there is a wide view from this point, from the western isles of Galway right round to Inis Meáin, seen just beyond Oileáin na Tuí or Straw Island with its lighthouse.

A little further along, in to the left, is the ruin of a church dedicated to St Ciarán who, after a period under the tutelage of St Enda, returned to the mainland to preach and eventually to found the great monastery at Clonmacnoise on the Shannon in the year 545. The building dates from the twelfth century and has some fine decorative features. The saint's holy well can be found nearby, a stream of clear water issuing from a limestone terrace—water that I can vouch for as a certain cure for a walker's thirst!

The Way continues west, and soon the rounded shape of Dún Eochla appears on the skyline to the left, with the ruins of the old Napoleonic signal tower nearby. A detour to see the prehistoric dún, the first of a number to be passed on Inis Mór, is worthwhile. It has a dramatically commanding position overlooking the north and east coasts of the island, and across to Inis Meáin, where a signal fire on the great fort there, Dún Chonchúir, would be easily seen.

A little further on, as a salt lake is reached on the right, the whitewashed houses of Cill Mhuirbhigh village can be seen on the high ground ahead. Fringed by a band of tall reeds, the picturesque lake is separated from the sea by a great bank of sea-rounded limestone cobbles. In winter a great variety of waders mingle with duck, whooper swans and mute swans on this sheltered water, attracting bird-watchers from the mainland.

The west side of the cobble bank forms a crescent-shaped bay, where the limestone terraces below the road look as if they were constructed as grandstand seating for the beach. Dominating the bay are the gaunt, roofless ruins of the kelp factory, built in the 1860s. Seaweed gathered laboriously from the beaches up and down the coast by the local people was processed here, and a variety of chemicals extracted, principally iodine. By paying poor rates for the weed collected, and using doctored weighing-scales, the company mercilessly exploited the local people for the five years the factory was in operation.

After the seaweed factory the Way turns inland and briefly follows the edge of a limestone terrace, below which is a gully, sheltering a lush and profuse growth of wildflowers and orchids. Soon a boreen is met that curves round to meet the white sandy beach at Port Mhuirbhigh. In the distance the stone fort of Dún Aonghasa can be seen rising from the clifftop on the far side of the island. Inis Mór is only 0.75 km (0.5 mile) wide at this point, and it is said that during a storm in the seventeenth century the sea came over the southern cliffs and briefly bisected the island.

Rejoining the road at the far side of the beach, pass an old fish-curing shed, used as the processing laboratory during the making of the epic 1930s film *Man of Aran*, which depicted the hard and dangerous life of the island's fishermen in their flimsy canvas-hulled currachs, and the fanciful hunting of great basking-sharks.

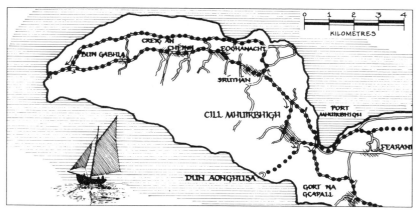

The Way continues uphill past the village of Cill Mhuirbhigh and the Dún Aengus Hostel; down to the right, through fragrant pastures of wildflowers, is Clochán na Carraige, the best-preserved Early Christian 'beehive' dwelling on the island. In buildings such as this, St Ciarán and St Enda and their fellow-monks would have lived.

As the village of Sruthán, birthplace of the writer Máirtín Ó Direáin, is reached, another great stone fort can be seen on the high ground to the left. This is Dún Eoghanachta which, in spite of having lost its outer walls over the centuries, is in an excellent state of preservation. It is said to have been the fortress of the Eoghanacht Árann Mhór, a warrior clan descended from the third-century kings of Munster.

Now the route follows a boreen down to the shore. Up to the right can be found a densely packed group of ecclesiastical ruins called Na Seacht dTeampaill (the Seven Churches). Only two of the buildings are in fact churches, the larger one, of massive construction, suggesting a date about the ninth century and dedicated to St Breacán, and the building shoehorned into a limestone gully, suitably named Teampall an Phoill (the Church of the Hollow); the other five buildings are probably monastic houses. The scattered graveyard around the buildings contains the remains of three high crosses, a number of 'leapacha' or saints' burial-places, and a curious stone inscribed VII Romani, believed locally to mark the graves of seven Romans but more likely a memorial to people who went as pilgrims to Rome.

As the Way veers inland onto another terrace, the village of Eoghanacht and Creig an Chéirín can be seen strung along the road above. Primroses, herb Robert, violets and cushions of saxifrage are abundant along here in late spring and summer, and the bulbous limestone terrace above the road becomes like a grey, linear Ayres Rock before the boreen tops an almost imperceptible rise, and the end of the island comes into sight. A slender black-and-white-striped lighthouse stands on the second of two storm-swept rocky islets offshore.

The walled fields at the roadside seem even smaller here than elsewhere on the island; the proportion between the volume of the walls and the volume of the scant soil they surround must be a remarkable figure. Built to clear the ground for cultivation, these walls also protect precious crops from the Atlantic gales. There are about 1,500 km (932 miles) of dry-stone walls on Inis Mór, which must amount to almost the same figure of worker-years of heavy labour it took to build them.

Soon a T-junction is met; the Inis Mór Way turns left to return to Cill Mhuirbhigh. Down to the right is Cladach Bhun Gabhla, the westernmost beach on Inis Mór. It is not really a beach but a stony shore where a few fishermen still keep their currachs, looking out across 0.5 km (0.3 mile) to Oileán Dá Bhranóg or Brannock Island. The road winds steeply uphill to higher ground and to the most westerly of the Aran villages, Bun Gabhla. The houses here are few and tiny; one in the background to the right is a typical traditional cottage, with very few tiny windows and a rye-grass thatch. Grey-backed crows as big as ravens quarter the fields on rigid wings, on the look-out for titbits. There are choughs about here also; when I passed I was amazed to see a flock of eighteen of them sporting and jinking through the air, and mobbing a grey-back.

As the road begins a long downhill stretch, Port Mhuirbhigh can be seen ahead, with the village of Fearann an Choirce along the hill beyond it. The scattered houses of Creig na Chéirín merge into the next village, Eoghanacht, as a school and church are passed. Continuing downhill through the village of Sruthán, join the outward-bound route again, until the Dún Aengus Hostel is reached, where the Way turns to pass through Cill Mhuirbhigh. Look out for a handball alley, built with massive blocks of stone on a floor of limestone bedrock smoother than the finest concrete.

The route now ascends towards the south, where the skyline is dominated by the buttressed stone ramparts of Dún Aonghasa, past the finest house on the island, Kilmurvey House. This was built in the last century by James O'Flaherty, owner of the biggest farm on the islands, and overlooks what must be the islands' biggest single field. Mrs Joyce runs a very comfortable guesthouse there now, where I stayed when I passed. In the grounds of the house are the well-preserved ruins of a tiny eighth-century church, Teampall Mac Duach.

The road, which now becomes a track, is followed up to Dún Aonghasa. I recommend, however, that you not approach the fort directly by this route: it is far more spectacular to ascend it from the cliffs to the east. To do this, bear left a few hundred metres short of the first ramparts until you reach a great bite out of the high cliffs, called An Sunda Caoch or Blind Sound.

Inis Mór is a great slab of limestone that tilts at a shallow angle towards the north. While it shelves gently into the sea along the north coast, here on the south coast it is like the front line in a primordial battle between sea and land. Great cliffs stubbornly resist the constant battering of the Atlantic, although in places weaker layers have eroded severely, creating massive and terrifying overhangs.

Crowning the highest point of these cliffs is the elaborate and impressive Dún Aonghasa (the Fort of Aonghas). The abrupt and uncompromising cut-off made by the cliffs makes it seem to the non-expert eye that there was once a complete circular building here and that erosion of the cliffs in the succeeding millenniums has consigned half of it to the Atlantic. There is one low-lintelled entrance through the rampart into the central space, which is bare except for a wide natural slab of limestone raised 0.5 m (1.5 feet) out of the tight wiry grass that carpets the ground.

Even with today's sophisticated archaeological methods it has not been established when or by whom Dún Aonghasa was constructed or what the precise purpose of the building was, whether religious or military. This mystery gives the place another dimension, particularly if you manage to visit Dún Aonghasa early in the morning or late in the evening, before or after the tourist hours. The titanic wall construction, the ambience of the enclosed space, and above all the stark and spectacular siting of the structure on the brink of the cliff cannot fail to impress.

Leaving the cliffs and Dún Aonghasa, retrace your steps to Cill Mhuirbhigh, and behind the beach turn southwards to reach the prosperous-looking village of Gort na gCapall, where the novelist Liam O'Flaherty was born. Another of Aran's natural wonders can be found under the cliffs not far from the village. Poll na bPéist is a perfectly rectangular hole about 30 m (100 feet) long, like a natural swimming-pool, in the broad limestone slab at the foot of the cliffs. No trace of the monolith that came from the hole can be seen. The pool is connected at depth to the sea, which provides exciting foaming and boiling of waters when the tide is rising. The name Poll na bPéist means the Hole of the Worm or Serpent.

Turning left in Gort na gCapall, the Way goes eastwards again along Bóthar na gCreag (Road of the Crags), rising through increasingly desolate surroundings. Here lush grassy fields contrast remarkably with those immediately adjacent, where the cold grey stone pavement is relieved only by the vigorous growth in the grikes or cracks between the slabs.

After climbing steadily up a series of limestone terraces, some of which display architectural features like string courses of a straightness and section that would not be out of place on a cut-stone building, the boreen levels out to follow a long straight. Off to the left, in an area called Baile na Sean (Village of the Old), are numerous stone dwelling-sites, ruined ring-forts and other structures, suggesting that in spite of the unsympathetic and desolate surroundings that exist today, things may have been different a millennium ago.

Soon the last rise is topped and Cuan Chill Éinne or Cill Éinne Bay is in view below, the flat sandspit with its airstrip extending into it, and Oileán na Tuí with its lighthouse off the eastern point. The Way now follows the boreen steeply down, and then south again along the west side of An Turlach Mór, a rich pasture enclosed east and west by 8 m (25 foot) cliffs. The sheltered turlough, which becomes a lake in wintertime, is rich in plant and insect life and provides a good habitat for an abundance of birds, from herons and grey wagtails to curlews and cuckoos in season. Soon the southern edge of the island is reached at An Aill Bhriste (the Broken Cliff), a large section of cliff that is in the process of parting company with the land. From this scary point walk east along the cliffs towards Dún Dúchathair, perched on a promontory about 0.75 km (0.5 mile) away.

The cliffs here are dramatically undercut by the sea, and it is not a comfortable place for those who suffer from vertigo, particularly where the fort is entered on the east side, across a 1.5 m (5 foot) space between the end of the rampart and the cliff edge.

Dún Dúchathair (the Black Stone Fort) is thought to date from the same period as Dún Aonghasa. Unlike the latter, however, it has the remains of some substantial corbelled stone buildings within it, from one of which a passage leads out under the terraced rampart. The sea makes a constant thundering noise as it eats into the foot of the cliffs, and one can feel an aural pressure shock almost as if the whole cliff is shaking.

The Way now heads back inland along the east side of the valley, and soon the village of Cill Rónáin comes into sight ahead. As the road drops steeply past the island's oil-fired generating station, the shore is reached. The road is now followed into the village to complete the Inis Mór Way.

THE INIS MEÁIN WAY

DISTANCE: 8 KM (5 MILES). WALKING TIME: 2 HOURS.

Inis Meáin is the second-largest island of the Aran group. The population of about 250 is mainly involved in farming and fishing, and there is a small knitwear factory exporting high-quality products. Inis Meáin has been less exposed to outside influences than the other two islands, and its Irish language and culture are probably better preserved. Patrick Pearse, Eoin MacNeill and John Millington Synge were all enthusiasts of Inis Meáin, and the cottage Synge rented for his visits is passed by the Way.

The Inis Meáin Way is mainly over quiet tarred roads and grassy boreens, and there are no real hills involved. Bed-and-breakfast is offered in a number of houses on the island, and evening meals are also available. Make sure to try the island's delicacy, its delicious floury potatoes.

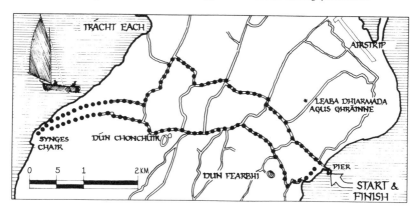

The Inis Meáin Way begins at An Córa, the pier on the east side of the island. Like giant beetle carapaces, the 2.75 (9 foot) tar-black currachs, the fishing craft of the west of Ireland, lie upended in rows near the slipway. These are among the last surviving descendants of one of the oldest type of craft used by man, the skin-hulled boat, known to have been used by Stone Age peoples. Not many years ago cowhide soaked in pitch was the material used to cover the delicate framework, but in recent times canvas and even fibreglass have taken over, just as the outboard motor has taken the place of the bladeless oars. The characteristic size and shape, however, have not changed for centuries.

Leaving the pier, head inland past the rock-strewn foreshore and turn left towards a small roofless building a couple of hundred metres away. In the 1830s the Ordnance Survey scholar John O'Donovan thought this building the most perfect of the primitive churches then in existence. The tiny oratory has the typical features of the eighth or ninth century: huge masonry, a low and narrow-lintelled west doorway, and a triangular-headed east window. It stands in a graveyard densely packed with commemorative stone slabs, where burials were carried out up to 1940.

Follow the wildflower-cordoned grassy boreen beside the little church as it winds steeply uphill in the direction of the stone fort that dominates the skyline. This is Dún Fearbhaí, a D-shaped fort with an internal space nearly 30 m (98 feet) across, commanding the north and east of the island. It has the typical dry-stone terraced ramparts of other Aran forts, and similarly its age is not known with any certainty. The view from the top of the walls is marvellous on a good day. To the north-west the undulating forms of the Twelve Bens and the Maumturk Mountains in Connemara lead the eye eastwards to the flatlands east of Lough Corrib, while Black Head, northern outpost of the Burren in Co. Clare, extends into Galway Bay to the north-east. To the east and south-east the coast of Co. Clare rises up to the impressive ramparts of the Cliffs of Moher, while in the foreground are the grey-and-green limestone layers of Inis Oírr.

The Way continues westwards on a level boreen into the village of Baile an Mhothair, passing the Telecom Éireann microwave station, its high-tech equipment hidden within a thatched roof and stone walls. A little further on is Inis Meáin's only pub, a long, low thatched building remarkable for its lack of garish advertising signs. Further along on the right is a shop where I bought the first 'wafer' ice-cream I had seen in many years. After this shop the dramatic silhouette of Inis Meáin's largest fort, Dún Chonchúir, looms on the horizon ahead.

Keeping straight on, pass Eaglais Mhuire Gan Smál (Church of Mary Immaculate), Inis Meáin's church, on the left. Its stained-glass windows, with colours rich and strong, were designed by Harry Clarke. The holy water font at the entrance is from an old fifteenth-century church, the site of which is across the road.

A little further on on the right is a thatched cottage in which John Millington Synge, writer and founder-member of the Abbey Theatre, spent the summers of 1898 to 1902. Synge's uncle had been the Church of Ireland minister on Inis Mór in the 1850s, so he would have heard much about the islands before he was urged by William Butler Yeats to seek inspiration there. He spent a short time on Inis Mór before moving to Inis Meáin and this cottage, where he eventually became accepted and liked and where he gathered the material for the first book about the islands, *The Aran Islands*, published in 1905.

Soon, the high walls of Dún Chonchúir can be seen up to the left. In Irish mythology, Conchúr was the brother of Aonghas, after whom the great cliff fortress on Inis Mór is named. Dún Chonchúir is a particularly awe-inspiring and well-preserved stone fort. The entrance through the main wall, 5.5 m (18 feet) high and 4.9 m (16 feet) thick in places, is protected by a spacious rectangular outer fortification. The oval internal space, overlooked by terraces and flights of steps common to the other big forts, measures 69 m (226 feet) at its widest and contains the stone bases of a number of substantial clocháns or beehive huts.

The outlook from Dún Chonchúir is even more impressive than that from Dún Fearbhaí, because here, close to the highest point of the island at 79 m (260 feet) above sea level, there is an almost 360-degree view of the horizon. In clear weather the top of Mount Brandon on the Dingle Peninsula can be seen 97 km (60 miles) away to the south, rising island-like from the horizon. Almost 3 km (2 miles) away across Sunda Ghrióra or Gregory's Sound, the cliffs of Inis Mór rise from an apron of white, foaming waves.

Surrounding Dún Chonchúir is a crazy maze of dry-stone walls, like the offspring of the great fort, enclosing tiny fields, some with beautifully manicured potato drills and others with long grass and a single, contented grazing cow.

Returning to the Inis Meáin Way, turn left and continue westwards. Just before a sharp bend, note the cottage on the hill ahead with walls decorated with pieces of mirror, which catch the light in a magical way. A little further on, the remains of a beehive hut can be seen in a field at the back of a little cottage on the left.

Steeply uphill, the Way follows the road as the high cliffs of Inis Mór come into sight ahead. Soon the tarmac comes to an end and the now grassy boreen bears round to the left, and narrows until there is only about a metre between the high stone walls on each side. Emerging into the open, the Way follows white-painted markings across rough and bare limestone pavements, rich with shell fossils, heading for Cathaoir Synge or Synge's Chair. Built by Synge himself, this dry-stone shelter near the cliff edge faces out over Gregory's Sound towards Inis Mór and the Connemara coast beyond. Here the writer spent hours each day, with 'the black edge of the North Island in front of me, Galway bay, too blue almost to look at, on my right, the Atlantic on my left, a perpendicular cliff under my ankles and over me innumerable gulls that chase each other in a white cirrus of wings'.

To the south along the cliffs is a remarkable natural phenomenon that can be found in a number of exposed locations on the islands: the storm beach. Over the ages, particularly violent seas have flaked great slabs of rock off the cliff edge and flung them ten or fifteen metres inland, where they lie, a fantastic geological jumble of a high-water mark. Between them and the cliff edge remains a zone swept absolutely free of loose matter.

The Way now returns along the cliffs at a lower level. Take care to pick up the correct route back: Aran field walls are extremely effective barriers, with a combination of flimsiness and height making them difficult to climb, so it is not easy to cut across a few fields if you go wrong.

There is a continual thunder of waves on the rocks below as you walk along here to join a green track that soon improves to a tarred road. The Way turns left through a wilderness of stone-walled fields, passing a left turn that leads to Trácht Each, Inis Meáin's western beach, and then loops around towards the island's water-storage tanks, two great concrete cylinders that seem to mimic the circular form of the stone fort on the skyline. Soon Inis Meáin's knitwear factory, a simple whitewashed building, is passed, and Dún Fearbhaí comes into view again at the eastern end of the escarpment.

Up a turn to the left, in a stone-surfaced field, can be found Leaba Dhiarmada agus Ghráinne, the bed of Diarmaid and Gráinne, a collapsed wedge-tomb possibly of the Late Stone Age. In Irish mythology Diarmaid and Gráinne were runaway lovers, hunted from one end of the country to the other by the legendary warrior Fionn mac Cumhaill, who wanted Gráinne for himself. The story must have been a popular one in rural Ireland; similar wedge-tombs all over the country are pointed out as the lovers' bed.

Our walk finishes where it started, at the pier. There is much more to see than is covered by the Inis Meáin Way in its 8 km (5 miles), and I would particularly recommend an exploration of the beach and harbour of the north of the island, and the lake and the beaches of the north-east.

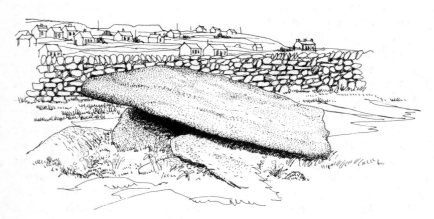

Leaba Dhiarmada agus Ghráinne

THE INIS OÍRR WAY

DISTANCE: 10.5 KM (6.5 MILES). WALKING TIME: 2.75 HOURS.

Inis Oírr is the smallest of the three Aran Islands but, being close to the coast of Co. Clare, attracts more visitors than Inis Meáin. The population of about 275 lives mainly by fishing and farming. Daffodil-growing is a new industry, and if you walk the Way in spring you will pass by blazing yellow fields of these flowers.

The Inis Oírr Way follows quiet tarred roads and boreens, with a number of opportunities to shorten or lengthen the distance walked. Inis Oírr has plenty of good guesthouse accommodation, in addition to a small hotel, a small hostel and a good camping park.

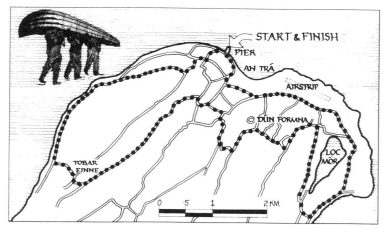

The Inis Oírr Way starts out from the island's main pier, where the ferries from Galway and Clare drop and collect their passengers. Turning east, the Way passes along the sea front through a picturesque scattering of nets, floats, winches, and beached boats, including many currachs of the west coast. The beach is ahead now, from where the cattle being sent to the mainland have to be floated out and hoisted aboard the supply ship offshore.

At the island Co-op offices the Way turns inland towards the hotel, Óstán Inis Oírr, and passes an easy-to-miss Bronze Age tumulus or burial monument called Cnoc Raithní (Fern Hill). It lay hidden by a burden of sand for three-and-a-half thousand years, until storms cleared the sand in 1885.

Dominating the whole scene here, citadel-like at the top of a series of grassy limestone terraces, is Caisleán Uí Bhriain or O'Brien's Castle, a fourteenth-century building rising out of the centre of Dún Formna, a prehistoric stone fort that dates at least from the first century. To their right can be seen the ruins of a signal tower of the Napoleonic wars.

The Way follows the road running along the back of the beach, and soon the island's graveyard looms up, high on the sandhill to the right. In the middle of the graveyard there is an amazing sight: a tenth-century church with fourteenth-century additions rising from a depression in the sand, the top of its gables hardly level with the ground around, dotted with tombstones. In the same conditions that exposed the Bronze Age tumulus, this church was inundated with sand over the centuries; even when it was completely buried, the local people continued to bury their dead around it. The church is dedicated to St Caomhán, a brother of St Kevin of Glendalough. He was the most celebrated of the Aran saints after St Enda and was especially venerated by seafarers, who believed him capable of miraculous power over storms. This is a peaceful and thought-provoking place, surrounded by centuries of Inis Oírr's dead. Nearby is a shrine that is said to cover the saint's grave.

The Way continues eastwards past the airfield, with the village of Formna clustered on a limestone promontory up to the right, and soon the road deteriorates into a grassy boreen that winds its way through stone-walled fields of wildflowers. An Loch Mór (the Big Lake) now appears ahead, with a strange saw-tooth escarpment behind it. Stone-built columns for drying seaweed can be seen on the skyline and along the roadside.

The Way follows the boreen uphill onto the next limestone terrace. The strange and gaunt rust-gold profile of a wrecked ship, the *Plassy*, comes into view ahead, incongruously perched on the limestone clifftop. The ship ran into difficulties during a storm in 1960 and had to be abandoned when it was driven aground. Later it was picked up by the Atlantic waves and deposited on the clifftop, where it has rested to this day, a testament to the power of the sea.

Ahead now is the lighthouse, built in 1857, marking the southern point of the island. Soon the Way follows the boreen inland again, passing through a ravine of lush vegetation and gently ascending towards the village of Formna between field walls that in places are nearly 3 m (10 feet) high. Formna is a cosy, old-fashioned village of closely gathered cottages, through which the boreen meanders.

The Way now turns south, and over to the right the signal tower built about 1800, standing at the highest point of the island, comes into view. Inis Oírr's oil-fired electricity generating station, constantly humming, is passed, before the Way follows a daisy-strewn boreen across another tiny bee-loud valley. Rising again and passing the Telecom Éireann building, the limestone walls of which are rich in fossils, the Way approaches the highest point of the island.

A couple of hundred metres downhill on a rock promontory is the stone fort called Dún Formna, unique among those of the Aran Islands in that it has a medieval tower-house built within it. The O'Brien clan, descendants of the eleventh-century high king Brian Boru, ruled the Aran Islands seven hundred years ago. They had one tower-house on Inis Mór and, making use of the Iron Age stone fort as a ready-made bawn, they constructed this three-storey tower about the end of the fourteenth century to dominate the beach below.

There is a marvellous view from the fort's ramparts, out across Galway Bay, where to the north-west Errisbeg rises like an island from the sea, while further east the serrated profile of the Twelve Bens leads the eye east past the Maumturks to the plains of east Galway and the Burren of Co. Clare.

Returning to the Way, follow the road south past the ruined signal tower. This was part of an extensive coastal network of buildings constructed during the Napoleonic wars to watch out for and repel an expected sea-borne invasion by the French. Observers on the towers kept in touch with the rest of the network by semaphore.

The Way now winds towards Baile an tSéipéil (the Chapel Village). The chapel, built in 1901, is on the left, a simple structure that in strong sunlight looks as if it belongs to a Greek island. Soon the tarmac comes to an end and the now grass-surfaced road turns south into a landscape of walls. Very little green can be seen from some angles; all around is the backdrop of stone walls stretching into the distance, so tightly placed that the tiny pastures between them are hidden. In summertime the wildflowers of the verge perfume the route, while larks keep up a song on all sides; in winter the constant thunder of the sea accompanies the sight of great waves smashing on the ragged shore of Inis Meáin 3 km (2 miles) away.

After heading south for 1 km (0.6 mile), the Way turns right to reach the shore again, passing Tobar Éinne (St Enda's Well) in a stone-walled enclosure. Between two low walls in the shape of an S lies a pool of clear water. Beside it in a niche is a cup for the use of pilgrims in drinking the water, regarded as being beneficial and curative. St Enda founded a monastery on Inis Mór and is said to have come to Inis Oírr to pray on occasions; nearby are the scant remains of a clochán or dry-stone corbel-roofed dwelling that the saint is said to have used.

The Way now follows the shore back towards the north of the island. To the left is the characteristic Aran phenomenon of the storm beach. The road descends along the coast, dropping down terrace by terrace through natural rock gardens of wildflowers. Passing by a low limestone cliff whose rounded top and frequent ivy-covered, tower-like structures give it the look of a medieval town wall, the Way ascends again. Down to the left is a tiny harbour, where at low tide the sea uncovers astonishing rock formations, ruby-studded with sea anemones.

As the path climbs gently, houses soon begin to appear again, and the Way passes near the roofless church of St Gobnait, Aran's only woman saint. It is a tiny building with very thick walls and is thought to date from the eighth or ninth century. There are some very early stone-slabbed graves beside it, and nearby are the remains of a clochán.

The road is followed downhill again, through a narrow alley past Tigh Ned (Ned's House), one of the island's three pubs, to the sea front and the end of the Way.

2
THE BALLYHOURA WAY

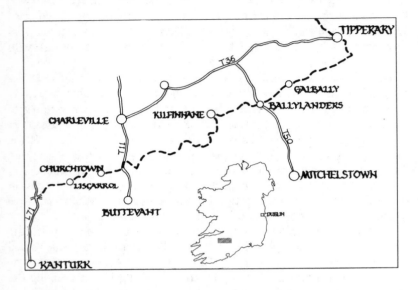

A year after the Irish defeat at the Battle of Kinsale, the last remaining loyal Irish chieftain in the area, Dónall Cam Ó Súilleabháin Béarra, 'the O'Sullivan Beare', isolated and surrounded by enemies, abandoned his territories in December 1602 and set out for sanctuary in the north. Leading four hundred fighting men and their families, a thousand in all, his aim was to reach the territory of Ó Ruairc of Breffni in Co. Leitrim. Some were killed during the constant skirmishes they endured along the way, others died from hunger, fatigue and exposure, and only a sad group of thirty-five reached Leitrim two weeks and 500 km (311 miles) later.

This terrible journey has taken its place among Ireland's epics, and a long-range walking trail covering the route is being planned. One section of the route, from St John's Bridge, north of Kanturk in Co. Cork, to Limerick Junction in Co. Tipperary, 80 km (50 miles) away, has been inaugurated as the Ballyhoura Way.

How to get there
The nearest town to the western end of the route is Kanturk, Co. Cork, 260 km (162 miles) from Dublin and served by the table no. 242 Cork–Newmarket bus.

Maps and guides

The route straddles three Ordnance Survey 1:127,000 (0.5 inch to 1 mile) maps: nos 18, 21 and 22. An excellent fold-out map and guide describing the route in detail is available from Ballyhoura Fáilte Society Ltd, Education Centre, Kilfinnane, Co. Limerick.

Enquiries

Ballyhoura Fáilte Society, Kilfinnane, Co. Limerick; telephone 063 91300

Liscarroll Castle

STAGE 1: ST JOHN'S BRIDGE TO BALLYHEA

DISTANCE: 22 KM (13.5 MILES). WALKING TIME: 5.5 HOURS.
This section is entirely on tarmac, mostly quiet, rolling country roads but always with the danger of meeting a speeding tractor: take care at bends. The lush Cork countryside and the villages of Churchtown and Liscarroll, the latter with its massive castle, do, however, compensate. Ballyhea has limited bed-and-breakfast accommodation.

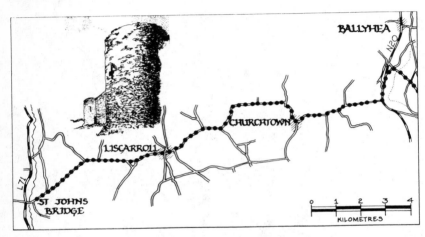

The Ballyhoura Way starts at a nondescript crossroads 6.5 km (4 miles) north of Kanturk, distinguished only by a grocery shop and filling-station. The route follows the road eastwards across St John's Bridge over the narrow River Allow, said to be where O'Sullivan Beare's party ran into an ambush when fording the stream. The ambushers were probably a party sent out from Liscarroll Castle 6 km (4 miles) to the east, and when they finally withdrew they left four of the Irish dead and many wounded.

The Way wanders eastwards through pleasant if uneventful countryside. The high and rich hedgerows of elder, ash and whitethorn do not allow much of a view in summertime other than occasional glimpses of the Boggeragh Mountains to the south-west and the Ballyhoura and Galty Mountains ahead.

Although O'Sullivan Beare's party avoided Liscarroll, the Ballyhoura Way drops steeply to reach the village, still dominated by its thirteenth-century castle. It is a spectacular building, in size (it is the third-largest of its kind in Ireland) and in being almost intact. Covering an area of about 2,500 sq. m (0.6 acre), it has circular towers at the corners and a fine gatehouse, and its walls in places reach to 12 m (40 feet) above the cottages of the village.

In 1641 English forces held out in the castle for almost two weeks against the repeated attacks of an Irish army of 7,000 foot soldiers and 500 cavalry, backed up by artillery, before surrendering. The delay allowed Lord Inchiquin to assemble an army sufficient to attack and defeat the Irish, and the castle was back in English hands within another week.

The key for the castle can be obtained from Mrs O'Brien at O'Brien's pub in the main street.

Continuing eastwards from Liscarroll, pass a donkey sanctuary which had a field full of worn-out but contented-looking donkeys when I passed, and the Way continues to meander uneventfully towards the Ballyhoura Hills, until 6.5 km (4 miles) further on the village of Churchtown is reached. The village dates from the middle of the nineteenth century, when the pleasant limestone houses and the market-house were built in place of the previous village, which was destroyed in 1832 during the Whiteboy agrarian riots. Near here the well-known horse breeder Vincent O'Brien and the poet Seán Clárach Mac Dónaill (1691–1754) were born.

A short distance on, pass the great nineteenth-century castellated gateway of Burton Hall on the right. Destroyed in the wars of 1641 and 1690, the present building was erected in 1792 and has been occupied by the same family for nearly two hundred years.

The route continues to join the busy Cork–Charleville road after nearly 4 km (2.5 miles) and, turning left, follows it for 3 km (2 miles) till it reaches the hamlet of Ballyhea.

Ardpatrick

STAGE 2: BALLYHEA TO BALLYORGAN

DISTANCE: 24 KM (15 MILES). AGGREGATE CLIMB: 400 M (1,312 FEET). WALKING TIME: 7.5 HOURS.

This stage takes you through the Ballyhoura Mountains and down to the hamlet of Ballyorgan (the Village of Ó hArgáin—nothing to do with music or physiology!) in the sheltered valley of the Keale River. Apart from 3 km (2 miles) on tarmac and 6 km (4 miles) on open moorland, the stage is all forestry roads. Arranging a drop at the beginning of the boreen west of the forest will shorten the stage by 4 km (2.5 miles) and save walking on that busy Cork road. Lantern Lodge in Ballyorgan, where red deer are farmed, provides excellent bed-and-breakfast and evening meals. Ballyorgan has no regular bus service.

Follow the road south-wards out of Ballyhea and turn up the first side-road to the left. Carrying on straight uphill, the route follows a grassy boreen which, after crossing one tarred road, continues to meet another and, turning left and uphill, within minutes bears right onto another boreen. The 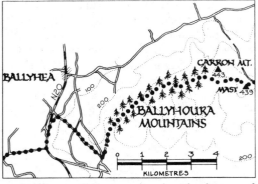 hedges on each side, festooned with woodbine, are lined with clumps of hedge bedstraw and tall spears of foxglove in summertime.

Soon the boreen becomes a forestry road and the route turns east and uphill. Great clumps of Michaelmas daisies were in bloom at the roadside when I passed here, and I was nearly as astonished at these as I was by the myriad butterwort that lined the verges in places. The butterwort is an insectivorous plant and traps tiny insects in the viscous liquid in its leaves before absorbing them. Another plant that surprised me in the profusion with which it grew was the common spotted orchid; extensive stands of it lined the road in all its varieties of colour, from reddish-purple to white.

After a long stretch without much of a view it is a relief when a clearing is reached where trees have been harvested, presenting an extensive view over the plains to the north. The town of Charleville can be seen on the left in the distance, and Kilmallock to the right.

Soon after, the rocky summit of Carron Mountain makes the first of a number of welcome appearances ahead as the route meanders through further stretches of thick forestry. Then, abruptly, the route leaves the forestry road, turning right to follow a break in the trees steeply uphill to reach open moorland and continue along the southern flanks of Carron Mountain, the craggy summit of which, surmounted by an ancient burial cairn, is worth a short detour to visit. According to my map, you pass back and forth over the border of Counties Cork and Limerick three times over the next kilometre of the route.

A telecommunications mast can be seen ahead to the east; the route now winds towards this landmark, first along a forest margin and then across open ground to meet a rough track that cuts through the heather to reach it.

There is a new vista ahead now, the dramatic horizon of the Ballyhoura Mountain Park. The route ahead can be seen as a scar through the moorland, dropping and then rising to reach the nearest of the sandstone tors, called Castle Philip. Leaving the mast and its fenced enclosure, the Way descends into the flat valley along a path on top of a low turf bank. Down to the left the moorland turns into rich meadows as it reaches the plain, while to the right, beyond a newly carved forestry road, the landscape with its scattered young trees has a look of the African plains, and one almost expects to see herds of giraffe and zebra at any moment! When I passed I was satisfied to see a hen harrier coasting slowly and eagle-like along the bottom of the valley, searching out prey.

Take care along this pathway; I'm told that no sooner was it created than someone rode a horse along it, leaving a legacy of ankle-twisting holes hidden in the grass. As the path levels out, the ragged skyline seen ahead from the telecommunications mast resolves itself into an impressive array of strangely shaped sandstone outcrops, the largest of which looks a bit like a multi-storey building that has fallen on hard times.

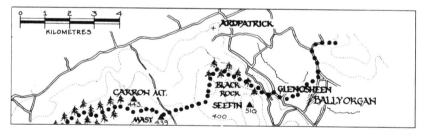

Now the route veers to the left to pass by the nearest outcrop, Castle Philip, and descend again. Soon a young forest is entered, and within minutes a forestry road is met and followed downhill.

Straight ahead, rising from the plain, is a rounded green hill with a line of trees and a ruin on its summit. This is Ardpatrick, the remains of a monastic settlement said to have been founded by St Patrick. The stump of a round tower stands outside the walls of a graveyard that surrounds a seventh-century church ruin. The graveyard has been in constant use for at least 1,300 years; up to recently coffins were carried up the steep hill on the shoulders of mourners, but today a special hearse-like trolley, hitched to the back of a tractor, bears the dead to their last resting-place, which a local told me is the best graveyard in Ireland, because it is nearest to Heaven! O'Sullivan Beare and his party spent the third night of their epic journey near here, resting and nursing their wounds.

As the route bears round towards the east the town of Kilfinnane comes into view ahead against the backdrop of the Slievereagh Hills, and a little later the great rugged eastern slope of Black Rock can be seen above the trees. The forestry road becomes closely hemmed in by trees again, and there is little to look at other than the wildflowers; along this stretch there were extensive bunches of pink wood scabious when I passed. Indeed, it is the sheer abundance of wildflowers in the Ballyhoura area that makes that aspect memorable for me.

As the forest clears away on the left it reveals a series of hills extending to the horizon. In the middle ground a strange and gaunt tower rises from one hill; this is Oliver's Folly, a castellated gazebo built by the local landlord during the Great Famine to give employment.

The highest summit in the Ballyhoura Mountains now comes into view: Seefin, at 519 m (1,700 feet). Just after this the route leaves the forestry road and climbs a rough path through the trees. Crossing a wooden bridge over a mossy, rock-filled gorge, the path meanders through a beech wood to reach a grassy forestry road, and in minutes re-enters the trees to descend to a car park and the public road.

After a couple of hundred metres on tarmac, the route follows a steep and narrow pathway down to the immaculate hamlet of Glenosheen. On the left is the house where the antiquarian Patrick Weston Joyce and his brother, the poet Robert Dwyer Joyce, spent their boyhood.

The route follows the public road south-eastwards from Glenosheen, and immediately after a fork in the road it enters a grass-covered forestry road, teeming with young rabbits when I passed. After a couple of minutes the road comes out into the open where the forest has been harvested, and the Galty Mountains can be glimpsed ahead. Over to the left on a hill, Oliver's Folly can be seen, closer now.

A wooden bridge over the Keale River is crossed, and the clover-surfaced forestry road ascends gently into a pleasant mixed wood with rhododendron and elder squeezing between ashes and conifers. Within five minutes the Way reaches the public road again a couple of hundred metres north of the little hamlet of Ballyorgan, the end of this stage.

STAGE 3: BALLYORGAN TO GALBALLY

DISTANCE: 21 KM (13 MILES). AGGREGATE CLIMB: 325 M (1,070 FEET). WALKING TIME: 6 HOURS.

This stage takes the Way over wooded Benyvoughella Hill to the town of Kilfinnane and on uphill again through the woods of Slievereagh, before passing through Ballylanders to reach the village of Galbally. Other than 6 km (3.75 miles) on boreens and forestry roads, this stage is all on public tarred roads. The stage can be easily broken into shorter walks to explore the pleasant hillsides and towns of the Ballyhoura area. Kilfinnane, Ballylanders and Galbally all have bed-and-breakfast accommodation. Galbally is served by the table no. 340 Shannon–Galbally bus and the table no. 328 Limerick–Mitchelstown bus; both buses also serve Ballylanders.

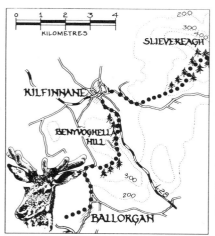

The Way heads north from Ballyorgan along the public road, passing on the left the castellated gateway of Castle Oliver, a Scottish baronial mansion. This was the birthplace of Marie Gilbert, who in the 1830s became an 'exotic dancer' and listed among her lovers the composer Liszt, the Viceroy of Poland and Lord Ranelagh. She completely infatuated King Ludwig 1 of Bavaria and, staying with him for a year during which she virtually ruled the country, provoked the revolution of 1848.

The road is followed for another 1.25 km (0.75 mile) until at a sharp bend the route turns onto a forestry road and heads up along the northern flanks of a forested hill. It's a pleasant stretch along here, looking out over rich hedged grasslands (watch out for two galláns or ancient standing stones in fields below), the meadow-grassed verges decorated with stands of orchids and herb Robert in summertime. As the route rises towards Benyvoughella Hill, a fine vista opens up behind, out past Oliver's Folly and the rounded hill of Ardpatrick to the plains between Charleville and Kilmallock. Reaching the ridge, the route turns towards the north for a few minutes, past a group of farm buildings, with the Galty Mountains appearing again on the eastern horizon; the forested Slievereagh Hills, through which this stage of the Ballyhoura Way passes, can be seen to their left.

The Way now descends and enters the forest, heading north on a long enclosed straight. The brief enclosure adds to the sense of arrival when the road reaches open ground at the northern end of this ridge, with great views out over south Tipperary. As the forestry road becomes a grassy track, the town of Kilfinnane with its tall church spire comes into view at your feet, before the route descends to reach the public road and, turning left, enters the town. A lofty Norman motte is passed on the way in, built, it appears, in the middle of a much earlier ring-fort with three concentric earthen rings.

Kilfinnane is clearly in the process of renewing itself after a long sleep; many of the nineteenth-century shops and houses, like Molly Bloom's Restaurant, have been carefully restored, while others, suspended in a state of picturesque decay, are awaiting renewal, like the sandstone-arched market-house, last repaired in 1836. There are a number of good pubs here; I recommend O'Shaughnessy's for its pints and atmosphere.

The route leaves Kilfinnane by following the road opposite the motte and dropping downhill first and then rising gently eastwards towards a hill crowned with a tall stand of Scots pines, called the Palatine Wood. The name recalls the German Protestant refugees who settled here in the seventeenth century, part of a colony of about 1,200 established near Rathkeale, Co. Limerick. It took them a long time to settle in, and for many years they kept very much to themselves, wearing their own traditional dress and speaking only German. But gradually they did merge into the community, and today local surnames like Switzer, Steepe and Alton, combined with a characteristic neatness that makes some cottages and gardens in the area stand out, are all that remain of the Palatine past.

Further along the road, just under a dramatic sandstone crag that bursts through the hillside up to the left, the Way leaves the road to follow an overgrown boreen. As the boreen rises towards the forest that clothes the southern slopes of Slievereagh, the roofs of Kilfinnane come into view behind, backed by wooded Benyvoughella Hill. As the corner of the forest is reached, the route crosses the fence and continues uphill along the forest margin to reach a forestry road.

Soon the road takes the Way out into the open, and the summit of Slievereagh, from this angle looking like a miniature Benbulbin, appears ahead. The route will pass between the summit and the rounded wooded hill to its right.

The forestry road bears round, taking our route into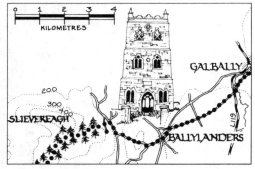
the heart of these hills, and passes through pleasant and open areas where it will be some time before the young trees cut out light and view. Bunches of shredded-looking ragged robin grew along the verge when I passed, beside clumps of lady's bedstraw.

The highest point of this stage is reached when the summit of Slievereagh, now quite impressive-looking and a temptation to climb, is to the left of the road; then the Way descends towards the east, with the lofty Galty Mountains filling the horizon ahead. Winding round a hillock, and just before Slievereagh disappears from sight behind, the Way abruptly leaves the forestry road, turning down a steep and narrow—and easily missed—path through the trees.

Reaching a gravel road, the route turns left and promenades along, with great views out to the Galty Mountains, before dropping downhill to reach the public road at Glenbrohane. To the left is a Catholic church, recorded as having been built in 1819 at a cost of £600. The Way turns right and takes the second left, to descend gently between high hedges, until an unusual squat church tower appears in the distance, announcing that the village of Ballylanders is not far ahead.

The long main street of Ballylanders is dominated by that church tower, which belongs to an unusual nineteenth-century building now in ruins. Built in local sandstone with strange ogee-type windows, it is quite massive, and looks as if it will be standing when the modern church in the village is long gone!

Leaving Ballylanders and continuing north-eastwards on the public road, again glimpse the Galty Mountains, seeming now much closer. At the highest point of the hill a strange pond is passed on the right, before the road drops downhill, crossing the main Glen of Aherlow road and the River Aherlow before reaching the village of Galbally.

Galbally was in former times a strategically important place, dominating the only pass into Tipperary from north Cork, and it was here all the chiefs of Munster were summoned by Lord Carew in 1601 to a meeting during which he appointed Lord Barry to take his place as President of Munster. The village, a past winner of the Tidy Towns competition, is centred on a broad market square surrounded by colourfully painted nineteenth-century houses, to one side of which is a carved limestone monument to the illustrious flying columns of the old IRA.

The Galty Mountains

29

STAGE 4: GALBALLY TO LIMERICK JUNCTION

DISTANCE: 23 KM (14 MILES). AGGREGATE CLIMB: 200 M (650 FEET). WALKING TIME: 6.5 HOURS.

This stage lingers along the southern flanks of Slievenamuck, a long, narrow ridge running eastwards into Co. Tipperary, before crossing it, dropping into the Golden Vale and passing through Tipperary town to reach Limerick Junction. I found that a 10 a.m. start from Galbally will allow non-purists to make a welcome lunch stop at the Aherlow House Hotel. The stage consists of 2.5 km (1.5 miles) through open meadows, 6.5 km (4 miles) on busy tarred roads to Limerick Junction and the rest on forestry roads. Tipperary has a wide range of hotel and bed-and-breakfast accommodation available, and is served by the table no. 347 Limerick–Tipperary bus, the table no. 55 Limerick–Waterford Expressway bus, and the table no. 342 Tipperary–Shannon bus.

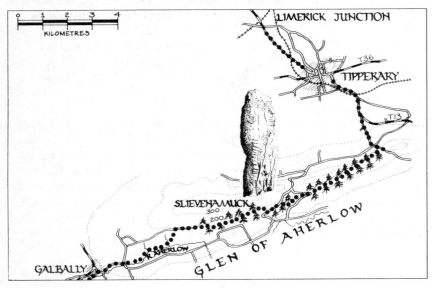

Leaving Galbally, the ruins of an ancient church can be seen on the higher ground to the left. A picturesque pub and some houses a short distance on suggest that the original town of Galbally may have extended along this road, ending over the county border in Co. Tipperary at a ruined fifteenth-century Franciscan church, which soon appears ahead against a backdrop of the Galty Mountains. This building is all that remains of Moore Abbey, probably built after the original abbey, founded in the early thirteenth

30

century, was plundered and burned in 1472. Suppressed in 1540, it was burned again in 1569, and the friars who returned to pick up the pieces were massacred a year later. Even as late as the twentieth-century War of Independence it was under threat, when the British forces, concerned about the cover it offered for ambushes, attempted unsuccessfully to blow it up.

Here at Moore Abbey the route takes a long-awaited and welcome break from the tarmac and follows the banks of the River Aherlow through a series of pastures and meadows into the western end of the Glen of Aherlow. Electric fences are common along here, so take care: they can give you an uncomfortable jolt. There were plenty of fish in the river when I passed, disturbing the water in slow-moving stretches with their leaps for flies. Herons were also in evidence, taking off ponderously with a harsh squawking call when disturbed.

The route meanders along with the river, negotiating a few patches of nettles (be careful in summertime if wearing shorts!) and in one place a patch of giant hogweed. About 2 km (1.25 miles) further on, after crossing a stile that bridges a ditch, the Way turns left and uphill through the fields, following a series of stiles. As the route climbs the western foothills of Slievenamuck, the Galty Mountains across the valley seem to increase in height and fill the sky to the south. Almost 1 km (0.6 mile) from the river the Way reaches a gravel road and, turning right, follows it through a farmyard. After the farm a meadow is crossed diagonally uphill to reach and follow a track that becomes a pleasant shaded boreen as it drops downhill again.

About 0.5 km (0.3 mile) after leaving the farm, keep a careful look-out for a narrow gap in the hedge to the left, which takes the route through trees to meet and follow a forestry road, thickly enclosed by trees. This is quite a long stretch in the trees, with the road rising and falling as it continues eastwards. Again, be vigilant and look out for the place where the route leaves the road, turning right to drop steeply along a long and narrow fire-break and reach the public road.

The Way now goes uphill, and before long passes the Aherlow House Hotel, where I recommend taking a break. Why not order sandwiches and refreshments, and relax awhile on the terrace of the hotel, which commands a stupendous view of the Glen of Aherlow and the mountains beyond. The glen, as an important pass in ancient times between the plains of Tipperary and Limerick, was the site of many battles. Its remoteness and seclusion made it a frequent retreat for outlawed Irishmen over the centuries, and the caves in the foothills of the Galty Mountains sheltered many a Volunteer 'on the run' during the War of Independence.

Continuing on the Way, note the 2,000-year-old ogham stone standing beside the hotel car park, looking decidedly out of place! Beyond the hotel the route enters the forest again and then, just before reaching another tarred road, turns up a narrow track and into a mixed wood. Continue eastwards to reach a car park near a 5 m (16.5 foot) statue of Christ the King, erected in 1950 overlooking the glen and the pyramidal Galty Mountains beyond.

The route now enters the forest yet again and follows a road through an informal plantation of Scots pine, birch, rowan and holly, the last two probably descendants of the trees that grew in the great woods that clothed these parts before they were cleared in the sixteenth and seventeenth centuries. Soon the highest point in the Slievenamuck ridge is passed up to the left, and the road comes out into an open harvested area, giving the last great views back to the Galty range.

After another stretch through the trees the road starts to descend again, and it is a pleasant surprise to leave the trees and find yourself looking out over the plains of Co. Tipperary, with the grey-roofed town of Tipperary clustered round a tall church spire in the middle distance.

The Way follows the forestry road up and down another couple of times before it finally drops down past some water-storage tanks to reach the public road and, continuing downhill into the lush vale of Tipperary, meets and follows the main road into Tipperary town. I understand that there are plans to take this section of the route off the road and along the bank of the Arra River into the town; it will be a very welcome change when it occurs.

Like many Irish towns, Tipperary grew up around a Norman castle, possibly founded by King John, and a religious foundation, in this case an Augustinian priory. Today it is a bustling market town with a long main street, beside which is a fine bronze statue on a limestone base of the writer and Young Irelander, Charles Kickham.

The Ballyhoura Way leaves the town and follows the wide and busy road for 4 km (2.5 miles) to Limerick Junction, which consists of a series of railway cottages, a pub and a racecourse at Ireland's largest railway junction. It is not known for certain where O'Sullivan Beare dropped from the comparative safety of the high ground and crossed the hostile Tipperary plains, heading for the next hills 32 km (20 miles) to the north, the Slievefelim Mountains. We do know, however, that for eight hours his band fought a running musket battle with columns of enemies, until darkness fell and they had a brief respite while they camped near Soloheadbeg, close to where Limerick Junction is today.

32

3
THE BARROW WAY

The Barrow is the second-longest river in Ireland, rising close to the centre of the country in the Slieve Bloom Mountains in Co. Laois and flowing north, east and then south to join the Rivers Nore and Suir before entering Waterford Harbour 191 km (119 miles) from its source. After the Norman invasion the Barrow became an important trade conduit into the interior of Ireland, and most of the towns on it grew up around castles or monasteries established at fords or crossing-places. Later it became the boundary of the Pale, beyond which English law could not be enforced among the unruly natives.

When the navigable Barrow was linked by canal from Athy with the Grand Canal, via Monasterevin and Rathangan, the south-east of Ireland was linked into the commercial network created in the midlands by the Grand and Royal Canals. The last lock of the system, and the end of the towpath, is at the ancient monastic settlement of Saint Mullin's in Co. Carlow, where the Barrow becomes tidal.

The Barrow Way follows the canal and river towpaths of the Barrow and is 109 km (68 miles) long. It officially begins at Lowtown, near Robertstown, in Co. Kildare; for convenience, however, I describe the route from Robertstown onwards, making it possible to link the Grand Canal Way (see page 122) and the Barrow Way and walk from Ringsend in Dublin to Saint Mullin's.

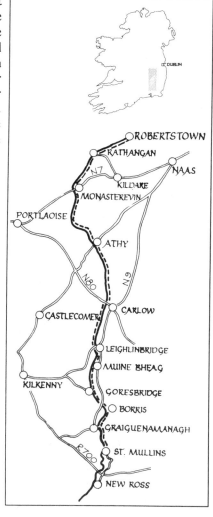

How to get there
Robertstown is 44 km (27 miles) from Dublin. The table no. 120 Dublin–Edenderry bus serves Brockagh Cross, 1.6 km (1 mile) north of Robertstown.

Maps and guides
The route is covered by the Ordnance Survey 1:127,000 (0.5 inch to 1 mile) map nos 16 and 19. The Inland Waterways Association (19 Duke Street, Dublin 2) have produced, with the assistance of the Office of Public Works, an excellent guide to the Barrow Line, and is available in most good bookshops.

Enquiries
Canals Section, The Office of Public Works, 51 St Stephen's Green, Dublin 2; telephone 01 6613111

Muine Bheag

STAGE 1: ROBERTSTOWN TO RATHANGAN

DISTANCE: 14 KM (8.75 MILES). WALKING TIME: 3.5 HOURS.

This section of the Kildare Way heads south-west with the canal, past Ballyteigue Castle into the open flatlands of Kildare, and on to the old town of Rathangan. Nearly 5 km (3 miles) are on tarmac roads, and the rest on good canal towpaths; it is a great route for a brisk walk on a summer's morning, when the herons, hawks and kingfishers which frequent the canal-side are active. There are some listed bed-and-breakfast houses in Rathangan, which has no public transport service.

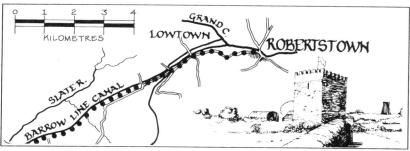

Leave Robertstown and follow the road on the south side of the canal westwards. A few minutes out of the village, the road parts company with the canal, and loops around past a late Georgian farmhouse with a fine doorcase and fanlight to rejoin the canal again.

Soon a tall bridge appears ahead and a public house called the Travellers Rest is passed. To the south, stark against the sky, the Hill of Allen with a tower on its summit comes into view, with its western flanks eaten away by quarrying. After a long straight stretch, the Milltown feeder canal which joins the Grand Canal here is crossed by Huband Bridge. A strange bridge this, with the inscription 'Huband Bridge 1788' engraved in stone on one side and a plaque stating 'Greene Bridge 1799' on the other.

A little further on, Ballyteigue Castle is reached, a tiny but solid-looking tower-house of probably the fifteenth century. It is said that Silken Thomas, the rebel son of the Earl of Kildare, took refuge here in 1535 shortly before his capture and eventual beheading at Tyburn. After Ballyteigue the route parts company with the tarmac, and follows the grassy towpath along the canal.

The canal now curves out into very open countryside on an embankment 6 m (19 feet) above the surrounding countryside. A few minutes after leaving the last houses at Cloncumber behind, the canal crosses the Griffith Aqueduct over a tributary stream of the Slate River, which parallels the canal about 0.8 km (0.5 mile) away. This is a great place for seeing herons, their dagger-like beaks at the ready as they stand sentinel at the stream's edge watching and waiting for a meal to come by. Soon the canal embankment begins to sweep around to the right, scrubland and patches of bog taking the place of the surrounding pastures.

The towpath here was well cropped by ponies and donkeys when I passed, making an excellent surface for walking. Like the 'Long Acre' of old, the open road where farmers put out their animals to graze, the canal banks must provide a particularly rich diet of grass and herbs.

Just before reaching a two-storey house between some red-roofed barns and the canal, an old canal milestone can be found to the left of the track. It has an Ordnance 'arrow' mark on its top, and on its two faces towards the canal is engraved 'To Dublin 24 mls' and 'To Monasterevin 7 mls'. Along here, some farmers own land on both sides of the canal, and to avoid the long detours (having to travel nearly 6.5 km (4 miles) to get twenty yards!), rectangular flat-bottomed boats, of a type that would not inspire me with confidence, are used and poled gondola-style across to the far bank.

Before long as a tall Late Georgian farmhouse comes into sight ahead, Glenaree Lock and Bridge are reached. This is a busy place in the summer season when the pleasure barges and boats are making their way to and from Rathangan. The lock-keeper here told me that upwards of one hundred and fifty craft would be expected to use this lock over the Easter weekend alone.

Leaving the bridge behind, the canal winds westwards towards what appears to be an inpenetrable wall of conifers. When I last passed here, the banks of the canal had just been rebuilt by dredging material from the canal bed, and the mucky ground was scattered with fresh-water clams, similar to the common otter shell one finds on the sea shore.

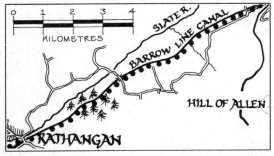

Soon a wide gap opens up in the wall of trees ahead, a broad reservation through which the canal passes. Here between the densely planted coniferous trees, a silence descends, broken only by the occasional twittering of blue tits and the indignant scolding of a disturbed wren. Down one of the forest fire-breaks when I passed I saw two foxes at play for a few moments, until seeing me, they melted into cover.

As the canal leaves the wood, the skyrocket-shaped tower of the church at Rathangan can be seen in the distance, and shortly afterwards the shapes of the great grain silos on the east of the town come into sight.

Rathangan is a pleasant, neat Georgian village that winds up a hill to where the original rath or ring-fort from which it takes its name can still be seen, ringed with beech trees beside the old church. Occupation of the place by the clan Uí Failge, as early as the sixth century, is recorded. The Fitzgeralds built a castle here in the twelfth century, which was visited by Edward Bruce of Scotland in 1315, and changed hands over and over again during the ensuing centuries until it was demolished two hundred years ago.

The present town was built up during the construction of the Barrow canal line in 1791, and it owes its charm in part to the many fine Georgian town houses erected then and still well preserved today. The Church of Ireland church is a fine Gothic revival building built on the site of an Anglo-Norman establishment, and the unusual old Italianate Catholic church, burnt down some time ago, has been refurbished as a community centre. The poet William A. Byrne and the author Maura Laverty were born in Rathangan.

Heron

STAGE 2: RATHANGAN TO MONASTEREVIN

DISTANCE: 11.2 KM (7 MILES). WALKING TIME: 2.75 HOURS.

This stage follows the canal from Rathangan through open countryside to Monasterevin, where although it crosses the Barrow by way of an aqueduct, it is still 24 km (15 miles) short of joining it at Athy. My own outstanding memory of this stretch, walked in July on comfortable if sometimes overgrown grassy towpaths, is of the abundance of wildflowers and orchids along the way, and the constantly perfumed air. Monasterevin has limited bed-and-breakfast accommodation, and is served by the table no. 124 bus (Dublin–Portlaoise–Mountmellick) and the table no. 8 and 12 Expressway Services between Dublin and Cork and Dublin and Limerick.

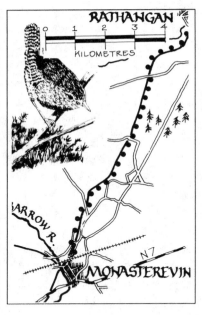

Crossing to the right-hand side of the canal after the bridge into the town, follow it south-westwards along a grassy towpath. The grey-slated roofs of Rathangan are clustered on the far side of the Slate River to the right, which is hidden from the canal bank by an overgrown meadow. Beyond, stately Georgian houses rise from the trees above the town.

Not far from the town the canal drops through the twenty-third lock and passes under Spencer Bridge, which bears a plaque stating the date of its erection, 1784. Note how the bridge has been built in such a way as to provide an extra few inches' space for the lock's balance beams to open fully. Beyond Spencer Bridge continue on the right-hand side, although for this stretch both sides are passable.

In the distance to the right now can be seen the cooling tower of the turf-burning power station at Portarlington, Co. Offaly, and beyond, the hill-like Slieve Bloom Mountains. Almost immediately the canal is in the open countryside, with very few houses in sight. In summertime, when I walked here, the canal was fringed with frothy blossoms of strong-perfumed meadowsweet, around which black lacy-winged damselflies flitted. Watch out for hares, hawks and herons, all of which were plentiful when I passed; in fact I saw twelve adult herons and five kestrels in the 11 km (7 miles) between Rathangan and Monasterevin.

The towpath soon deteriorates into a path, winding through long grass, which in summertime, although rich in wildflowers, can be very wet. This linear meadow following the canal must be similar to pastures in the old days, long before the use of fertilisers became common. In addition to a wide variety of flowers, look out for spotted orchids, pyramidal orchids and the tall purple spears of the unusual-smelling fragrant orchid.

Just before reaching Wilson's Bridge, the towpath veers a little away from the canal and follows a green boreen, before reaching a gate onto the road. From the crown of the bridge Dunmurray Hill can be seen to the east while the Slieve Bloom Mountains and the cooling tower at Portarlington are now quite clear to the south-west. Cross the bridge and continue on the left bank of the canal along a grassy track.

Soon a wedge of coniferous wood, fringed by a cordon of birch and ash, is passed on the left; there is a heronry in this wood, so it is a good place to see the birds. The boundary with Co. Offaly is less than a kilometre to the west now. After the wood the tall shape of the next bridge on the canal, Umeras Bridge, comes into sight, and as it is approached extensive patches of yellow water lilies in the still waters protected by clusters of reeds can be seen. Just before the bridge there is a marvellously photogenic thatched cottage nestling in the trees.

From Umeras Bridge looking towards the south-west, Ballythomas Hill and Kilteale Hill, the first of a string of limestone hillocks west of the town of Stradbally, called 'hums' by geologists, are in sight. Continue southwards along the left bank of the canal, leaving good farmland behind, replaced by boggy meadows and copses of trees. The next bridge is McCartney's Bridge, beside which is a scenic cluster of cottages including the lock-keeper's, dating from 1784. Crossing to the right bank of the canal now, continue south towards Monasterevin, a little over 1.5 km (1 mile) away.

A few hundred yards beyond McCartney's Bridge on the left bank is a substantial mill complex, with some Georgian features such as a fine door-case and fanlight, suggesting how long it has operated here. A little distance after the mill, the tower of the church in Monasterevin is in sight ahead. At the next bridge, called High Bridge, cross over to the left bank, and follow the road past Ballykelly Gaelic Football Club into Monasterevin. On the edge of town, past the derelict canal harbour, there is an unusual density of bridges as the Barrow River, the Grand Canal, the railway line and the Portarlington road all converge. An unusual feature here is the curious counter-balanced steel lifting-bridge over the canal, operated manually by the lock-keeper.

The stage ends here where the Barrow Way follows the canal towpath as it swings around to the right and is taken across the Barrow River by an aqueduct. A broad street parallel to the river, lined on one side by a tall terrace of Georgian houses, and on the other by their gardens, leads a short distance to the centre of the town. In one of these gardens is a monument to Gerard Manley Hopkins, a native of the town. Further along is a plaque commemorating a local priest who was hanged from a tree shortly after the 1798 Rising, for ministering to the rebels.

In the sixth century, St Evin of Cashel, one of the ruling Eoghanacht sept of Munster, founded a monastery near here, from which Monasterevin takes its name. The settlement had probably fallen into disuse by the twelfth century, when the Cistercians built an abbey 1.5 km (1 mile) to the south, on land granted to them by Diarmaid Ó Díomasaigh, King of Offaly, where the local 'big house', Moore Abbey, now stands.

Originally, the village grew up around the commerce brought by the Cistercian monastery; after the suppression it hibernated for a couple of centuries, passing into the ownership of Viscount Loftus of Ely and then the Moore family. The Grand Canal reached Monasterevin in 1776, and the town was linked by canal to the River Barrow at Athy in 1791, each of which developments brought a new lease of life to the place.

The Irish tenor, Count John McCormack, leased Moore Abbey between 1927 and 1942, during which time many well-known international figures such as the boxer Gene Tunney, the opera singer Lucrezia Bori, and the evangelist Bishop Fulton Sheen, came for visits. Some scenes from the Hollywood movie John McCormack starred in, *Song of my Heart*, were filmed on the banks of the Barrow at Moore Abbey.

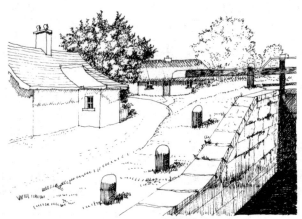

At McCartney's Bridge

40

STAGE 3: MONASTEREVIN TO ATHY

DISTANCE: 22.5 KM (14 MILES). WALKING TIME: 5.5 HOURS.

Almost half of this stage is on tarred side-roads and the rest on grassy towpaths. For those who wish to cover a shorter distance, the pleasant village of Vicarstown, which has accommodation, marks the half-way point of the stage.

At the time of writing Athy has limited bed-and-breakfast accommodation, so it might be prudent to book ahead if you wish to stay there. The town is served by the table no. 7 Dublin–Clonmel Expressway bus, and is on the main Dublin–Waterford rail link.

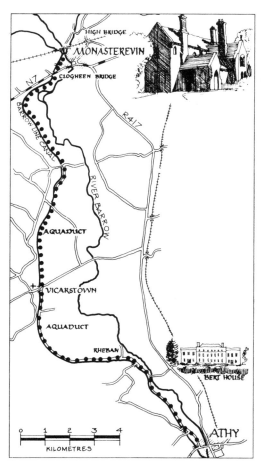

Although the Barrow proper is met at Monasterevin, the river is not navigable until it reaches Athy, so the Barrow Way continues to follow the Barrow Canal for this stage. The left bank of the canal is followed across the aqueduct over the river. The aqueduct was built in 1826 when a plan was being considered to connect the coal-mining town of Castlecomer, nearly 48 km (30 miles) to the south, with the Barrow line. The plan was never carried out, although a 20 km (12.5 mile) section was opened to Portarlington in 1830.

Heading south, the route crosses Moore's Bridge to the right bank of the canal before meeting the main Limerick road, after which it reverts to the left bank. Soon the noise of traffic is left behind as the path becomes a grassy track decorated with daisies, yarrow and mint, and passes from Co. Kildare into Co. Laois. Along here the western bank is thickly wooded, with hazel, willow and ash trees heavily

41

overhanging the canal. The thick cover provides living quarters for many shy herons, which can often be glimpsed ahead, rising on their great wings and wheeling away as they are approached.

At Fisherstown Bridge the road that crosses the canal is said to follow one of the ancient routes across Ireland. Where it crosses the Barrow 1.5 km (1 mile) to the east, the bridge is called Belan Bridge, from the Irish 'bialann', suggesting that once there was the equivalent of a roadside eating-house here. After Fisherstown Bridge the towpath becomes a tarred road again as far as Courtwood Bridge, less than 1.5 km (1 mile) further on. One of the limestone hillocks to the south-west provides the spectacular setting for the extensive but ruined fortress of Dunamase, scene of many sieges and battles until destroyed by the Cromwellians in 1650. To the west the Slieve Bloom Mountains rise blue from the horizon, and in clear weather the Wicklow Mountains and their highest summit, Lugnaquillia, can be seen to the east.

Soon the towpath is a grassy track again, following the canal over a tributary of the Barrow by the Grattan Aqueduct, named after Henry Grattan. The nineteenth-century parliamentarian had a residence nearby at Dunrally, built within a great Iron Age ring-fort, on the banks of the Barrow. The canal water along here was perfectly clear when I passed, displaying a luxuriant growth of water plants carpeting the shallow bottom.

Less than 2.5 km (1.5 miles) after crossing the aqueduct the towpath reaches Vicarstown. Formerly a canal harbour of some importance, as the picturesque group of disused stone warehouses suggests, Vicarstown is today a pretty hamlet, with two fine pubs, Turley's and Crean's, one on each side of the canal. Crean's also provides bed-and-breakfast accommodation. To the south-west at a distance of 6.5 km (4 miles) lies the town of Stradbally.

After Vicarstown the towpath follows a tarred road for much of the remaining 11.25 km (7 miles) into Athy. Two of the 'hums' noticed earlier, Kilteale Hill and Hewson Hill (the latter named after the commander of the Cromwellian force that 'slighted' or de-roofed Dunamase Castle), are now clearly visible to the right, while ahead, tree-covered Bawn Hill rises from the flat countryside. The canal crosses another aqueduct 1.5 km (1 mile) from Vicarstown, this one over the Stradbally River.

Ballymanus Bridge is passed before the canal loops round towards the east and crosses the county border back into Kildare. After about 1.5 km (1 mile), past a residence called Rheban Cottage, look out for a tower-house incorporated into a farmhouse a few hundred metres from the road. Built in the fourteenth century, the tower-house was held by Eoghan Rua Ó Néill (Owen Roe O'Neill) during the Confederacy wars in the 1640s. In the early twentieth century, during construction work on the farmhouse that adjoins the castle, a skeleton hand was found in the wall clasping half a dozen coins of fifteenth-century date!

After Bert Bridge, across rich farmland and the hidden Barrow can be seen the broad expanse of Bert House, a seven-bayed Georgian mansion. Soon the industrial buildings of Athy come into sight ahead, and the town is entered shortly after.

Like other towns along the Barrow, Athy grew up around a ford, and the subsequent Norman fortifications were built to protect this. The first bridge was built over the Barrow in 1417; the current one, overlooked by White's Castle, dates from 1706. Its age seems to be confirmed by the shining glass-like finish of the little limestone seat built into the parapet, polished by almost three hundred years of travellers' backsides!

White's Castle, Athy

STAGE 4: ATHY TO CARLOW

DISTANCE: 21 KM (13 MILES). WALKING TIME: 5.25 HOURS.
The Barrow River is finally joined here at Athy, to take the Way out of Co. Kildare and into the northern part of Ireland's second-smallest county, Carlow.

Carlow is an ideal centre for exploring the midlands, and has an independent hostel as well as a good range of guesthouses, hotels and restaurants. The town is served by train from Dublin and by the table no. 130 Dublin–Kilkenny bus and the table no. 4 Dublin–Waterford Expressway bus.

At Athy the towpath finally joins the River Barrow, not seen since it was crossed by aqueduct at Monasterevin. Leaving Crom Dhu bridge in the centre of the town—named after the ancient god Crom Dubh—follow a footpath through an attractive linear park along the east bank. The towpath is rejoined beyond a narrow stone bridge called the Horse Bridge, where in the old days the horses that towed the barges crossed.

The Barrow was made navigable by excavating short sections of canal or 'lock cuts' around places where the river flowed over rapids, terminating in locks to take vessels down to the lower level. After a railway bridge the first of these canal sections is met, and the towpath follows the canal. Between the canal and the river here is a broad thistle-covered island, teeming with goldfinches and reed warblers when I passed. A counter-weighted lifting-bridge further on gives access to the island, shortly after which the canal rejoins the river after dropping through Ardreigh Lock.

Soon the river becomes slow moving, flowing broad and glass-like through a landscape of rich meadows and fields of barley that stretches into the distance on all sides.

About forty-five minutes out of Athy the roar of a weir can be heard as the next section of canal is reached. At over 3 km (2 miles), this stretch leading to Levittstown Lock is the longest lock cut on the Barrow. The long island created can be reached by frequent bridges, and from the first of these, a narrow livestock bridge, Mount Leinster can be seen to the south-east.

The towpath for a while becomes a pleasant boreen with a screen of young trees separating it from the canal. When I passed here I walked through a sea of yellow ragwort, each flower-head covered with black-and-yellow-striped cinnamon caterpillars. To my delight, an otter burst out of a clump of reeds ahead of me and bounded across the path and into the water without a splash.

After passing a road bridge Levittstown Lock is reached, beyond which are the remains of a massive six-storey castellated malting mill, burned down in 1942. As the river meanders out into the open again the bank of pastured hills to the west of Carlow town comes into sight ahead.

The next bridge, Maganey Bridge, is a fine seven-arch stone construction, with granite-ringed circular niches over each buttress. To the left a couple of hundred metres away is a shop and a pub called the Three Counties, referring to the fact that Laois, Kildare and Carlow meet close by.

The towpath continues past Maganey Lock and enters Co. Carlow. Here when I passed, I saw my first kingfishers since leaving Monasterevin, shocking iridescent blue flashes rocketing past, just above the river's surface. Herons I had met frequently, and I had learnt to look out for one at each weir, where they like to stand awaiting fish ascending the cascade. By this stage I was becoming used to water-hens also and their flapping, splashing, panic-stricken escapes to the far bank on my approach.

Two tributaries join the river along this stretch, the Greese and the Lerr, and the towpath is carried over them by humped-back bridges. The river broadens out soon after crossing the Lerr, the opposite bank an impenetrable jungle-like wilderness. As the river sweeps round to the right, the tall chimney of Carlow's sugar factory comes into view over the trees. On the opposite bank can be seen a nineteenth-century mansion called Knockbeg House, now a boarding-school run by a religious order.

After another section of canal is passed the Carlow sugar factory is in view ahead, with a church spire in the background. It is hard visually or aurally to ignore the factory, as the towpath passes within a hundred metres of the massive buildings, but once we are clear of it the approach to Carlow town is very fine indeed, sweeping peacefully and gently to the right towards the slender spire of St Mary's Church.

After an ancient burial ground called the 'Graves', which slopes down to the river's edge, the river bears round to the right to reach the old town centre, dominated by the surprisingly massive bulk of what remains of Carlow Castle.

Carlow is a bustling midland town serving an extensive area of rich farmland. Like the other towns on the Barrow, it grew up around a river crossing-point, where in 1180 a motte-and-bailey was built by the Norman knight Hugh de Lacy. Early in the twelfth century a substantial castle, the ruins of which now tower over the old town, was built by William Marshall, and subsequently, as Carlow grew in importance as a Pale frontier town, the expanding settlement was walled. Carlow was frequently attacked by the native Irish, and Norman officials who were obliged to settle in the town had to be paid danger money! The town changed hands regularly over the centuries, and was burned to the ground twice. After surviving centuries of military action, Carlow Castle was almost completely destroyed in 1814 when, in an attempt to refurbish it as a mental asylum, explosives were used to enlarge the windows, resulting in the collapse of most of the building.

Carlow County Library was once the property of George Bernard Shaw, who inherited the building from his great-grandfather, Thomas Gurley. In his later years he signed over the building to the urban district council as a gift, saying he thought of himself as an absentee landlord, having spent only one day out of his eighty-eight years in the town!

The Old Gaol, Carlow

STAGE 5: CARLOW TO MUINE BHEAG

Distance: 20 km (12.5 miles). Walking time: 5 hours.

This stage can be broken at Leighlinbridge, 13.5 km (8.5 miles) from Carlow, where there is a good pub and restaurant called the Lord Bagenal. A grassy towpath on the west bank of the river is followed (with a brief interruption at Milford) as far as Leighlinbridge, and for the last few kilometres to Muine Bheag the towpath reverts to the east bank.

There are a number of registered guesthouses in Muine Bheag, which is served by train from Dublin and by the table no. 130 Dublin–Kilkenny bus.

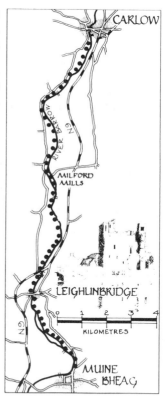

Leaving Carlow, cross the old bridge to Graigue (also called Graiguecullen) and, turning immediately left, follow the towpath past the old warehouses and the Carlow Lock. Soon the towpath crosses the county border into Laois, and the river follows a series of wide and lazy meanders. The first lock after Carlow, Clogrennan Lock, has gates made from steel, which do not have the same look of robustness as the old timber ones. Just beyond a fine curved harbour after the lock is a strange quadrangular structure with round towers at each corner, growing out of what looks like a late eighteenth-century house.

The river now bears round to the left, and Cloydagh Church, built in 1801, appears on a promontory ahead, beside its finely sited presbytery. Off to the right now is Clogrennan Demesne, where the ruins of Clogrennan Castle, scene of many battles in the sixteenth and seventeenth centuries, can be found. Near here the defeated King James is said to have encamped on his way south after his defeat at the Battle of the Boyne.

At Milford the massive and castellated Alexander's Mill comes into sight on the eastern bank. In the early nineteenth century this was a busy harbour, where a hundred people were employed in malting and in the corn mills. Nearby were coal mines and lime quarries, which provided additional cargoes for the barges. In 1891 Carlow was the first inland town in Ireland to have electric street lighting, and it was at the hydroelectric station in this building at Milltown that the electricity was generated. In 1990 a new turbine in the refurbished mill went into operation, feeding power into the national grid.

The Barrow Way

Follow the road and canal past the bridge over the Barrow, and a couple of hundred metres on, the route passes through a brick-arched gateway and crosses the canal by a lifting-bridge. Nearby is a white house called The Locks, where accommodation can be obtained.

Soon a substantial wooded island divides the river again, and when the island is passed, Mount Leinster can be seen in the distance straight ahead. Nearly 1 km (0.5 mile) away on higher ground, traffic whizzes to and fro on the main Carlow road. When I walked this stretch I was glad it had been recently mown, as the wide cut was bounded by walls of shoulder-high nettles.

Shortly after another island is passed, the Leighlinstown by-pass bridge can be seen ahead, and beyond it rises the tower of Leighlinbridge Church. Before reaching the by-pass, the river goes over another weir and the towpath bears round to the right to follow the canal past Rathvinden Lock and under the road to reach the village of Leighlinbridge.

Leighlinbridge is an immaculate narrow-streeted village that somehow survived being on the main Dublin road until the by-pass was built in the 1980s. The southern side of its buttressed bridge, garlanded with great clumps of pink-flowered valerian when I passed, dates from 1320; it may have been the first bridge to be built across the Barrow. It is very likely that King Richard II led his tired and hungry army across this very bridge in 1399 in pursuit of Art MacMurrough Kavanagh's guerrilla forces.

The bridge at Leighlinbridge is overlooked by Black Castle, dating from the fifteenth century but built on the site of a Norman castle of 1181. Some of the bawn walls of the castle, and possibly the original bawn gate, can be seen just off the street on its east side.

The Barrow towpath leaves Leighlinbridge on the east bank along a path like a well-kept linear lawn. A few minutes out of the village Mount Leinster with its television mast appears again off to the left. On the west bank, but not visible from the river, is the earthen-banked hill-fort of Dionn Rí (Dinn Rig), ancient citadel of Leinster.

A short distance out of Leighlinbridge the roar of a weir is heard, and the river divides again, the towpath following a canal section. A fine brick-arched livestock bridge connecting the central island is passed, and soon afterwards the public road to Muine Bheag can be seen a couple of hundred metres to the left. Rathellan Lock is reached before the river bears round in a broad sweep towards the town of Muine Bheag, the needle-like spire of its church rising above the skyline.

Muine Bheag was founded near the end of the eighteenth century by Walter Bagenal; although Muine Bheag is now its official name, most people still refer to it as Bagenalstown. Walter Bagenal wanted the architecture of his new town to rival Versailles, but the rerouting of the coach road that passed through the place must have dampened his ardour. Although it is a very pleasant town, the only remnants of Bagenal's dream are some fine Late Georgian houses and the broad Doric portico of the courthouse overlooking the Barrow.

STAGE 6: MUINE BHEAG TO BORRIS

DISTANCE: 18.5 KM (11.5 MILES). WALKING TIME: 4.75 HOURS.
Borris is not on the Barrow but about 2.5 km (1.5 miles) to the east of the river. The town of Goresbridge, Co. Kilkenny, is passed 10.5 km (6.5 miles) out of Muine Bheag. Bed-and-breakfast is available in Borris, and for those who need something more than pub grub, Step House on the main street is an excellent restaurant. Borris has no scheduled bus service.

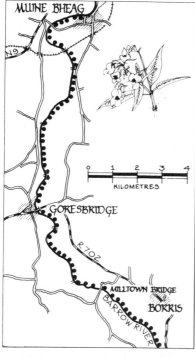

The Barrow Way leaves Muine Bheag along quays that suggest what a busy harbour it was in the heyday of the canals. Past the lifting-bridge at Muine Bheag Lock is a functioning water mill.

A few minutes out of Muine Bheag a great mansion called Malcolm Villa can be seen overlooking its heavily treed demesne on high ground on the far side of the river. A little further on there is a return to the prosaic as Muine Bheag's noisy meat processing factory is passed on the left.

Now pass beneath Royal Oak Bridge as the river swings round to the left and south, its banks a profusion of balsam when I passed, into whose cover numerous waterhens hurried as I approached. Nearly thirty minutes out of Muine Bheag the river passes under a limestone railway viaduct, on the far side of which Brandon Hill, which will overlook the rest of the route as far as Saint Mullin's, comes into view.

The towns, bridges and locks of the Barrow Way, and particularly the locks, are the punctuation marks of our walk. The lock-keepers' cottages, built over two hundred years ago, all vary, with no two the same. Many of them are today unfortunately in a state of ruin, roofless and overgrown. The cottage at the next lock on the Barrow, however, Fenniscourt Lock, is one of the exceptions. It is a comfortable and homely little place, almost lost under a cloak of ivy, with a garden gateway bridged with roses leading to its bright red front door. The grass around the lock is lawn-like in its neatness, and the little island between the canal and the river has a row of nine great old plum trees.

The next lock, nearly 2.5 km (1.5 miles) further on, also has an ivy-covered cottage, but this one is in a sad state of ruin. The far bank, a heavily wooded demesne with tall specimen trees, is now in Co. Kilkenny. At the next weir nearly 1 km (0.5 mile) further on is an exquisite Georgian farmhouse called Barraghcore House, surrounded by lawned gardens that slope down to the far river bank. Beside it is a great stone-built mill with a castellated parapet and a disused malting kiln, a high, square building made of brick and stone.

Soon there are glimpses of Mount Leinster over to the left and Brandon Hill straight ahead, before Upper Ballyellan Lock is reached, and a promenade-like towpath follows the river into the village of Goresbridge.

An old church with a pinnacled tower, standing overlooking the river, is a lone representative of Goresbridge's past as the village is approached; the place seems surrounded by busy and prosperous-looking industrial plants. There are a few pubs in the neat main street, some of which serve sandwiches and tea.

After Goresbridge and Lower Ballyellan Lock are passed, the river is forced towards the south-east by the first outcrop of high ground in its way since it turned south at Monasterevin. From here on, the valley of the Barrow narrows increasingly as the river flows south to squeeze between Brandon Hill and the southern Blackstairs Mountains, the many-pinnacled ridge of which comes into view as the next meander of the river is rounded.

When I passed here in August the river banks were a profusion of butterflies, of which painted ladies and peacocks gave the best displays, gliding for long stretches on the still air and performing elegantly bobbing mating aerobatics. A startlingly black mink crossed the track in front of me about twenty metres ahead, paused, and looked at me for a moment before slinking nonchalantly into the long grass on the landward side of the towpath.

Fifteen minutes after passing Ballyteigelea Lock the bridge over which the road to Borris passes comes into sight ahead. To get to the village, pass under the bridge, climb to the road, and follow it for nearly 1 km (0.5 mile). Borris Idrone (it is pronounced 'Burris' locally) is an attractive village of fine cut-stone houses and cottages. At the top of the main street are the imposing castellated gates of Borris House, seat of the MacMurrough Kavanagh clan, one-time kings of Leinster. One of the most colourful characters in the family was Arthur MacMurrough Kavanagh who, despite being born in 1831 with six-inch stumps in place of arms and legs, was an expert horseman, marksman, fisherman and yachtsman, in addition to being a Member of Parliament, Lord Lieutenant of County Carlow, and a magistrate. He was known to hold his magistrate's court in the courtyard of Borris House, enthroned on a stone seat, wrapped in a long black cloak and with a pet bear on a chain. He was a benevolent if conservative landlord, and was responsible for much of the village of Borris as it is today.

STAGE 7: BORRIS TO ST MULLIN'S

DISTANCE: 19 KM (12 MILES). WALKING TIME: 4.75 HOURS.

This last stage takes you via the historic town of Graiguenamanagh, to the ancient monastic settlement of Saint Mullin's. Graiguenamanagh is 12 km (7.5 miles) from Borris and well worth exploring. If you are taking your time you might like to divide this stage in two, staying overnight at Graigue, which has bed-and-breakfast accommodation. The only accommodation at St Mullin's is Mrs O'Dwyer's Teach Moling, a picturesque, rambling old house on the river bank, where a stream tumbles through a rock garden into the Barrow. Mrs O'Dwyer also runs a small restaurant and specialises in excellent fresh salmon dinners. St Mullin's has no scheduled bus service.

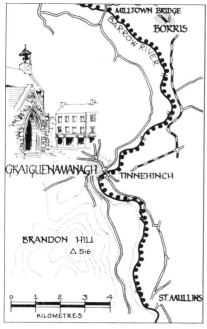

Return to Milltown Bridge from Borris, and follow the towpath southwards on a broad grassy path, which gets flatter and more like a lawn the nearer you get to Graigue. The silver, silent Barrow is a soothing influence for most of the way, although shortly after leaving the bridge, the growing roar of a weir can be heard ahead. Past the weir a narrow island divides the rushing river from a quiet canal stretch, which the towpath follows up to the stone-built channel and sturdy timbers of Borris Lock. Near the lock-keeper's cottage a track leads up through the wooded demesne of Borris House to the village. Fishermen can be met at any point along here, casting out into the water, and often with two or more rods spread out near them. Good-sized trout can be taken on this stretch, as well as bream, rudd, perch and pike.

For over 1.5 km (1 mile) the towpath is bordered on the left by the woods of Borris House demesne, then the trees begin to thin out beyond where the Dinin stream, tumbling down to the Barrow through moss-covered boulders, is crossed by a stone-built three-arch bridge.

The next lock is Ballingrane, from the Gaelic Baile na Greine or the Place of the Sun, and it certainly lived up to its name the morning I passed, when the picturesque, dormered lock-keeper's cottage was festooned with the thick pink flowers of wild raspberry. Although derelict, the house was in good condition inside, and passing fishermen who used it for shelter had scratched records of their catches in the soft lime plaster of the porch. From these I learned that a P. Brooks caught fourteen fish on 14 April 1987, and a P. Roe had a bag of twenty-seven in July 1988, while in 1989, during the rod-licence dispute, a B. McGarry left a sad and brief note, 'not able to fish'.

Soon a wrecked river-barge appears perched on the far bank, prow in the air and sinuous helm nearest the river's edge. One wonders at the stormy conditions that must have prevailed the day or night this heavy forty foot craft took its last voyage.

As the river now broadens, a conifer-crowned ridge ahead blocks the way south, and it swings around towards the west as the next weir, and a canal section leading to the much photographed Clashganna Lock, come into sight. The public road comes close to the Barrow here, 60 m (196 feet) or more above the canal.

After Clashganna, the Barrow broadens out, coaxed into a new south-westerly direction by a steep, craggy tree-clad cliff. Near the next lock, Ballykeenan Lock, the ivy-covered ruins of a medieval tower-house can be seen on the far bank. The wealth of shrubs, trees and wildflowers along the banks here ensure a colourful journey whatever time of year you happen to pass; when I passed, showers of snowy may-blossom covered the thorn bushes, and the gorse was already in startling yellow flower, filling the air with its coconut fragrance. Later in the year the acres and acres of yellow flags in places along the riverside make a spectacular show.

Brandon Hill comes briefly into view ahead as the Barrow curves around a bend called the Devil's Elbow, on its last few hundred metres into Graiguenamanagh, the slated roofs of which are dominated by the bulk of Duiske Abbey. Arriving at Tinnehinch, the little village on the Carlow side of the river, the fine old seven-arch bridge has to be crossed to reach the town of Graiguenamanagh in Co. Kilkenny. The design of the bridge is attributed to the architect George Semple, among whose other works still existing are the spire of St Patrick's Cathedral and St Patrick's Hospital in Dublin, the latter built using funds bequeathed by Jonathan Swift and completed in 1749.

If you have time to spare, Graiguenamanagh is well worth exploring. The name means 'the Grange of the Monks', and the present town has grown up from an extensive Cistercian abbey which was founded here in 1207 by William Marshall, Earl of Pembroke, a veteran of the Crusades. He inherited the title Earl of Pembroke and extensive lands in Wales and Ireland by marrying the daughter of Richard de Clare, or Strongbow, who led the Norman invasion of Ireland. Strongbow himself had come into ownership of the Irish lands by marrying Aoife, daughter of Diarmuid MacMurrough, King of Leinster, who had been instrumental in bringing about the Norman invasion.

Funding the establishment of a Cistercian settlement was the most practical way in those days to exploit undeveloped countryside, turning it from a wilderness into productive farmland. The abbey church built here was the biggest Cistercian church in Ireland, and although the building was mainly constructed from local stone and timber, the decorative stonework is a yellow limestone shipped here specially from Dundry Hill in Somersetshire.

Graigue is a town of narrow winding streets and decorative shopfronts, its people clearly very conscious of the history and antiquity of their place. Their concern for the character of the town is evidenced by the care with which the older buildings, their features and decoration, are maintained, and only a relatively small amount of poor contemporary work is to be seen.

The abbey church and its grounds are well worth a visit. The Cistercian abbey was dissolved in 1536, and the town absorbed the extensive buildings bit by bit; there is hardly a house or shop within a hundred metres of the church today, particularly on the river side, that did not utilise sections of wall of the original abbey. The church was restored rather badly in the nineteenth century, destroying remains of the original vaulting and columns that got in the way. A 'rescue' restoration was carried out in the 1980s, which, although not going very far, re-establishes something of what was before.

Leaving Graiguenamanagh, follow the towpath along the east side of the river, past a quayside often busy and bustling in summertime, when it is lined with moored barges and launches pausing for a while in their trips up or down the river. Behind the lock-keeper's cottage at Tinnehinch Lock, hidden by the trees, is a ruined castle, built in the fifteenth century to guard an ancient bridge that spanned the Barrow at this point before the present bridge was built. This castle, called Tigh na hInse (House on the River Bank), gave Tinnehinch its name.

A great bank of trees clothes the steeply rising ground on the far side of the Barrow now. The north-eastern slopes of the granite outcrop that is Brandon Hill force the river to turn eastwards for a while, towards the Blackstairs Mountains. In places bare, rounded rocks rise above the surface of the water in midstream as the defile of the Barrow narrows to become a great gorge. The summit of Brandon Hill is visible most of the time now, over the treetops on the far bank.

At Carriglead Lock the former keeper's cottage has been beautifully restored and extended. Not far beyond the lock, look out for a granite boulder at the side of the towpath shaped and placed exactly like a seat, overlooking the river. The waters of the Barrow are flowing with more haste now, as if sensing the nearness of the sea, and one wonders at the difficulties the bargemen had to deal with coming upstream. For stretches such as these, winches sited along the river bank were used to wind the barges up, metre by metre.

About 6.5 km (4 miles) from Graiguenamanagh the last lock on the Barrow navigation system, called the Sea Lock—although the sea is still a long way off—is reached. After this point the river rises and falls with the tide reaching upstream from Waterford Harbour. To celebrate its importance, the lock-keeper's cottage here is quite a ceremonial little building, with a stone pediment-like gable and a simply decorated central doorway.

After the next bend, what remains of industrial St Mullin's, a disused mill, comes into view, beyond which a terrace of white-painted houses curves down to the shrubs and ornamental trees of the park-like river bank. Here at St Mullin's the towpath ends; the gorge through which the Barrow flows is so narrow and wooded that it is no longer possible to follow the river bank.

St Mullin's is a magical place, some of the magic coming from the ambience of its riverside location and the rest emanating from the ruined churches and ecclesiastical buildings in the graveyard high above the river. It is said that the well-preserved Norman motte-and-bailey near the graveyard, constructed in the early 1170s, was built on the site of a prehistoric tumulus, evidence of the religious significance of St Mullin's in pre-Christian times.

St Brendan is said to have selected the riverside site for a monastery, Christianising the pagan shrine; the nearby and dominating Brandon Hill, once a centre for celebrating the pagan festival of Lúnasa, is named after him. St Moling, who founded the monastery, was said to be of the blood of Leinster kings, and is documented as being Archbishop of Ferns in the year 632.

St Mullin's

4

THE BEARA WAY

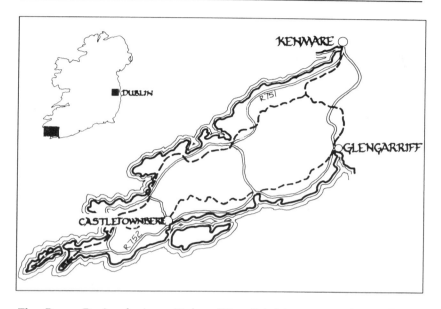

The Beara Peninsula is a 48 km (30 mile) long, mountainous finger stretching into the Atlantic from south-west Ireland, shared by Counties Cork and Kerry. Lesser known than its neighbours the Iveragh and Dingle Peninsulas, it is, like them, a magical world of mountains and lakes surrounded by a picturesque sea coast. The extremities of the peninsula are remote and unspoiled, and it is only the existence of Castletownbere's busy fishing industry that has brought the place into the twentieth century. Castletownbere would not be what it is today but for the existence of Bere Haven, a deep and protected sound between Bere Island and the mainland, where the British Atlantic fleet used to anchor in times gone by. Today you are more likely to see a fleet of eastern European Fish Factory ships moored there in wintertime; when I was there I counted no less than twenty-eight great vessels at anchor. A local person told me that the town's population is often swelled by 5,000 or more by these ships. The Beara is home to a friendly people, most of whom, to the visitor, seem to be called O'Sullivan, and those that are not are Harringtons!

The Beara Way is a circuit of the peninsula following side-roads, boreens, bog roads and mountain tracks, taking in all that is special about the place. While there are a few stretches along the very edge of the Atlantic, one is never very far, even on the mountainous parts, from the sea, and the route includes a thrill unique to the Beara—a spin over the sea in a tiny cable-car. I found the stretch from Kenmare to Bonane a long and monotonous bit of tarmac, and I suggest the alternative signed route, via Dromaghty Lake to Bonane, which I describe, is preferable.

How to Get There
Glengarriff is 320 km (200) miles from Dublin and 90 km (56 miles) from Cork, and is well served by Bus Éireann.

Maps and Guides
Discovery Series map nos 84 and 85, and *The Beara Mapguide*, published by Cork/Kerry Tourism cover the route.

Enquiries
Beara Tourism and Development Association, Castletownbere, Co. Cork; telephone 027 70054

Ard na Gaoithe, Bere Island

STAGE 1: GLENGARRIFF TO ADRIGOLE

DISTANCE: 16.8 KM (10.5 MILES). AGGREGATE CLIMB: 231 M (750 FEET). WALKING TIME: 5 HOURS.

Starting in scenic Glengarriff, this first stage introduces walkers to the wildness of the Beara mountains, taking them up through a pass between Sugarloaf (575 m—1,887 ft) and Gowlbeg (359 m—1,178 ft), and along an old medieval road with great views out across Bantry Bay before descending to the village of Adrigole. 8.8 km (5.5 miles) of the stage are on tarmac, 2.4 km (1.5 miles) on boreen/track, and 5.6 km (3.5 miles) on mountain paths. Glengarriff has a good range of bed-and-breakfast accommodation, an independent hostel open part of the year, and plenty of places to eat. Johnny Barry's pub, among others, serves good food all day at very reasonable prices. There is some bed-and-breakfast accommodation in the Adrigole area, but limited opportunities for evening meals, so arrangements should be made in advance. Glengarriff is served by the table no. 44 Cork–Killarney Expressway bus and the table no. 46 Cork–Glengarriff Expressway bus. Adrigole is served by a local bus (O'Donaghue's), and by an extension of the table no. 46 Expressway bus on Fridays and Sundays.

The grandeur of the manner in which the mountains meet the sea at the head of Bantry Bay, in a wonderland of rocky, wooded islets, has made Glengarriff a tourist attraction since travel for pleasure became popular. It's a colourful place, with old-fashioned shops with display-shelves covered in oil cloth, and a pub called the Blue Loo! William Makepeace Thackeray, William Butler Yeats and George Bernard Shaw are among the writers that have stayed here; the latter stayed at Eccles Hotel, founded in the eighteenth century and still doing business, a warm and comfortable place where you may be served oysters on the house when you buy a drink!

The Beara Way leaves Glengarriff following the L61 towards the serrated profile of Shrone Hill, crossing a bridge over the Glengarriff River. A hundred metres downstream are the picturesque remains of an older structure called Cromwell's Bridge, although it is doubtful that the Protector ever got this far. Local tradition has it, however, that the Cromwellian army transported

57

heavy guns across the river here en route to Castletownbere and Dursey.

Further out the road, Glengarriff Harbour comes into view to the left, with its centrepiece, Garnish Island. Garnish is an exquisite paradise of magnolias, rhododendrons and camellias, a small masterpiece of garden design, established by a man named Annan Bryce in the early twentieth century and designed by Harold Pinto. Boat trips can be arranged to visit this fantasia of miniature Japanese gardens, martello tower, pavilions and lily ponds, where George Bernard Shaw's play *St Joan*, first performed in New York in 1923, was written.

A little over 2.4 km (1.5 miles) out of Glengarriff the route turns off the main road, taking a narrow road to the right that rises and falls like a roller-coaster as it penetrates westwards into the Magannagan Valley. Great bulbous outcrops of bedrock, clothed in rhododendrons and gorse, protrude from the ground on all sides like dug-in dinosaurs. To the right, the sheer bare rock of Shrone Hill's flanks form the northern side of the valley, while to the left and ahead are two cone-shaped hills, Gowlbeg and Sugarloaf, between which the Beara Way passes.

A little more than 1.6 km (1 mile) up the track the route goes left and passes the lonely, reed-fringed Magannagan Loughs. Peat cuttings in this area have exposed the roots of pine trees that grew here before the bog formed, over four thousand years ago. The track climbs slowly to pass through a small wood of birch and conifer, where pine martens have been seen in recent years. These rare and beautiful creatures, resembling a large stoat or weasel, are carnivores and prey on rodents and small birds. The pine marten's mating procedure is a long drawn-out and spectacular affair with lots of growling, squeaking and purring as the male drags the female from place to place by the scruff of the neck!

The pathway meanders upwards through a scattered coniferous plantation towards the pass between Sugarloaf and Gowlbeg. A spectacular high waterfall, the infant Magannagan stream, can be seen and heard on the right as the route ascends into very dramatic terrain, below the towering bare grey rockfaces of the Sugarloaf.

At the pass, a great view across Bantry Bay opens up, as the track, indistinct in places and very boggy when I walked, bears around towards the south-west. Whiddy Island, on the far side of the bay, stretches long and flat, while ahead, Bear Island comes into view. Across the bay Sheeps Head stretches into the Atlantic, behind which Mount Gabriel and Knocknamadree, the two highest points of Mizen Head, can be seen in clear weather. The second and largest of the two sea inlets that can be seen below is Adrigole Bay, the destination of this stage.

Soon the track becomes a more formal route when it becomes bounded in places by old stone walls; this is the old road west, and is called Cromwell's Road. The route descends into surroundings that become increasingly green and fertile, while far ahead, the spectacular swirling geology of Adrigole Mountain and Hungry Hill come into view. Up to the right the fields are patterned with the just perceptible shapes of lazy beds, ancient cultivation ridges which date back to at least a century and a half ago.

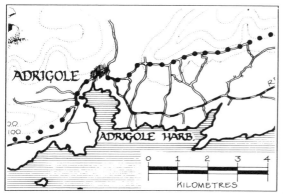

Soon the first house to be encountered since entering the Magannagan Valley appears far up to the right. A thunderous stream and waterfall, shrouded in holly and ash trees, are crossed over by a medieval stone-arched bridge that seems to grow out of the bedrock to throw its gothic span across the water.

The route joins and leaves the gorse-strewn track a couple of times before it becomes a green road, and soon after, a tarmac side-road. Crossing another ancient bridge, the remains of a ring-fort can be seen up to the right. Ring-forts, of which all that usually remains today is a circular earthen bank, were the farmsteads of the first millenium; this one has a clearly defined ditch which could be turned into an effective moat by the diversion of the nearby stream.

Soon a standing stone of prehistoric origin, one of many hundreds surviving on the peninsula, can be seen down to the left. The purpose of such stones seems to have varied from grave-marker and ritual use to the more prosaic purpose of scratching stone for cattle. A little further on, you can take a detour from the route to see another megalithic monument, this time a wedge-shaped gallery grave, which can be found in a field a couple of hundred metres north of the road. The road rises and falls gently, while Hungry Hill comes into view again ahead, a great rampart of vegetation-bare mountain dominating the horizon. On the left some stone gables and fragile-seeming Gothic arches are all that remain of Massmount Church.

Now Adrigole Harbour, biting deep into the landmass, comes into view below, backed by the twisted and swirling geological formations of Adrigole Hill. Downhill the route drops, between hedges of fuchsia, montbretia and rhododendron, and meeting the main road, follows it to the village of Adrigole.

STAGE 2: ADRIGOLE TO CASTLETOWNBERE

DISTANCE 21.75 KM (13.5 MILES). AGGREGATE CLIMB: 369 M (1,200 FEET). WALKING TIME: 7 HOURS.

This stage brings you up along the southern flanks of Hungry Hill into a desolate valley, and crosses two boggy ridges, two more valleys and many streams, to reach Castletownbere. It can be a strenuous stage, and more formidable than it looks, particularly after wet weather. The rewards, however, of views and surroundings are great. 6.4 km (4 miles) of the stage is on tarmac, and the balance on mountain tracks and open ground. Castletownbere has plenty of accommodation and a number of good places to eat out, including the excellent Cottage Restaurant where they serve seafood of exceptional quality, and McCarthy's Pub, where they serve great toasted sandwiches. The Beara Hostel, out near the ruins of Dunboy Castle, also offers camping. The town has no Bus Éireann service, but the Berehaven Bus Service has regular connections to Glengarriff, Bantry and Cork.

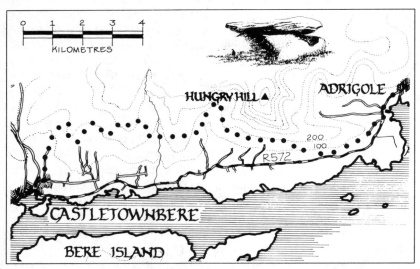

The Beara Way leaves Adrigole on the main Castletownbere road, and crossing Reen Bridge, heads gently uphill. Over to the right now can be seen the Mare's Tail waterfall, said to be the highest cascade in Ireland, which has been a tourist attraction since the mid-eighteenth century.

A short distance further uphill the Way turns right onto a grassy holly-lined boreen that wends its way gently up and out onto the open rocky hillside. Reaching a high point, a new view is seen out over Bantry Bay—a cluster of islands to the south, one of them topped by a lighthouse.

The route is now following what seems to be an ancient road carved out of the bulbous sandstone bedrock that gradually makes its way uphill between great house-sized boulders, with thatches of ivy and holly. The route soon becomes less clear, and follows winding, sometimes indistinct, paths and boreens, crossing a couple of streams, before it climbs steeply uphill towards looming Hungry Hill (693 m—2,251 feet).

If you become detached from the route around here, remember the main Castletownbere road is only a few hundred metres away to the south. The eastern end of Bere Island comes into view ahead now, with a Napoleonic wars signalling tower crowning its highest point. The island is separated from the mainland by Bere Haven, a broad, safe anchorage. It was here that part of an ill-fated French invasion fleet anchored in December 1796, to escape the worst of the easterly gales sweeping the coast. It was a powerful assembly of fifteen vessels, one of which, the *Indomptable*, had a devastating armament of eighty guns. The ships carried over 6,000 men-at-arms (the original force numbered 14,000) who, if they had come ashore, would have greatly outnumbered the available crown forces. After days of waiting in vain for the weather to improve, however, the invasion was called off and the armada upped anchor and returned to France.

The next attempt at invasion was to have taken place in May 1798, under the command of an up-and-coming commander-in-chief named Napoleon Bonaparte, but at the last minute orders were changed, and the fleet sailed instead for Egypt.

As dome-like Holly Hill comes into sight straight ahead, the town and fishing port of Castletownbere can be seen beyond it. The route now bears around to the right, and terraced south-western flanks of Hungry Hill appear ahead like a surreal giant staircase. A grassy valley is crossed and the route ascends and descends, crossing cascading streams, before passing a small reed-bounded lake where mallard and moorhens swam amongst water lilies when I passed.

From here, looking up, Hungry Hill looks a cruel, remorseless mountain; with the exception of a geological fault line, which takes a stair carpet of vegetation all the way to the top, little else survives on the cold bare rock. The green road soon becomes a track bearing round to the right to ascend the valley to the west of Hungry Hill, past a series of astonishing rocks that look like a fossilised school of stranded whales. There are few places singularly more desolate than this valley, a landscape of sandstone outcrops with tiny patches of boggy vegetation between, surrounded on three sides by high, forbidding volcanic escarpments.

West of Hungry Hill the track descends briefly, and reaching a clear stream, the route turns south again. Some peat is still cut in this area; look out for bleached roots and trunks of ancient trees excavated during peat-cutting. Two insectivorous plants can be found in this damp area where little nourishment is available from the soil. The sundew is a tiny reddish plant,

61

usually much enlarged in photographs for description purposes, so you expect it to be bigger. The butterwort is a light-green, star-shaped plant fairly common in boggy wet terrain. Both plants trap and absorb tiny insects and flies. The other rarity you may see in these parts is the Kerry Slug, which differs from most common slugs in that it has white spots; the only other places it is found are northern Spain and western France.

Crossing the stream, the route rises again over boggy ground crossed by little cascades, and as the lake passed earlier comes into view on the far side of the valley, a green road is joined which winds up the next ridge, an extension of Holly Hill, seen earlier. In clear weather Mizen Head, beyond Sheep's Head, comes into view to the south before the bare top of the ridge is reached.

Another deep valley opens up ahead, with a further ridge beyond it. Dropping steeply down through rough terrain the route reaches the strong flowing Owgarriff River which, the first time I walked here, after heavy rains, was impossible to cross safely. At the time of writing, plans for the erection of a footbridge are well under way. If, however, you are stopped by deep waters here, you can backtrack one hundred metres to the last gate passed, go through it and head southwards on a green road which will take you to a tarmac road, and thence to Castletownbere in a few miles.

Across the river, however, the route climbs nearly 200 m (650 feet) onto the barren southern slopes of Maulin (629 m—2,044 feet) through terrain which was very boggy when I passed, slowing progress considerably. The wonderful broadening views to the south-west, and the feeling that the Way must be coming near to finally descending to Castletownbere, are consolations—until the route turns to climb again. It is only a brief ascent, however, and after a couple of loops the route begins to descend along a series of ancient and very wet bog roads crossing heather-covered, almost featureless bog where only ancient standing stones and Cappaghvuckee Boulder Dolmen relieve the landscape. Weaving and winding, the Way descends with a great view of the harbour of Castletownbere ahead, and the track becomes a gravel road as the route passes, bordered by clumps of rhododendrons, through farmland, to reach tarmac and enter the town.

Casteltownbere is a bustling town and fishing port that owes its existence to the broad sheltered natural harbour provided by Bere Island, which was formerly a base for the Royal Navy's Atlantic fleet. The ruins of Dunboy Castle, one of the premier strongholds of the O'Sullivan Beare clan, are near the town. In June 1602 the castle was besieged by a sea-borne force under Sir George Carew. Cannons soon reduced the superstructure to ruins, and the surviving Irish moved to the thick-walled cellars of the castle and continued a stubborn resistance. Finally, an attempt by the defenders to blow up what remained of the castle failed, and the seventy survivors were taken prisoner, only to be hanged a few days later. Near Dunboy Castle are the extensive ruins of a great Victorian extravaganza of a house, Puxley Manor, a mixture of many architectural styles. The Puxleys were a Welsh family who settled on the Beara Peninsula in the early eighteenth century, and there are many local stories about their relationship with the descendants of the erstwhile lords of the area, the O'Sullivans. Daphne du Maurier's novel *Hungry Hill* is said to have been largely based on these feuding families.

Near Hungry Hill

STAGE 3: THE BERE ISLAND CIRCUIT

DISTANCE: 21.7 KM (13.5 MILES). AGGREGATE CLIMB: 380 M (1,235 FEET). WALKING
TIME: 7 HOURS.

*This stage consists of a double loop covering the most interesting aspects of
Bere Island, from the wedge tombs and galláns of the prehistoric
inhabitants to the Martello towers and shore batteries of more recent times.
The island is 10 km (6 miles) long and 4 km (2.5 miles) wide, and protects
a deep-water anchorage that has been taken advantage of by seafarers for
many centuries; as recently as 1990, during a long winter storm, 98 ships
from all over the world availed of its shelter at one time or another. The
place's strategic importance, evidenced by the many remains of military
buildings, and the fact that it continued under the control of the British
Army until 1938, has brought it many visitors of note over the years, from
Sir George Carew, President of Munster in the sixteenth century, to
Winston Churchill and Eamon de Valera in the twentieth century.*

*Two ferries give access to the island. One, a car-ferry, operates from the
centre of Castletownbere directly across to the island, and the other
operates from the 'Pontoon' east of the town to the island's main village,
Rerrin.*

*Some bed-and-breakfast accommodation is available on the island, and
there is a good restaurant and two pubs.*

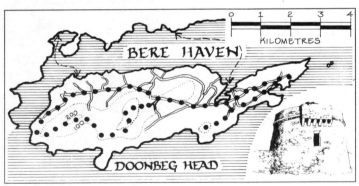

Starting in the picturesque village of Rerrin, the route follows the road
north as it winds along the shores of Laurence Cove. When I walked here in
summertime, hedges were hung down with lush foliage, and great rounded
hydrangeas bloomed everywhere. Laurence Cove House Restaurant is
passed on the right before the road takes the route winding uphill to reach
and pass through a scattered military barracks, built originally by the
British Army. The Irish Army now uses the surviving buildings for accom-
modating companies of soldiers in training; I was passed on the road by a
platoon of fully equipped, black-faced commandos, all of whom gave me a
great salute!

Beyond the barrack buildings the eastern end of the island comes into view, and an old gateway, festooned with barbed wire, marks the entry to the Lonehort Battery, one of the great gun emplacements built when the island was fortified in 1899 to protect the Royal Navy's dreadnoughts at anchor in the Haven. These great iron warships were extremely vulnerable when they were undergoing routine maintenance. Their steam boilers, which powered not only their engines, but also their gun turrets and ammunition delivery systems, could take more than a day to fire up, and if they were not protected, a raiding warship could cause mayhem. A series of batteries armed with six-inch guns were built on the island to cover both sides of Bere Haven; here at the Lonehort Battery, the last surviving two of the old, long-barrelled guns can still be seen beyond the protective fosse that surrounds the battery.

Turning right near the gateway, the route follows a gorse-lined track past Lonehort Harbour, the rocky shore of which provides shelter for cormorants hanging their wings out to dry. Straight ahead, atop one of the island's many hills, is one of the two Martello towers remaining intact on the island, and dating from the time of the Napoleonic wars.

The gable of a ruined house on the right contains a mysterious stone on which is carefully carved the date 'June 1854', leaving all who pass here to wonder at the significance of it. It is only one of the many derelict houses that are scattered across the island; another, more recently abandoned, can be seen on the left further on with surreal, smoke-shaped, wind-sculpted shrubs growing from its chimneys. When I passed, the hedgerows along here were decorated in profusion with thyme, clover, fuchsia and cornflowers, all combining to produce a very heady perfume.

The collapsed remains of a grand megalithic construction, Ardragh Wedge Tomb, are passed soon after on the right, fourteen great slabs of rock erected during the Bronze Age. The rocky and hilly nature of Bere Island is very apparent from here as you look west now towards the cross on the highest point, near which the route will pass. The main route takes the second turn to the right after the wedge tomb; if you keep straight on here you can follow a worthwhile spur to the Martello Tower on Ardragh Hill 1.2 km (0.75 mile) away. It takes you by a winding narrow road to reach a grassy track, an overgrown military road, which rises up Ardragh Hill from where there are wonderful views back over Rerrin, the east end of the island and the mainland beyond. Bog asphodel, common butterworth and orchids decorate the track as it takes you up into a high marsh past a little lake and a ruined watch tower to reach the Martello tower, which is in a good state of preservation. To the north of the tower is a geological rift, a great water-filled cleavage in the bedrock of the land that is so regular as to look man-made.

Back on the main route, follow the road north to reach a T-junction. Rerrin is now to the right, but the route turns left to follow the road as it rises and falls between high hedges and passes to the south of another hill topped by a Martello tower. From the rocky flanks of the hill there are fine views down along the south coast of the island, and ahead to the Holy Year Cross on Knockanallig, the island's highest hill.

As the road swings around and crosses a saddle called Ard na Gaoithe, the return loop is passed coming from the left. Nearby is a prominent, 3 m (9 foot) high standing stone or gallán, erected some time in the mists of prehistory at precisely the centrepoint of the long and short axes of the island. Below to the north, the village of Ballynakilla with its little church and cluster of houses comes into view, and offshore, the superstructure of a merchant ship which sank in 1982 is usually visible at low tide. As the route passes to the north of the Holy Year Cross there are extensive views across Bere Haven to the mainland, dominated by Hungry Hill. On the right now, looking out over this great vista, is O'Sullivan's, one of Bere Island's pubs.

Dropping downhill beyond the pub, Castletownbere comes into view across the water and, west of it, rising from a grassy platform, the ruined Puxley mansion can be seen. Ahead to the left rises the next and last of the island's hills, this one topped by a curious heap of stones, the remains of a Napoleonic wars' signal tower. Soon the turn right to the 'West End' ferry pier is passed, but the route continues straight ahead between hedges that are a rich treasury of wildflowers and herbs. When I walked in summer great spears of purple loosestrife counterpointed frothy heads of meadowsweet beneath hedges of fuchsia and honeysuckle.

The tarmac road comes to an end near another set of shore batteries, and the route crosses a stile and continues southwards along a track that was once a military road. More ruined pill boxes and military bunkers, some converted for agricultural use, are passed before the route turns abruptly up to the left and follows a faint and winding path through a rocky wilderness. The sound, where the gap between the mainland and the island narrows to a few hundred metres, comes into view ahead now, beyond the shattered concrete and rusting iron of the Ardnakinna Battery, its armoured bunkers today providing shelter for a few sheep.

The winding pathway leads uphill over a series of neatly constructed steps cut into the exposed rock until an old grassy road is reached and followed to Ardnakinna Point, the south-west corner of the island. The white-painted lighthouse here, built in 1850, was made redundant in 1860, but a number of incidents in the 1950s led to it being re-activated again in 1965. The view out over the tower is rewarding, a series of rounded promontories extending south-westwards to terminate at Blackball Head, topped by the next Napoleonic signal tower, fifteenth in the line from Cork, which passed messages between Bere Island and Dursey Island.

There is a temptation here to drop down to the lighthouse and follow the coast eastwards, but the route turns and climbs inland through pathless but well-signed moorland. The broad expanse of Bantry Bay stretches below, with Sheep's Head at the far side. As the route climbs, the rocky skeleton of the land is bared as great slabs of sandstone protrude from the grassy sward.

At the highest point of this hill lie the ruins of yet another signal tower, struck by lightning in 1959 and further damaged by a storm in 1964, to such an extent that it had to be demolished. The views from here are quite magnificent: the coastline of the mainland backed by great mountains fills the northern vista, while to the west the heights of Dursey Island are in view over the distinctive shape of Crow Head.

The Way drops boggily downhill over clumps of butterworth to meet and follow a stony track for a short distance. A grassy valley is crossed to reach another track which brings you winding southwards into a place called Pairc Nua. The remains of a number of prehistoric dwelling sites have been found in this natural amphitheatre of rock, grass and heather, and nearby there is a large cairn which is much older than the local tradition which holds that it was a Great Famine burial place. The winding track heads uphill into craggy wild west country, a desolation of sundered rocks, to a marvellous arrival on the northern side of Knockanallig, at 258 m (846 feet), the island's highest point. There is a track up to the summit to the right, but our route continues north-east past the great concrete Holy Year Cross, erected in 1950 at a cost of £300, before descending steeply to pass the Ard na Gaoithe gallán mentioned earlier. When the track reaches the tarmac road, return along it to Rerrin and the starting point, less than 3 km (1.9 miles) away.

Ardragh Wedge Tomb

STAGE 4: CASTLETOWNBERE TO ALLIHIES

DISTANCE: 13.6 KM (8.5 MILES). AGGREGATE CLIMB: 339 M (1,100 FEET). WALKING
TIME: 4.5 HOURS.

*This stage crosses the peninsula to the old mining village of Allihies
through surroundings which vary from open moorland to thick forestry.
The arrival at the highest point under Knockgour Mountain is a great
moment, with a tremendous view westwards across Ballydonegan Bay and
out into the Atlantic. 7.2 km (4.5 miles) of the stage are on tarmac, 2.4 km
(1.5 miles) on paths, and 4 km (2.5 miles) on forestry roads. Allihies has
bed-and-breakfast accommodation and a popular independent hostel;
there is another hostel a mile outside the village. The Atlantic Restaurant
and B & B serves seafood and you can get simple meals in O'Neill's pub.
There is no public transport serving the village.*

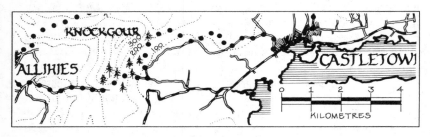

The Beara Way goes west out of the town past the Silver Dollar pub,
following a sign for a stone circle. The road turns inland and winds gently
uphill, with Bere Island and Bere Haven coming into view behind. 1.6 km (1
mile) from the town Derrinataggart Stone Circle is reached. Like many of
the prehistoric monuments on the Beara Peninsula, this one, a ring of
twelve wafer-thin slabs leaning towards each other in a prayerful manner,
has been little disturbed since its construction millenniums ago.

The Way continues uphill into open country and, leaving the tarmac,
follows a gravel track out over moorland, with long views all round. Soon
the route turns abruptly left off the track close to where, when I walked, the
rusting hulk of an old bulldozer lay. An almost pathless route is followed
across hillocks covered by thick grassy hummocks, intersected by deep
rivulets and patches of bog; take care walking here in summertime, when
the thick growth of grass hides the holes.

Within about fifteen minutes the route rejoins tarmac and goes right at
the next two junctions, before it takes you up into rugged and rocky open
country. The Way climbs between bluffs, crossing stiles and streams to reach
a fence, where it turns left to meet and follow a track. Soon the Way enters
forestry and follows boggy paths and fire-breaks to reach a track through a
natural rock garden of great bulbous bluffs and fantastic geological

formations, rich in growths of herbs, heather and gorse.

The tarmac is reached again briefly at Knockoura, and the route follows it southwards. The craggy sea inlet of Pulleen Harbour comes into sight ahead, before a right turn brings you up a series of forestry tracks and fire-breaks on to the wooded eastern flanks of Knockgour Mountain.

Soon after the route levels off, tarmac is reached and the Way begins to descend again with great views ahead. To the north, beyond Knockgour, the western end of the Slieve Miskish Mountains can be seen dropping ruggedly towards the sea and ending in Cod's Head. Broad Ballydonegan Bay fills the scene ahead while, to the right, as the road descends, the village of Allihies can be seen as a cluster of colourful buildings climbing a ridge. Out of the rocky terrain above the village the gaunt remains of some of the old mine buildings rise. Another stark and gothic engine building and chimney can be seen straight ahead as the route meets a junction and goes left.

The Way now drops down a very narrow boreen, past signs warning about open mine shafts in the area, and crosses a bridge to rise to meet a main road. Here the Beara Way divides; to the left is Stage 5, the Allihies to Dursey spur. To complete Stage 4, however, the route turns right towards broad Ballydonegan Strand, one of the few beaches on the Beara Peninsula. It is a man-made beach, made up of thousands of tons of fine-grained minerals, by-products of the Allihies mines that have built up here since production began nearly two hundred years ago.

The Way turns away from the beach and climbs towards the stepped multi-coloured gables of Allihies. Copper-mining has been going on in the Allihies area since prehistoric times, but only began in earnest early in the nineteenth century, when the local landowners, the Puxleys, established the mines on a 'modern' basis. In the thirty years after they were opened, the mines produced nearly 90,000 tons of copper and a small fortune for the Puxleys. The rugged mountains above the village must be honeycombed with shafts, judging by the number of mine openings there are; it is said that one of the mines contains a cavern with a lake which had to be crossed by a rowing boat. Allihies today is a colourful and busy holiday place with an off-the-beaten-track feel.

STAGE 5: THE DURSEY SPUR

DISTANCE: 25.75 KM (16 MILES). AGGREGATE CLIMB: 720 M (2,300 FEET). WALKING
TIME: 9 HOURS.

*This stage is a looping scenic coastal walk that takes you out along the
cliffs south of Ballydonegan Bay with marvellous views across to Lamb's
Head on the Iveragh Peninsula, and on to Crow's Head, before returning to
Allihies via Dursey Island and Garnish Bay. The stage includes an exciting
and memorable ride on Ireland's only cable-car across Dursey Sound to the
island. There are a number of houses offering simple bed-and-breakfast
accommodation along this stage where walkers are made very welcome,
but there are no restaurants and you should make arrangements in
advance for evening meals. There is no public transport serving the area.*

The road is followed south-westwards towards the Barness Gap past some
disused copper mine shafts; when I passed here in very heavy rainfall a
spectacular geyser was spouting out of an air-vent to one of these. As the
road nears the sea again, the route turns right onto a boreen lined with high
fragrant hedges and climbs gently along the flanks of a hill called
Knockahulla. To the right, frequent deep crevasses with crashing seas reach
in towards the boreen from the sea cliffs. As the boreen peters out, the route
turns steeply uphill across open country, over ground that is likely to be
boggy in wet weather. On the way, look out for a large boulder with a raised
earthen area above it, surrounded by a kerb of stones, probably a megalithic
boulder burial.

Levelling out, the
route contours along
about 125 m (400
feet) above sea level,
heading for a green
road slicing along
northern flanks of
the second of the two
hills before you. The
outlook from this
point must be one of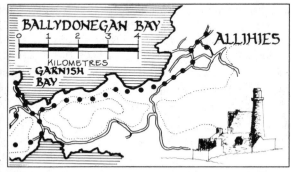
the finest in the country. Garnish Point at the western end of this great
bight is in view ahead now, and beyond it, a signal tower atop a hill marks
the first sight of Dursey Island. Looking back across Ballydonegan Bay, the
mountainous backdrop to Allihies stretches a ragged arm north-westwards
towards Cod's Head, beyond which the landmass of the Iveragh Peninsula
forms the horizon, terminating in the mounded Deenish and Scariff Islands.

The green road provides a comfortable grassy carpet to walk upon, and
soon the corner is rounded and the shores of Dursey Island come into view.

The patchwork of fields rising from the Garnish shore, each one a different shade of green, makes a wonderful backdrop to the wave-fringed sea. The route now descends past a few farmhouses to reach the main Dursey road, turns left, and after thirty metres, turns right down a narrow lane. The laneway winds steeply up the eastern slopes of rounded Crow Head, and the route passes through a farmyard and a couple of fields to reach open moorland. Head for the little building at the top of the hill; to the right, the island of Dursey seems moored to the mainland by the pylons that support its tiny cable-car. To the east Black Ball Head extends its bulbous promontory into the sea, topped with yet another Napoleonic signal tower like that on Dursey.

The little structure on top of the hill is one of the hundreds of look-out posts built along Ireland's shores during World War II, where soldiers watched day and night for signs of an invasion by either the Axis or the Allied forces. As the route descends to the level, low-lying, outer part of the headland, look out for a series of low undulations in the ground running across the narrowest part of the headland; these are the remains of a substantial system of banks and ditches constructed to fortify the headland as a promontory fort during the Iron Age. Nearby is a seemingly meaning-less pattern of stones scattered on the ground used to spell out 'EIRE' in huge whitewashed letters to inform early transatlantic aircraft where they had made their landfall.

These letters may have been the last thing seen by the crew of a German reconnaissance Ju88 which came this way by mistake one foggy day in 1943, crashing into the hill and scattering wreckage into the sea below. Local tradition suggests that legless pilots were not unique to the RAF, as the unfortunate pilot was found to have artificial legs. A few days after, a local fisherman pulled in the catch of a lifetime, two parachutes made of eighty yards of pure silk, a valuable commodity in wartime.

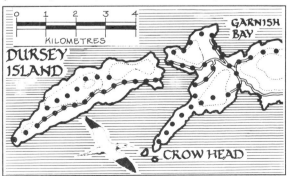

You can walk out to the end of the headland, but the main route drops down to the right to meet a boreen returning inland and meeting a tarmac road just beyond a farmhouse. The route now follows the road over the side of the hill. In the fields on both sides there are megalithic boulder burials, prehistoric hut sites, and a ring-fort, evidence of earlier inhabitants of this place. Meeting the Dursey road again, the route turns left and descends to the cable-car station. A sign here indicates that Moscow is 3,310 km away to the east, while New York is 5,280 km to the west!

The trip across to Dursey in the cable-car is an exciting added attraction. It is suspended by a series of rusty cables from two pylons and carries its passengers over the 200 m (656 foot) wide Dursey Sound, 22 m (72 feet) above the waves. The tiny box-like cabin, with room, I was told, for six persons or one person and a cow, has two bench-seats and four tiny windows. When I was there, it was equipped with two Lourdes holy-water bottles hanging by a string in a corner and a St Christopher prayer selotaped to the wall!

On the island, the route follows a road westwards; the island's tiny pier is passed after a few minutes, and shortly after the ruins of a church surrounded by a cemetery. Here the remains of some of the O'Sullivan Beare clan lie buried beneath a pyramidic monument; nearby is a gravestone commemorating islander Timothy Harrington, who died in 1919 aged 104. Further on, a grass-covered islet close to the shore called Illaunbeg was the site of the principal O'Sullivan Beare castle in the area before 1602, when it was captured by the English and loyal Irish, and the three hundred men, women and children who had taken refuge there were put to death.

It is a quiet place, Dursey; the symphony of calls from its gulls, choughs, wheat-ears and stonechats provide soft background music as you walk. The road is bounded by beautifully made stone walls, clothed with herbs and wildflowers, exuding a heady perfume in summertime.

After fifteen minutes the route climbs to pass through the first of the two hamlets on the island, Ballynecallagh, a cluster of traditional slated cottages, mostly derelict. The post office doesn't differ from any of the other cottages, and is identified by the telephone box in the front garden! When I passed, a sign on the post box requested that it should not be used to post letters for the moment as there was a bird nesting in it!

The route passes between two texturous stone gables, one of them colonised by great green cushions of rock sea spurry and a lone veronica, and rises gently along the bracken-clad flanks of the island. Uphill, a cluster of ancient standing stones can be seen near the barely discernible remains of an old military road, while downhill, a ruined cottage surrounded by old cultivation drills is gradually but surely being absorbed by the landscape. The lazy-bed patterned fields to the left, bounded by beautifully crafted stone walls, soon drop steeply away, and submerged by thick bracken, shelve ever steeper towards the sea below. In good weather, Sheeps Head can be seen 24 km (15 miles) away to the south, stretching into the Atlantic, and beyond, low lying and blue-grey, is Mizen Head. Look out for gannets coasting along the wavetops; these great seabirds probably come from the gannetry on the famous Skelligs rocks.

Around the next corner another cluster of cottages appears ahead, surrounded by a patchwork of fields. Beyond the first two houses, the route turns to the right to climb towards the signal tower. But first, it is worthwhile taking a ten-minute walk to the westernmost end of the island. The road becomes green with grass before it is reduced to a path through rock-strewn heather, bejewelled with wildflowers. It is a wonderful final arrival at the point with, to the north-west, the Skelligs rising uncompromisingly from the ocean, the confusion of bulbous blue headlands and hills that is the Iveragh Peninsula, and the vastness of the Atlantic Ocean stretching before you.

Retracing your steps towards the mainland, rejoin the route again and follow it as it climbs towards the old signal tower, built in the early nineteenth century to provide early warning of a French invasion. From the tower, the all-round views are hard to surpass.

The route descends back towards the mainland but instead of rejoining the road, heads up over the next hill, loud with meadow pippits when I passed. An indistinct path takes the route down through boggy ground to meet a track on the far side, and turning left, curves around the flanks of the next hill, before rejoining the road back to the cable-car station.

On the mainland again after another thrilling cable-car trip, the route ascends the grassy hillside to the north of the cable-car station, climbing steeply to reach a craggy ridge. Dramatic high cliffs are followed around a deep rounded bay, before the route descends towards Garnish Point. When I walked here the sea was rough and streaked with foam, and a succession of great combers rolled in thunderously from the Atlantic to break spectacularly over the rocky islands offshore. Passing a tiny protected harbour the route reaches Garnish post office, before the Way ascends to join the Dursey road and return to Allihies.

Dursey Island

STAGE 6: ALLIHIES TO ARDGROOM

DISTANCE: 24 KM (15 MILES). AGGREGATE CLIMB: 338 M (1,100 FEET). WALKING TIME: 7 HOURS.

This stage includes a variety of surroundings, with a dramatic start climbing the copper-rich crags above Allihies, a meander along the shores of Coulagh Bay, and finishing with a promenade along a grassy ridge high above Ardgroom Harbour. The stage includes nearly 6 km (3.5 miles) across open moorland, 7.2 km (4.5 miles) along a rocky shore, 4.8 km (3 miles) on mountain tracks and the balance on tarmac roads. The total distance can be halved by doing Allihies to Eyries (11.2 km—7 miles) and Eyries to Ardgroom (12.8 km—8 miles). Either way, pick-ups may have to be arranged from Eyries and Ardgroom, because they have no registered accommodation. Both of these pretty villages have a couple of pubs, and are served by a local bus service (O'Donoghue's), and in summer a limited service by the table no. 282 bus is run to Castletownbere.

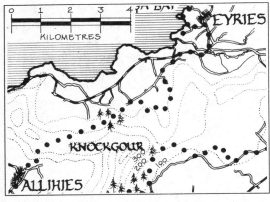

The route heads uphill out of Allihies village towards the towering crags, and leaving the road, passes a sign warning of the danger of open mineshafts. With the gothic silhouette of one of the old engine buildings ahead, the route crosses a stile and follows a faint path through bog asphodel climbing past the old magazine building, built in the 1830s, where the blasting powder for the mines was stored.

The great copper deposits at Allihies were probably first exploited by Bronze Age miners, who scraped out, using deer's antlers, the copper-rich quartz outcrops exposed on the surface of the rocks, and extracted the copper by crushing the quartz with rounded sea-cobbles. Although copper was probably mined periodically after this, it was not until the richness of the ore was spotted in the eighteenth century, and the Puxley family of Castletownbere invested substantial funds in its extraction in the early nineteenth century, that it was mined seriously. A thousand people, men, women and children, were being employed by the 1840s, with mainly Cornish miners working underground, and the Irish on the surface. The wages of 1 shilling and 2 pence per day for a man compared very favourably with those of a farm labourer, who probably got no more than 4 pence per day.

The route soon joins a gravelly road that winds up through a moonscape of rugged rocks into the heart of the mountain. As the highest point is reached, the road goes through a pass and ahead is Coulagh Bay, bounded to the north by Kilcatherine Point and the island of Inisfarnard. The route gradually descends along the mountain's flanks into farmland at Aughabrack to reach tarmac, beyond which it bears right along a boreen. If the boreen is followed southwards it will lead you back 6.4 km (4 miles) to Casteltownbere. The route, however, bears around left again to rejoin the tarmac road left earlier.

The Way meets the main Eyries road and follows it 1.6 km (1 mile) to the picturesque village of Eyries. As the village is reached the route turns left and descends towards the sea. Where the Kealincha River broadens to enter the sea, the route follows the shore around to the north, past a tiny lagoon fringed with reeds and water lilies. The tightly cropped grassy duach here is scattered with outcrops of thyme and purple saxifrage and speckled with stars of yellow tormentil in summertime.

The Way crosses a series of meadows and stony foreshores as it follows the coast northwards along Coulagh Bay. The shore is a narrow margin along which the sea has exposed sheets of fissured rock and piled up smooth rounded cobbles; when I passed, wagtails and turnstones scurried about the water's edge investigating clumps of seaweed while wheat-ears flitted ahead from fence-post to fence-post. Eyries Island soon comes into sight offshore, a long low-lying rock with a green covering of pasture scattered with sheep.

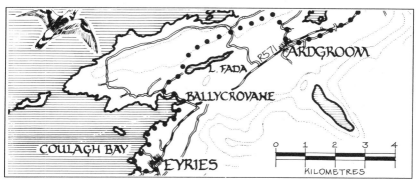

Eventually the track climbs gently onto low boulderclay cliffs as it approaches Ballycrovane Harbour. The ruins of an old coastguard station are passed before a boggy section is crossed, and in minutes the Ballycrovane Ogham Stone, the tallest in the British Isles, comes into sight ahead piercing the skyline. The route crosses one more bit of foreshore and a field to reach a tarmac road which brings you down to Ballycrovane Harbour. The ogham stone is a massive 4.7 m high slab of shist raised in pre-Christian times, with ogham writing honouring an unnamed celebrity who was the son of Deccada and the grandson of Torani.

The route follows the tarmac which winds along the sea shore; if you continue on this road, it will take you uphill to see An Cailleach Bheara, the Old Woman of Beara, a craggy outcrop of rock that resembles a woman with a basket on her back, or the face of an old woman, whichever you happen to see. In pagan times, which on the Beara one feels were not so long ago, the Cailleach was a goddess of the harvest. About 0.45 km (0.75 mile) from the harbour, however, the Way turns right down a narrow side-road signed 'Lough Fada'. When the lake comes into sight ahead and the tarmac ends, the route crosses a stile and climbs through rocky and boggy terrain on to the flanks of a low hill parallel to the lake.

There is not much of a pathway here; the route steps up the hillside along ridges of exposed bedrock with very boggy ground, rich in common butterwort, bog asphodel and bell heather, in between. Ahead, the outliers of the Slieve Miskish Mountains make a dramatic backdrop, particularly Skellig, a conical hill which looks more than its 220 m (714 feet), which seems to stand guard over a pass leading up to the beautiful Glenbeg Lough. Looking ahead along the line of the lake below, the cluster of buildings that can be seen a few kilometres ahead is Ardgroom village.

Before drawing level with the eastern end of the lake, the route takes a turn uphill to reach a green road, a great relief after the previous few hundred metres. Soon a tarmac road is reached and briefly followed, before the route turns off it onto a muddy track following the ridge of the hill. The Kenmare River comes into view now to the left ahead, with the wooded inlet and islands of Parknasilla easily identifiable on the far side. Ahead is Ardgroom Harbour with Killnakilloge Harbour beyond it. These havens, together with Dursey Island, were major pilchard fisheries in the seventeenth century. The pilchard is a fish of the herring family which was caught in enormous quantities off parts of the British Isles during the seventeenth and early eighteenth centuries; in 1767 at St Ives in Cornwall 245 million of the fish were caught in a single day.

When the route draws level with Ardgroom village over to the right, a gully is reached; here the Way descends the hill to meet the public road and follow it into Ardgroom.

Ardgroom

STAGE 7: ARDGROOM TO TUOSIST

DISTANCE: 19.5 KM (12 MILES). AGGREGATE CLIMB: 420 M (1,360 FEET). WALKING TIME: 6.25 HOURS.

This stage takes the Way over the county border into Co. Kerry, and includes two pleasant hillwalking stretches. Tuosist is a small scattered village with a pub, shop and post office about 1.5 km (1 mile) off the route. Accommodation in the area is scarce, but I particularly enjoyed the hospitality of Mary O'Shea at the Lake House, which overlooks one of the Cloonee loughs. In addition to accommodation, the Lake House has a comfortable pub and serves good food. Tuosist is not served by public transport.

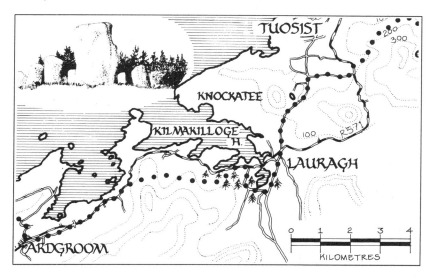

The route turns left at the Holly Bar and follows a narrow road that climbs to overlook Ardgroom Harbour, the Kenmare River and the Iveragh Peninsula beyond. Up to the right are the dramatic summits of Tooreennamna, Tooth Mountain and Coomacloghane, outliers of the Slieve Miskish range straddling the Cork and Kerry border. After wet weather, the flanks of these peaks are marbled with many silvery cascades. The many standing stones, cairns, stone circles and hut sites scattered across these uplands suggest that there was a substantial population here in prehistoric times.

Soon the main Kenmare road is joined again and shortly after crossing the boundary of Counties Cork and Kerry at Glashananinnaun Bridge, the route leaves the road and crosses a stile. Not far from the road, the very faint traces of an old droving road are met and followed, up and eastwards over a dip in Drung Hill, the rocky ridge ahead.

After a short climb a pass scattered with great cubist blocks of stone is reached, and ahead the droving road becomes clear as a broad green band descending into the valley beyond and up the ridge on the far side. One wonders at the engineering works involved in making such a road; up to 5 m (16 feet) wide, it is well constructed, and bounded by a drainage ditch with a protective bank. Roads of this sort are often many centuries old, and were built for the safe and swift movement of large herds of cattle and sheep to market places.

The route now enters a broad, deserted and silent valley, overlooked by Knockaveacal or Tooth Mountain, 518 m (1,685 feet) high. With the exception of a couple of cultivated fields near a lone green-roofed cottage up towards the head of the valley, it is a desolate place, a place of birch groves, rushing streams and great bulbous rocks that protrude from the grass like fossilised stranded whales.

On the surface of forest-fringed Kilmakilloge Harbour below the even, serried rows of fishfarm floats can be clearly seen, but at this distance they seem to merge with the natural surroundings. The picturesque harbour woodland is at its densest and richest around Derreen House, where the 400-acre exotic gardens feature giant red cedars and hemlocks, thickets of bamboo and tree ferns, and many varieties of rhododendron. The gardens, which are open to the public, were planted over many years at the end of the nineteenth century by the fifth Marquess of Lansdowne, whose terms as Governor-General of Canada and Viceroy of India gave him the opportunity to bring back and plant many species new to Ireland.

The route follows the old road over the hill bounding the eastern side of the valley, where a coniferous wood comes into view. To the right ahead, on a platform of ground, a megalithic monument can be seen consisting of an impressive group of standing stones, which were already ancient when the old road you walk was new; only Knocknastumpa and the other peaks that look down on them are older. Further on there is another similar monument, this time a stone circle. It is difficult not to wonder at what these monuments were used for; however primitive some might regard the peoples who built them, there is a clear and assured purposefulness about their layout and construction, and after all, how many of modern man's memorials will last as long?

The route descends into the next valley with a stone wall bounding the forest to the left. Crossing a stream by stepping stones, be vigilant for an abrupt turn off the green road and over the wall into the trees, where the Way descends a winding and sometimes steep jungle-like pathway close to a series of waterfalls, to reach the main Kenmare road.

Turning right, the road is followed under a canopy of Scots pines, turning to the right at the next junction, and passing a picturesque woodland lake to the left. Soon the Croneshagh River is crossed, rushing on its way to the sea from Glanmore Lake, deep in a valley between the Caha and Slieve

Miskish Mountains. Climbing briefly, the road winds and weaves up and down before descending towards Lauragh, with views to the left of Tooth Mountain.

Soon after passing a fine old forge with a horseshoe-shaped doorway, the route passes Smith's Sheebin pub and grocery shop, a popular watering place for travellers. The main road to the Healy Pass which crosses the mountains to Adrigole is passed, and the Owensna River is crossed, before the route completes the loop to the south and reaches the main Kenmare road again. Crossing the road, the Way climbs tarmac through forestry and out onto the open hillside, and the ragged cone of Knockatee appears ahead. It is a lush and rich countryside here; rhododendrons and palm trees shelter the picturesque cottages passed at the roadside. Climbing gently all the time, these are soon left behind as the rocky skeleton of the land bursts through a wilderness of gorse and bracken.

The Way levels out at a pass between Knockanouganish and Knockatee, which looks massive ahead now although it is only a little over 300 m (1,000 feet) in altitude. Looking back, there is a wonderful view of Kilmakilloge Harbour with its wooded fringes. As the route starts down the northern side of the pass, look out for the lonely and beautiful Gowlawn Lake east of Knockatee.

Down the route drops into farmland again and turning right, the road is followed back to rejoin the main Kenmare road, with a new series of mountain peaks forming the backdrop, the closest being Knockgarrif (448 m—1,459 feet) and Knockgarrane (420 m—1,357 feet), near which the route passes a little further on. After a short distance on the main road, the route crosses a stile and heads uphill. This stage, however, ends at Tuosist, which is about 1.5 km (1 mile) further along the road.

Standing Stones

79

STAGE 8: TUOSIST TO KENMARE

DISTANCE: 18.5 KM (11.5 MILES). AGGREGATE CLIMB: 520 M (1,690 FEET). WALKING TIME: 7 HOURS.

This is a richly varied stage which includes some glorious hillwalking in scenic Gleninchiquin and a stretch along the shore of the Kenmare River before crossing the bridge into the town of Kenmare. There are about 10 km (6.25 miles) on tarmac involved, and the balance is across open moorland.

There is a wide range of accommodation available in Kenmare including an independent hostel, and the town is served by the table no. 44 Cork–Killarney bus and the table nos 270 and 282 Kenmare buses.

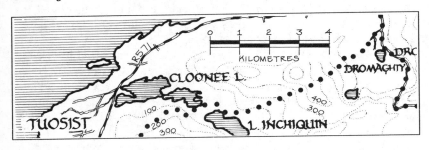

Retrace your steps from Tuosist to rejoin the route, which heads uphill into a rocky wilderness where the faint shapes of lazy beds, remains of man's agricultural efforts long ago, can be seen on level stretches of ground. The route, as it rises towards conical Knockgarrane, keeps to the left of a stream and passes a circle of stones that are the remains of a prehistoric dwelling. The really wet ground here was positively overgrown with common butterworth when I passed: although a rare plant elsewhere, it certainly lives up to its name here. As altitude is gained, a new section of the Kenmare River and the coast beyond comes into view, while to the south, the view is deep into the heart of the Slieve Miskish, peak piled on peak.

A soggy saddle, where bog asphodel competes with butterworth, is reached below Knockgarrane, and from here there are great views across to Iveragh; the wooded inlet up to Blackwater Bridge can be easily identified, and to its right in the trees the castle of Dromore in visible in clear weather. The arrival at the eastern side of this damp saddle is a great moment. Below stretches the broad glacier-created valley of Gleninchiquin, on the floor of which glitter Lough Inchiquin and the upper Cloonee Lough. The lakes are divided by a narrow neck of land, at the east end of which, even from this height, a prehistoric stone circle with a great central gallán can be seen. At the head of the valley a great waterfall called Ishaghbuderlick on the old maps but known locally as the Cascade, pours down from a higher lake called Coomeenaloughaun. The Beara Way can be seen stretching ahead, up a narrow tarmac road on the far side of Lough Inchiquin.

The route descends to reach a track to the left of a couple of stone-built farmhouses, and follows it between an avenue of spiky foxgloves, as it winds down through pleasant groves of trees. Soon the neck of land between the two lakes is reached and crossed. Two fast-flowing rivers, flowing through such flat-sided channels in the bedrock that they could be man-made canals, are also crossed by bridges, before the road on the north side of the lakes is reached and followed eastwards along the banks of Lough Inchiquin. In the distance the great waterfall can be seen streaking the steep end of the glen; after wet weather it is particularly spectacular. Soon the road forks and the route goes uphill to the left. The other road takes you to the waterfall 'amenity area' where there is a tea-house and walks have been laid out around and over the Cascade.

The Way rises high above the lake with ever-broadening views to the south and west, and before long the road deteriorates to a track. Crossing a stile and stream, the route turns uphill across boggy trackless moorland to head for the pass between two hills, overlooked by Knocknagorraveela to the south.

As you ascend, there are great views opening up behind. Above Lough Inchiquin in a scooped-out coomb, Cummeenadillure Lough comes into view, its name recalling the time when eagles soared above these hills; to the south is a 615 m (2,000 foot) peak called the Eagle's Nest. Eagles were known to be in this area as late as 1870, but were deliberately wiped out; the favourite means of getting rid of the birds was to burn them out of their nests with torches fixed to long poles. How things have changed today, although there are no eagles left to protect.

The Maulagowna stream is crossed, and the route continues uphill through dense tussock-grass to reach the pass; the driest path near the top is against the wall-like rock to the left. The arrival at the pass is a worthwhile moment; yet another valley is before you, green and wooded in places, its centrepiece Dromoghty Lake.

The route descends steeply through a grassy gully to reach an extensive upland meadow, a typical booley or mountain pasture which would have been used since prehistoric times for summer grazing. From here, the low-lying, wooded Dunkerrin Islands and their neighbours across the Kenmare River look like a dark battlefleet at anchor. The meadow, whose waist-high summer growth can be slow going and will saturate you if you are walking after rain, is crossed towards a pinnacle of rock, east of which the route descends towards the valley.

A rocky spur painted with a yellow arrow provides temporary relief from boggy ground, but there is more of it at the bottom of the valley, where a stream and a stile are crossed to reach the Drumroe Stone Circle, a well-preserved prehistoric monument consisting of a Bronze-Age stone circle surrounding a boulder-capped burial place.

Beyond the stone circle the route follows a faint track that soon crosses a couple of small fields and a stream to reach tarmac by way of a stile. Turning left, the narrow road takes you north to meet a junction after 4 km (2.5 miles). A right turn here takes you on the alternative route back to Glengarriff. The Way, however, follows a winding road northwards that rises and falls as it parallels the Dromaghty River below to the left. Soon a crossroads is reached just short of Dauros on the main Kenmare road; here the route turns right, and rises into the townland of Killaha, with great views down to the Kenmare River, the Dunkerrin Islands and the Iveragh coast beyond. It is a pleasant road to walk, overhung in places with ash and birch, hedges ablaze with montbretia and clumps of dotted loosestrife in summertime. The fine, well-extended cottages and bungalows along here suggest that Kenmare is near, and 2.4 km (1.5 miles) after the crossroads the narrow road drops to meet the main road, and follows the wooded shore of the Kenmare River. Soon the twin curves of the Kenmare Bridge can be seen between the trees, and shortly after, the bridge, built in 1933 at a cost of £9,990, takes the route over to the town of Kenmare (see page 172).

Stone Circle, Kenmare

STAGE 9: KENMARE TO GLENGARRIFF

DISTANCE: 24 KM (15 MILES). AGGREGATE CLIMB: 550 M (1,790 FEET). WALKING TIME: 8 HOURS.

On the final stage, the Dromaghty area is returned to, and the route then crosses a pass to reach Bonane, from where the long-disused old road is followed back over the county border into Cork and the town of Glengarriff.

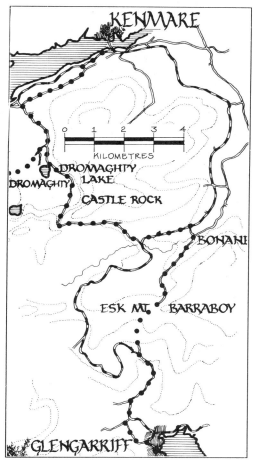

Return along the old high road to the junction where the route divided north of Dromaghty Lough, and continue straight in a south-easterly direction. Soon the picturesque lough is passed to the right, as the route follows a winding, switch-back side-road through leafy, ferny countryside with great mountain views on all sides. To the right are the cliffs below Knockgorraveela, and ahead are the spectacular serrated ramparts of Castle Rock cliffs, a carpet of recently cleared fields lapping at their foot like a bright green sea.

The road surface deteriorates as the route climbs into terrain like the wild west, with great bluffs all around. A pass is soon reached and the Way descends into country quite unlike that left on the mountain; copses of oak trees are scattered in a rough landscape below to the right; but for a few ancient stone walls and ditches there are few signs of man here. At the far side of this new valley, vehicles can be seen travelling along the 'Tunnel' road to Glengarriff, built by Ireland's Telford, the prolific Scottish engineer, Alexander Nimmo, in the 1820s.

The road descends to reach the 'Tunnel' road, turns left along it (it is a busy road, particularly in summertime, so take care) until after nearly 2 km (1.25 miles) the Old Presbytery bed-and-breakfast is reached beside a church, and the Way turns right, down a side-road. Bonane Bridge is crossed at the bottom of the valley and the road rises to meet a junction. Turning left will take you back to Kenmare in 14.4 km (9 miles), but our route goes right along a road thickly enclosed by high hedges and trees. A number of austere, stolid farmhouses are passed before the route climbs towards Barraboy Mountain and Esk Mountain which rise mightily ahead as if to block your way. Soon tarmac is left behind and the road becomes a rough bridal track fearlessly ascending the steep mountainside, giving wonderful views back over Esk Valley and the mountains beyond. This is the old road to Glengarriff, used until the 1820s when Nimmo built the 'Tunnel' road, which is longer but has an easier gradient. In the old days this road was too steep for horse-drawn transport, so travellers to Glengarriff or Kenmare had to order carriages to meet them downhill on the far side, or hire a half dozen strong locals to carry them over the top.

To the right of the bridal track at the top is a Mass rock that was much used in penal times. The track passes between Esk Mountain and Barraboy Mountain at an altitude of almost 369 m (1,200 feet), and entering the County of Cork, starts to descend towards Glengarriff. The views are wonderful on the descent: the silver spread of broad Bantry Bay, with Whiddy Island lying along its southern shore, the rocks, woods, mountains and valleys—all that is special about Irish scenery.

For nearly 0.8 km (0.5 mile), the route passes through a wood, before winding down to meet tarmac again and within minutes rejoin the main Kenmare/Glengarriff road. Just short of Glengarriff the route takes a short detour into the 300-acre Glengarriff Woods, thickly planted with sessile oak, arbutus, rhododendron, Scots pine and larch by the Earls of Bantry during the nineteenth century. The woods were taken in charge by the Office of Public Works in 1989 and are now run as a National Nature Reserve. The route returns to the public road, passing a marvellous old-world gate lodge, and enters the town of Glengarriff.

Castle Rock

5
THE BURREN WAY

The Burren is a partially eroded limestone plateau covering an area of 260 sq. km (100 sq. miles) in the north-west of Co. Clare. High ground is almost bare of soil and trees, a strange landscape of great flat slabs of grey stone divided by deep and narrow fissures called 'grikes'. The lush green and fertile valleys between the hills provide a dramatic contrast. Few rivers or streams interrupt the landscape; most of them run deep underground in caverns and tunnels, as can be experienced in a visit to the Aillwee Caves near Ballyvaghan.

This limestone country produces a surprising richness of wildflowers, including a number of Arctic and Mediterranean species not commonly found elsewhere in Ireland but here growing in profusion and sharing the same habitat. For those interested in wildflowers, May and June are the best months for walking in the Burren.

It is intended that the Burren Way will eventually complete a circuit of the Burren, but at the time of writing it is only about 45 km (28 miles) long, wending its way diagonally from Ballyvaghan in the north to Liscannor on

85

the west coast. I have broken the route into two stages, the first of 29 km (18 miles) to Doolin, and the second of 16 km (10 miles) from Doolin to Liscannor. Some 18 km (11 miles) into the first stage an escape can be made down 4 km (2.5 miles) to the coast road near Fanore, where accommodation is available.

The main way-markers on the Burren Way consist of an arrow cut in a slab of Liscannor stone and painted yellow. I found these markers broken in places, so take care at junctions.

How to get there
Ballyvaghan is 217 km (135 miles) from Dublin and 174 km (108 miles) from Cork, and is served by the table no. 50 Cork–Galway bus (summer only) and the table no. 423 Galway–Doolin bus. Liscannor is served by the table no. 337 Limerick–Doolin bus.

Maps and guides
The route is covered by the Ordnance Survey 1:127,000 (0.5 inch to 1 mile) map no. 14. A leaflet titled *The Burren Way* describing the route is produced by Shannon Development in association with Cospóir and can be obtained from Shannon Development, 62 O'Connell Street, Limerick.

Three local guides, *The Burren: a Rambler's Guide and Map*, *The Burren: O'Brien Country: a Rambler's Guide and Map*, and *The Doolin Guide and Map*, also cover parts of the route. They are rich in information and illustrations and are highly recommended for anyone walking in the Burren.

Enquiries: Tourism Group, Shannon Development, Shannon Town Centre, Co. Clare; telephone 061 361555

Cliffs of Moher

STAGE 1: BALLYVAGHAN TO DOOLIN

DISTANCE: 29 KM (18 MILES). AGGREGATE CLIMB: 400 M (1,312 FEET). WALKING
TIME: 8 HOURS.

*This first stage leaves the sea shore of Galway Bay and ascends gradually
into the hills of the Burren, first on tarmac and then following an old
droving road as it promenades high above the coast, to descend to the coast
again at the village of Doolin, renowned for its traditional music.
Ballyvaghan has hotel and bed-and-breakfast accommodation, in addition
to traditional cottages for rent. Doolin has lots of hostel and bed-and-
breakfast accommodation, but in the high season it is advisable to book in
advance. Nearly 20 km (12 miles) of this stage is on old green roads, some
of which can be quite wet in winter, and the balance on tarred roads. This
stage can be shortened to about 24 km (15 miles) by ending it at
Ballinalacken Castle, where there is accommodation available at
Ballinalacken House and where the table no. 423 bus can be connected with
to reach the plentiful accommodation of Lisdoonvarna, 5.5 km (3.5 miles) to
the south-east. The table no. 423 bus also serves the village of Doolin.*

Once a market town and centre of a herring and oyster fishery,
Ballyvaghan developed around an O'Loughlin castle, the faint remains of
which can just be made out on the little spur of land jutting into the water
in front of the rented cottage development.

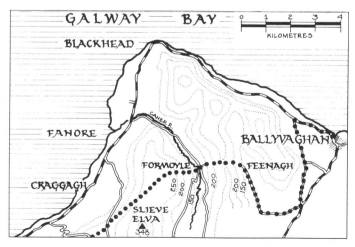

The Burren Way starts at the fountain in the centre of the village and heads
westwards along the coast road, passing the pier and Monke's pub, as good
for its shellfish as for its pints. To the north across the bay on a low-lying
spit of land stands Finavarra Martello tower, and beyond can be seen the
coast of Galway, its whitewashed houses glittering on a clear sunny day.

The road follows the shore, where oystercatchers and widgeon can usually be seen in good numbers and, in winter, brent geese. Looming up ahead is the steep terraced hillside of Ceapaigh an Bhaile, the eastern outpost of Black Head, which seems to be bare of vegetation although herds of cattle contentedly graze its slopes. Strongly built stone field walls, probably dating from a time when there was more soil and grass, run from the sea shore right up and over the brow of the bare mountain.

Nearly 1 km (0.5 mile) out of Ballyvaghan the Way turns off the main road onto a boreen and heads southwards along the mountain's flanks, climbing almost imperceptibly as fine views of Ballyvaghan and the coastline beyond open up. To the right is a thicket of hazel bushes, common all over the Burren, where they have colonised particularly inaccessible and uncultivatable places. They are at their most beautiful in February, when long yellow-green catkins hang in drooping tassels from their branches.

Soon the cylindrical sixteenth-century Newtown Castle is passed. An O'Brien tower-house, it grows from a pyramidal base which acts as four strong buttresses, and the design is possibly an early attempt to create a cannon-proof structure. In 1839 the occupier is recorded as 'Charles O'Loghlen, Prince of Burren'. Recently the tower has been carefully restored as part of the Burren School of Art.

Just over 5 km (3 miles) from Ballyvaghan the boreen meets the main Lisdoonvarna road, and turns right to follow a signpost for the green road and Lismacsheedy Cliff Fort. In a few minutes the gables of ruined Glenaraha Church can be seen on the left. Built in an ecumenical gesture by the Marquess of Buckingham in 1795, it fell into disuse when the new church was built in Ballyvaghan about 1860. Near the ruins can be found an earthen ring-fort. These constructions, found all over Ireland, were the common farm homesteads of the Middle Ages and earlier. The earth embankment would have been topped by a timber or thorn-bush palisade to keep out wolves and rustlers, and within the enclosure were the dwelling and farm buildings.

Shortly after, the ruins of another church can be seen on the left. This is Rathborney Church, dating from about 1500 and worth a detour. Built within a ring-fort, it has a finely carved limestone window on the east side and an unusual oval doorway.

As the road continues west it crosses Rathborney River, one of the Burren's few streams, which runs alongside for a while through a tunnel of hazel, blackthorn, and ivy, descending in frequent cascades. Mountain dippers patrol the clear water, bobbing up and down on rocks and diving to the bottom when a tasty morsel is spotted.

As the road ascends the valley it passes fields consisting almost entirely of bare limestone pavement, next to fields without a trace of stone, covered with lush green carpets of grass. When the end of the tarmac is reached, the Burren Way bears left to climb a rough green road going west. Back across the valley the grey circular stone construction of Caher Fhiodhnaigh can be seen to the left of a dwelling-house, to the right of which can be seen

Lismacsheedy stone promontory fort. As the route ascends, the mountain behind these ancient buildings begins to display its emphatically layered construction, unique to limestone areas such as this; the scale and parallel nature of these piled-up slices of rock can, when first seen, be astonishing. Look out for examples of fossils of the carboniferous era in the stones underfoot and in the dry-stone walls that line the green road. Corals that flourished in the shallow tropical seas millions of years ago have been frozen in time as round cobbles of blue-grey limestone with zebra spots of white, while traces of bivalves, similar to those found on any beach today, can be similarly detected imprisoned in the stone.

The green road levels out quite suddenly on a plateau, the top limestone layer of this particular hill. It is a moonscape of grey pavements with deep grikes dividing them. In places, whether by nature or human hand, loose slabs project vertically out of these grikes, as if in the process of being sucked into or ejected from the bedrock. The landscape has taken on an all-over grey tone now that there are no green valleys in sight; and all around are flat limestone summits similar to this one. The Way ahead is clearly visible for some distance, a walled green road winding up and over the next limestone ridge.

The south side of the plateau is reached abruptly as the green road passes through a gateway, and the rich, fertile Caher Valley stretching westwards to the sea appears below. On the left of the gate is a ruined stone fort called Caherandurrish. There is little left of the original walls; they seem to have been cannibalised to provide stone for other buildings within the fort, which were inhabited up to the nineteenth century. Local tradition suggests that the ruins housed at various times a chapel and a 'shebeen' or unlicensed drinking-house.

The Burren Way continues down into the valley, along which the Caher River meanders its way to the sea at Fanore. This is the only Burren river that does not disappear into the limestone bedrock at some stage during its course to the sea.

Meeting the public road and crossing the river, follow the green road uphill again past the ruins of Formoyle Church, which ceased to be used in 1870. Beyond the church is an old but well-built stone cottage, with particularly fine chimneys, the stones of which may well have originally adorned the church. This green road is an ancient droving road, the former importance of which is evidenced by its great width. The stones of the walls on each side are laid in beautiful solid and void chevron patterns. The age-old principle of their construction is simple and logical: the stones are set on their edges because in this way they are more secure from rocking, and the gaps between them prevent the wind from building up sufficient pressure to blow the wall down.

Nearing the summit of the hill, the cairn topping the Black Head massif comes into sight to the north, and beyond it glitters Galway Bay, with the coast of Galway beyond. Soon the terrain ahead comes into view, with to the left Slieve Elva, at 345 m (1,132 feet) the highest of the Burren limestone massifs. Legends tell of no fewer than seven battles fought here in the third century by the High King Cormac mac Airt. Slightly to the right ahead the Aran Islands should be visible, a chain of low-lying silhouettes extending into the Atlantic.

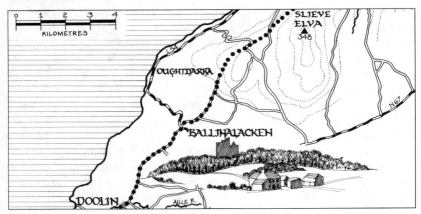

In the strange micro-climate of the Burren, an abundance of Alpine plants is found uniquely side by side with Arctic varieties. Picking wild-flowers is strictly forbidden, so you will not be able to try the old recipe using gentian: 'Wine, wherein the herb hath been steept, being drunk, refreshes such as are over-wearied by travel, or are lame in their joynts by cold or bad lodgings.'

At Ballyelly the village of Craggagh on the nearby coast comes into view, while below lie the ruins of the circular Faunarooska Castle, the main walls of which fell down a few years ago. A couple of hundred metres to the left here is Poll an Phúca, one of the entrances to the 'potholes', the labyrinth of caverns and caves that honeycomb the base of Slieve Elva and that attract explorers from all over Ireland and Britain. There are over 11 km (7 miles) of charted passageways to explore, some of them with features similar to those that can be more comfortably seen on a tour of the Aillwee Caves near Ballyvaghan.

The views down to the coast are great along here, with the land sweeping majestically down to the sea, the continual roar of which on rough days can be clearly heard at this height. To the north on a clear day it is possible to see the full length of the Galway coast as far as Golam Head.

Soon two more stone forts, Caher Mhaol and Caher Bheag, are passed on the left, before a tarred road is met. Turning right here leads down 4 km (2.5 miles) to Fanore, where bed-and-breakfast is available. The Way continues straight, leaving the tarmac again and crossing the western spur of Knockaun Mountain, where the northern extremities of the Cliffs of Moher come into view ahead. About 3 km (1.75 miles) to the south now can be seen the silhouette of Ballinalacken Castle, a typical

Irish tower-house, standing high over a grove of trees.

As a group of farm buildings is reached on the left of the Way, there is a dramatic change in the topography to the right: the flat pavements of limestone with their networks of stone walls suddenly drop away at a line of sheer cliffs to a deep and wild valley clothed in hazelwood. The valley is called Oughtdarra, whose impenetrable hazel thickets provide a safe habitat for a rich variety of wildlife. The area is one of the last remaining habitats in Ireland of the pine marten (sometimes called the tree weasel), probably our rarest mammal.

Soon the green road takes on a tarred surface and continues southwards over a series of hillocks. After a group of farm buildings, look out for a small lime kiln in a field on the left under an outcrop of rock. Kilns such as this were used up to the last century to make slaked lime for fertiliser and whitewash for walls.

The road now drops to the craggy promontory on which the spectacularly sited Ballinalacken Castle stands. An O'Brien castle, Ballinalacken is one of the best-preserved unrestored tower-houses in Co. Clare, and there are certainly few in a more strategic setting. Ballinalacken House, built beside the castle about 1840 and once occupied by the jury-rigging judge Peter O'Brien, known as Peter the Packer, has a dining-room and bar open to non-residents.

The Way follows the road to Doolin at Ballinalacken Cross; bearing left at the fork here leads to Lisdoonvarna, 5.5 km (3.5 miles) to the south-east. Lisdoonvarna is the only active spa town in Ireland, where people come to 'take the waters', and it retains a Victorian ambience. It is also famous for its Match-Making Festival in September, when men and women seeking a wife or husband, as well as those who want to look on, flock to the town.

Downhill the Burren Way continues, and after about 1.5 km (1 mile) the road rises and the Cliffs of Moher appear ahead; inland from them the conical-roofed Doonagore Castle can be seen. A rather exotic modern guesthouse is passed before reaching the Church of the Holy Rosary, built in 1830. The church bell here originally rang out over a tobacco plantation in Ecuador before being brought to Doolin and erected in 1971.

The hamlet of Roadford is the first bit of urban civilisation to be met since Ballyvaghan, and boasts a post office, a shop, a café, and a restaurant called the Lazy Lobster. Crossing the Aille River over a fine many-arched bridge, the road leads into the hamlet of Fisherstreet which, combined with Roadford, makes up the village of Doolin. This place has built up a considerable international reputation over the last twenty years as a vibrant centre of traditional music, and it attracts a steady stream of folk-music lovers from all over the world. There is rarely a night when good Irish music cannot be heard in one of the three pubs in the area, O'Connor's, McGann's and McDermott's. Doolin is also an embarkation place for the Aran Islands, the nearest of which, Inis Oírr, is only 8 km (5 miles) away.

STAGE 2: DOOLIN TO LISCANNOR

DISTANCE: 16 KM (10 MILES). AGGREGATE CLIMB: 200 M (660 FEET). WALKING TIME: 4.5 HOURS.

This stage takes the Burren Way up to the dramatic heights of the magnificent Cliffs of Moher, and on to Hag's Head before turning eastwards and dropping to the village of Liscannor. Except for the spectacular 6 km (3.75 miles) along cliff paths, the greater part of this stage is unfortunately on tarred roads. Walkers should remember that all cliffs are dangerous, particularly when the wind is high, and due care should be taken on this stage. Liscannor has some bed-and-breakfast accommodation and is served by the table no. 337 bus, which also serves the visitors' centre at the Cliffs of Moher.

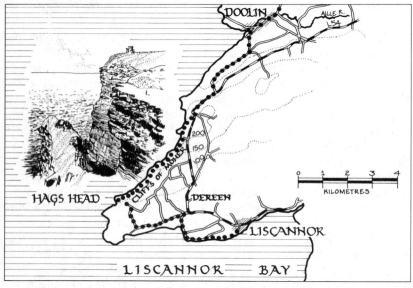

The Way follows the road as it rises out of the village and heads uphill again, with a panoramic view of the Doolin area opening up behind. It was intended, I understand, that the Way would continue straight here to follow the green road parallel to the cliffs, but problems of right of way arose, so the route follows the road as it turns inland and south, heading towards the picturesque Doonagore Castle, the fairytale silhouette of which now dominates the skyline ahead. This is one of two surviving circular tower-houses in Co. Clare; the other, Newtown Castle, is close to the Burren Way just south of Ballyvaghan. Built about the beginning of the sixteenth century, the tower was magnificently restored in the 1970s and is now a private residence.

Just under the castle the Way follows a narrow road uphill and out towards the sea, along a fine promenade with great views out to the Aran

Islands and the coast of Connemara beyond. Note the ruined cottages on the right roofed with great Liscannor stone slabs instead of slates. Soon the main road is joined again and the Way continues south-eastwards, climbing gently, until just before a sharp turn in the road the route crosses a stile through a wall on the right and heads uphill through fields towards the cliffs. The ground can be quite muddy here after wet weather, but to most walkers it will be a relief to be off the tarmac at last.

The deep indentation of Liscannor Bay comes into view off to the left as the route climbs, and then within moments the Burren Way reaches and follows what passes for the edge of the world in these parts: a margin of bare limestone slabs cantilevering sometimes metres out over the abyss. The height of the Cliffs of Moher above the sea, 200 m (656 feet) at this point, is awe-inspiring and breathtaking, as those brave enough to crawl prostrate to the edge to peek over will realise; far below, the tiny shapes of seabirds skimming the waves indicate the extent of the drop to the water. The dizzying precipices stretch on into the distance, promontory after promontory, down the coast to Hag's Head.

Nearby is O'Brien's Tower, built in 1835 by the legendary Cornelius O'Brien, Member of Parliament for Clare in the nineteenth century, as a comfortable and safe viewing stand for the cliffs, at their most splendid at this point. Inland from the tower today is a visitors' centre, with a shop, cafeteria, and toilets, always busy in summertime.

Myriad seabirds make their home on the thousands of tiny ledges provided by the strata of the cliffs. Up to early in the twentieth century the strange practice of harvesting both eggs and birds from the cliffs was carried on by local people, involving the lowering of a man on a rope at night with a bag hung around his shoulders and a lamp to dazzle the birds.

The cliffs also provided employment in the nineteenth century by yielding up fine flagstones that could be easily split into useful thicknesses, and quarries grew up along the cliffs where it was easiest to get at the stone. The flagstones, marked with distinctive fossil worm tracks, were shipped out of Liscannor and used in building work all over Ireland and Britain, notably in the Redemptorist church in Belfast and the Royal Mint in England.

The route follows the cliff edge, decorated in summer with clumps of fragrant thrift, bird's-foot trefoil and sea campion, down towards and past O'Brien's Tower. In clear weather the entire west coast of Clare can be seen stretching south-westwards; and often, beyond the point of Loop Head, the rounded blue form of Mount Brandon in Co. Kerry, 100 km (62 miles) away, is visible.

The path rises again after O'Brien's Tower; along here are the best vantage points on the cliffs for seeing the rich variety of birds that nest along this coast. Just below, a long cathedral-like rock with a roof of grass is where puffins gather. These colourful birds, who lay their eggs in burrows in the thin turf, are easy to recognise with their bright orange legs as they waddle about the grass. Guillemots, razorbills, kittiwakes and shags are here in their hundreds and often thousands, and the fulmar is always present, gliding beautifully and effortlessly back and forth. Small flocks of choughs squeal and cry as they coast along the cliff edge performing remarkable aerobatics.

To the left as the path rises, Liscannor Bay can be seen as it reaches inland to the broad expanse of Lahinch Strand. A number of old stone quarries are passed where pavements are exposed to view displaying the ripple patterns often found on a sandy beach left by a receding tide; the tide that left these ripples, however, went out 300 million years ago.

Take care in places along here to avoid coming in contact with electric fences, which can give an unpleasant shock. Ahead on this stretch, the signal tower and Hag's Head are in view most of the time. The hag concerned, named Mal, was supposedly washed up here after falling into the sea at Loop Head while chasing the champion Cú Chulainn; from this approach angle, the crag on the point resembles the head of an old woman gazing out to sea. Legend also has it that in ancient times where Liscannor Bay now is was solid land until, during a violent storm, the whole area, including a village and the Church of St Stephen, disappeared under the sea.

The 12 m (40 foot) signal tower at Hag's Head was built during the Napoleonic wars as one of a network of such towers garrisoned by military observers on the watch for a possible French invasion. At the signal tower the Way turns inland and descends following a track going south-eastwards from the head; the hill to the right is called Knockauniller (Cnoc an Iolair, Rock of the Eagle), a name that harks back to a time a hundred and fifty years ago when eagles soared above these cliffs. On the edge of Liscannor Bay ahead, the tall ruins of Liscannor Castle act as a signpost; the end of the Burren Way is nearby.

Meeting a gravel road that soon becomes tarmac, the route meanders eastwards; soon Cornelius O'Brien's memorial column can be seen off to the left, before the Way follows the tarmac down to and along the shore of Liscannor Bay. Watch out for a sign where the Way leaves the tarmac again and turns right into the fields to continue to follow the shore. The route continues eastwards, sometimes inside a wall that lines the cliffs, sometimes outside, along tiny cliff paths through the wildflower-rich grass, where care should be exercised, particularly in wet weather.

Ahead, Liscannor Castle reaches skywards; it was once occupied by Sir Turlough O'Brien, one of the Irish chiefs who, at the bidding of Sir Richard Bingham, the English Governor of Connacht, slaughtered any Spaniards who were fortunate enough to survive the storms that shredded the Spanish Armada and make it ashore on the Irish coast. He must not have been in residence when the galleass *Zuniga*, with three hundred sick and starving men on board, sheltered in the bay here in September 1588; after a week's rest the vessel put to sea again, eventually making it to Le Havre three weeks later.

The castle was owned in the seventeenth century by Daniel O'Brien who, after taking Clare's Regiment to Europe in 1691 to fight for the French, was made a French viscount and President of the Irish Brigade.

Shortly before the castle is reached, the Way turns left to reach tarmac again, and descends gently past a national school to reach the village of Liscannor, birthplace in 1841 of the inventor of the submarine, John P. Holland.

Puffin

6
THE DINGLE WAY

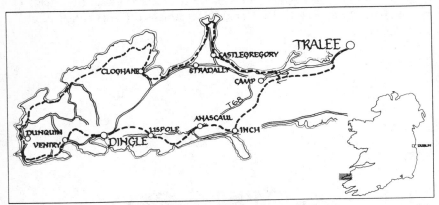

The Dingle Peninsula is the narrowest of the mountainous promontories of Co. Kerry that extend from the south-west of Ireland into the Atlantic. Unlike the others, however, its mountain backbone turns northwards at its extremity and drops dramatically into the ocean near Brandon Mountain (also called Mount Brandon), the second-highest mountain in Ireland. This neck of land contains more antiquities, beautiful beaches, exciting mountain peaks and dramatic scenery than many entire counties, and the Dingle Way has been planned to give the walker a taste for the place. As much as there is to see in the 153 km (95 miles) of the Way, when you have completed it you will know you have only scratched the surface.

The Dingle Way does not have to be walked in its entirety to enjoy it. The considerable by-road sections can be followed by car, leaving the really juicy bits for walking.

The way-markers on the Dingle Way are mainly the 'walking man' motif with arrow in yellow, although in some places where a post would not survive long, the yellow arrows have been painted directly onto stone walls or gateposts.

How to get there
Tralee is 306 km (190 miles) from Dublin and 117 km (73 miles) from Cork, and is well served by rail and by Bus Éireann.

Maps and guides
The route is covered by the Ordnance Survey Discovery Series 1:50,000 map nos 70 and 71. The route is included in *Walk Guide—Southwest of Ireland* by Seán Ó Súilleabháin, published by Gill & Macmillan.

There is also a locally produced guide, *The Dingle Way and the Saints' Road*, written and published by Maurice Sheehy, Ventry, Co. Kerry, and a Dingle Way Map-Guide, 1:50,000 (1.25 inch to 1 mile). Bord Fáilte information sheet no. 26G also describes the route.

Enquiries
Cork Kerry Tourism, Tourist House, Grand Parade, Cork; telephone 021 273251

Minard Castle

STAGE 1: TRALEE TO CAMP

DISTANCE: 19 KM (12 MILES). AGGREGATE CLIMB: 125 M (410 FEET). WALKING TIME: 5 HOURS.

The terrain on this stage varies from tarred roads to canal towpath, and from boreens to mountain tracks. The mountain track section, along the flanks of the Slieve Mish Mountains, is about 6.5 km (4 miles) long. There are fine views most of the way, and a feeling of being remote from civilisation, although the main Tralee–Dingle road is never much more than 0.75 km (0.5 mile) away. The hamlet of Camp, 0.75 km (0.5 mile) off the Dingle Way route, has a pub, a restaurant and limited bed-and-breakfast accommodation. A limited bus service is provided by the table nos 273, 275 and 281 buses from Tralee.

Tralee is a busy town full of winding, narrow streets linking tiny squares. Sometime in the nineteenth century someone tried, not too successfully, to put manners on the place by planning a few stately boulevards, such as Denny Street, but the charm of the town lies in the lack of any serious 'improvements'.

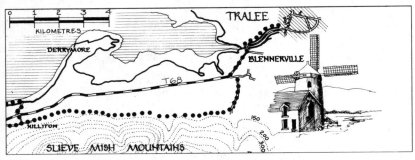

The Dingle Way starts at a crossroads a few hundred metres south of the Brandon Hotel on the south side of the town. The many peaks of the Slieve Mish Mountains line the horizon, stretching westwards out along the Dingle Peninsula. After a few minutes the route turns in to a small industrial estate and meets and follows the towpath of the old shipping canal westwards towards the sea. In the nineteenth century this was Tralee's sea port, and a vigorous boat-building industry was carried on in the grey-slated sheds on the right.

Ahead under the blue-grey massing of the mountains the unexpected and unmistakable form of a white-painted windmill comes into sight. This is the Blennerville mill, which the Way soon reaches by crossing the River Lee by an ancient narrow bridge. Built by Roland Blennerhasset in 1800, the great windmill was converted to steam power in the 1880s and, after lying derelict for much of this century, was renovated in 1987 and is now a museum.

The Tralee to Dingle Light Railway used to cross the road here in

Blennerville. The railway was constructed over the 52 km (32 mile) route in 1888, using a narrow-gauge rail to climb to an altitude of 207 m (680 feet) near Camp in a distance of under 6.5 km (4 miles), before descending to Dingle—quite a feat for a light steam engine. Like the many other light railways that sprang up in the nineteenth century, the system never made much money, but passenger services survived until 1939 and it didn't cease operation for goods until 1953. The only surviving engine is in a railway museum in Hartford, Connecticut. In recent years the stretch between Tralee and Blennerville has been revived as a tourist attraction.

About 4 km (2.5 miles) after leaving Tralee the Way turns left off the main road and heads up a narrow tarred road lined with honeysuckle, gorse, cornflowers and dog roses, towards the mountains. Just before a concrete bridge the Way turns to the right off the road onto a stone-paved pathway across the open mountainside. Clear of all trees and hedges, the vista back to the north is comprehensive and magnificent now. Blennerville windmill rises in the foreground, and the bulk of the Brandon Hotel can be easily distinguished among the glinting and grey-slated roofs of Tralee beyond. The rolling Stack Mountains—hills really, in Kerry terms—form the backdrop to the scene. From the mudflats west of the town Tralee Bay extends oceanwards towards the Atlantic, its northern shore terminating in Little Samphire Island. The bay was the centre of a significant oyster industry in the eighteenth and nineteenth centuries, yielding at times an astonishing ten to fourteen thousand oysters per day.

Although rugged in places, the mountain pathway is well constructed. Every so often tinkling streams cascade down from the heights through deep, lush ravines that groove the mountainside, but well-organised stepping-stones make crossings easy and dry. The noise of traffic on the road is replaced by the sound of the wind in the gorse, the song of meadow pipits and, in spring and early summer, the constant baaing of sturdy and thirsty lambs chasing their harassed and bedraggled mothers around the hillside. Cattle can also be met grazing on this open mountainside in summertime, a practice—called 'booleying'—that has been carried on in Ireland since ancient times. In the old days youths would be sent in summer to live with the cattle in the mountains and watch over them until autumn, daily sending the milk down to the lowlands.

At a place called Curragheen the Way crosses a boulder-strewn spur extending from the slopes towards the coast, piled up by the glacier that gouged out the deep coomb that can be seen in the mountain's flanks just ahead. The scattered sandstone boulders are of all shades of red imaginable, from deep red to pastel pink, some of them richly bejewelled with concretions of quartz, jasper, feldspar and olivine.

Soon a cascading stream is crossed by a bridge constructed with rails from the old Tralee–Dingle railway. Further west a disused reservoir, which once collected the clear mountain waters for the inhabitants of Tralee, is passed. Before drawing level with Derrymore Island, a grassy hook-shaped spit of land extending into Tralee Bay, the Way crosses another small river descending by a ravine from Baurtregaum.

Stradbally Mountain is now the dominant feature on the horizon ahead, poised over the low-lying peninsula of the Magharees. Across Tralee Bay is Samphire Island, behind which the village of Fenit can be seen. Beyond, the coast of north Kerry stretches into the distance, edged by Banna Strand, where on Good Friday 1916, Roger Casement was delivered by submarine back to his homeland, *en route* to the gallows in Pentonville Prison, London.

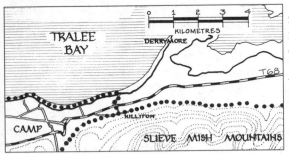

The Dingle Way now drops downhill to meet a boreen richly decorated with wildflowers, among which when I passed were the deep-orange stalks and spiky yellow flowers of bog asphodel. After a short stretch on tarmac the route follows an overgrown track perfumed with meadowsweet, herb Robert and foxgloves leading to the deserted village of Killelton.

It is difficult, even on the brightest and sunniest day, not to feel the sadness in this place under the peaks of the Slieve Mish Mountains. In the nineteenth century the entire village was evicted by the local landlord. Year by year since then nature has crept up on the buildings, cutting out the sunlight, rotting the timbers of the roofs, and spreading nettles, holly, fuchsia and ferns through the gaping doors and windows. The remains of Killelton are now swiftly deteriorating, and when I passed them the buildings were in a dangerous condition; in another ten years there will be little trace.

After crossing a stream, the Way passes by the ruins of one of the oldest churches in the country, once a structure like Gallarus Oratory, near Ballyferriter. Built in the seventh century and dedicated to St Eiltín, it gives the place its name, Cill Eiltín or Killelton. As the Way turns south now, the village of Camp with its church appears across the valley.

The boreen drops to cross the Finglas River by a series of great stepping-stones, and rises on the other side of the valley through a tunnel-like boreen to reach a crossroads. The Dingle Way carries on straight uphill, but for those finishing this section at Camp, the village is about 0.75 km (0.5 mile) to the right.

STAGE 2: CAMP TO ANASCAUL

DISTANCE: 17 KM (10.5 MILES). AGGREGATE CLIMB: 450 M (1,476 FEET). WALKING
TIME: 5.5 HOURS.

*Except for a little over 2 km (1.25 miles) on a green road at Inch, all this
stage is on tarred side-roads. At the highest point, both Tralee Bay and
Dingle Bay are in view, and the crossing of the peninsula from side to side
gives a fine sense of achievement. For those who wish to reduce the distance
there is accommodation to be had at Inch, about 12 km (7.5 miles) from
Camp. Anascaul has bed-and-breakfast accommodation and is served by
the table no. 275 Tralee–Dingle bus.*

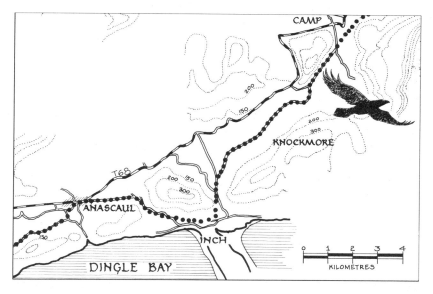

Leaving Camp and returning to the Way at the crossroads, turn to the right
and follow the road steadily uphill along the eastern flank of Corrin between
high fuchsia hedges. As altitude is gained, the hedges gradually drop away
like screens, exposing to view a dramatic wall of mountain slopes to the east.
The massif of Caherconree, at 827 m (2,713 feet) the second-highest summit
of the Slieve Mish, dominates all, its top often wreathed in cloud. Like most
big mountains, it has a presence that goes beyond its mere physical bulk and
height, and its often hidden peak adds to the sense of mystery.

Near the summit there is an Iron Age promontory fort, one of the highest
fortifications in western Europe. It occupies a triangular plateau of about
8,000 sq. m (2 acres), bounded on two sides by cliffs and on the third by a
stone-built rampart 100 m (328 feet) long, with a single entrance.

As the road reaches its highest point at over 200 m (656 feet), an
extensive panorama of Tralee Bay and north Kerry beyond can be seen

101

behind, while ahead the open moorland of a high valley stretches southwards, bounded to the east by Knockmore (572 m—1,877 feet) and to the west by Knockbeg and Knocknakilton, with Beenoskee (827 m—2,713 feet) and Stradbally Mountain (801 m—2,628 feet) beyond. In clear weather the great mass of mountains of the Iveragh Peninsula dominates the southern horizon.

The road is followed south-westwards as it descends across moorland, where extensive turf cutting is taking place. The Emlagh or Inch River is crossed as a little stream on its way to Castlemaine Harbour, and as the valley bottom descends gently it increasingly becomes greener and more fertile.

To the west the dramatic deep gash in the mountains that contains Lough Anascaul comes into sight as the Way passes briefly through a coniferous wood, heading for a pass between cairned Brickany Mountain and the westernmost portal of the Slieve Mish range. Dropping to cross the Emlagh River again, now a more respectable stream, Dingle Bay comes into view again, with the grey-blue backdrop of the Iveragh coast on the far side of the bay. Macgillycuddy's Reeks, including Ireland's highest mountain, the 1,039 m (3,415 foot) Carrauntoohil, are most prominent at the eastern end of the range.

Crossing a main road, the Way ascends again to skirt Brickany Mountain. Those breaking the stage at Inch should follow the main road downhill to reach the little resort after 1.5 km (1 mile). The Way, however, rounds the hillside, while a breathtaking view of the whole bay opens up, with the sand-duned peninsula of Inch Strand reaching almost clear across the bay, absorbing the power of continuous spuming rollers from the Atlantic. The Iveragh Peninsula presents a mountainous backdrop, with layer after layer of Paul Henry peaks reaching southwards and westwards to come to an almost abrupt end in the 691 m (2,267 foot) peak of Knocknadobar. When I walked here, a family of red-legged choughs, rare birds elsewhere in western Europe, planed and rollercoasted past me, calling to each other.

The fuchsia-lined road promenades round the southern side of the mountain, dropping and rising as it goes, until it meets the main road again, and the Way follows it uphill through a pass between Brickany and Knockafeehan. As Dingle Bay is left behind again and the highest point of the pass is reached at about 152 m (500 feet), the high mountain spine of the Dingle Peninsula comes into view again. Ahead is the cliff-ringed corrie that conceals dark and mysterious Lough Anascaul. The lake is mentioned in legends as being the scene of one of Cú Chulainn's exploits, a battle with a giant to defend the honour of a woman called Scál. The giant stood atop Knockmulanane, the eminence to the west of the lake, and Cú Chulainn positioned himself on Dromavally on the east side. For a while they argued, then they traded epic insults and finally began to hurl great boulders at each other. After a week of this, Cú Chulainn was struck by a lucky throw and fell to the ground. Scál, suddenly without her defender, jumped from the heights into the lake below and drowned, rather than face a fate worse than death with the unruly giant.

After a short distance on a boreen, the road to Anascaul is joined again, and shortly after it descends a long narrow section, very straight by Kerry standards, into the village of Anascaul.

Caherconree

STAGE 3: ANASCAUL TO DINGLE

DISTANCE: 22 KM (13.5 MILES). AGGREGATE CLIMB: 400 M (1,312 FEET). WALKING
TIME: 6.5 HOURS.

*About 14 km (9 miles) of this stage is on tarred side-roads, the rest being
wandering boreens and tracks and a short stretch of mountainside green
road. In clear weather the views across Dingle Bay and south-west along
the coast are very fine. The village of Lispole, where refreshments can be
obtained, is about half way to Dingle and is on the main Tralee–Dingle bus
route; bed-and-breakfast is available at Lisdargan, 6.5 km (4 miles) short of
Dingle. Dingle is well served by regular buses, and plenty of accommodation
is available in and around the town; in the high season, however, it is
advisable to book in advance. There were no restaurants in Dingle when*
Ryan's Daughter *was being filmed here in the 1960s, but today there are
twenty-four, some of them, like Fenton's and Whelan's, providing exceptional cuisine.*

*Anascaul is a typical Irish village, with a long main street and many
pubs. Three of them are worth noting for more than the beer they sell.
Hartnet's Corner or Ó Cinnéide's is a substantial building with an exterior
of very fine decorative plasterwork. The South Pole Inn at the western end
of the village was owned at one time by Tom Crean, who took part in polar
explorations with Scott and Shackleton. It has recently been refurbished in
the style that Tom Crean kept it, and has a South Pole display complete
with sound effects! Dan Foley's is well known for its decorative paintwork
and its larger-than-life proprietor, who in addition to being a publican and
a farmer has a reputation for being a magician and storyteller.*

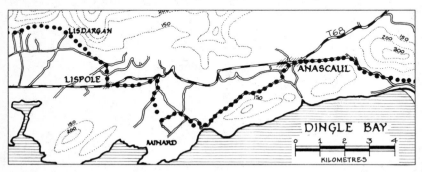

The Way follows the main road out of Anascaul, turns left onto a side-road,
and soon is wandering up along the northern flanks of Knockanaree. About
4 km (2.5 miles) out of Anascaul the road drops again to reach the coast at
Kilmurray Bay as ruined Minard Castle comes into view, perched
precariously near the water's edge. This bay is also called Béal na gCloch
(River-mouth of the Stones), the reason for which becomes obvious as the
Way reaches the shore. Where one expects a beach there is instead a great

ridge of astonishingly rounded sandstone boulders, looking for all the world like hundreds of seals resting at the water's edge. There is not a sharp corner to be seen: some of the stones are lozenge shaped, some egg shaped, some almost perfectly spherical. This unusual phenomenon is caused by tide action over the millenniums on the trapped boulders, and apparently at certain times during the rising and falling tides loud gunfire-like cracks are made by rocks striking each other.

Minard Castle was built about the middle of the sixteenth century, and must have been hardly a century old when Walter Hussey, head of one of the local Anglo-Norman families and a supporter of the Knight of Kerry, took refuge here in 1650 after being pursued by Cromwellian forces across the peninsula from Castlegregory. A siege gun was brought up, and from an emplacement on the cliffs the castle was bombarded and severely damaged, and Hussey was killed. The castle was abandoned, and before leaving, the Cromwellians mined the four corners and blew them out. This, surprisingly, failed to level the ruin, and it still stands cornerless today, looking dangerously unstable.

Leaving the shore, the Way follows a series of by-roads and boreens between fragrant hedges that in summertime are ablaze with deep-red fuchsia. Nearly 3 km (2 miles) after leaving Minard Castle the route reaches Aglish graveyard. Like most of the graveyards on the Dingle Peninsula, Aglish is a necropolis of mausoleums: coffins are not buried but placed on the earth inside a vaulted tomb.

After leaving Aglish the Way follows the road through two junctions and descends a narrow boreen towards the village of Lispole. A substantial stone-and-steel viaduct that once carried the Tralee–Dingle railway can be seen in the valley below, before the boreen brings you suddenly onto the village street.

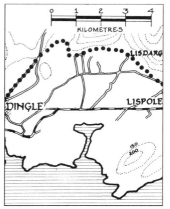

Lispole is a tiny village on the Tralee–Dingle road with a shop and a post office, named after a nearby earthen enclosure, Lios Póil. Leaving the village, the Way follows the road over the Poteen Bridge, so named because the Revenue men made a large seizure of poitín here a hundred years ago. Unlike most other rural areas of Ireland, Dingle has no real tradition of poitín-making, probably because of the availability of more exotic smuggled spirits during the eighteenth and nineteenth centuries.

After the bridge the Way heads north-west, following a side-road lined with crab-apple trees. At a crossroads a detour to the left of about 200 m (656 feet) will take you to a large earth-banked lios surrounding a ruined eighth-century church, one of very few in Ireland dedicated to St Martin. He was a French saint who was the son of a Roman soldier and had a great reputation for learning and piety. When he died in the year 400 he was bishop of Tours.

Nearly three-quarters of an hour after leaving Lispole the Way turns into the fields to reach a narrow boreen and continue towards the north-west. In wet weather the ground is extremely muddy and anoints walkers with the miasma of the Irish countryside!

The boreen meets tarmac again just before the hamlet of Lisdargan, but leaves it behind again to follow a narrow boreen along the 120 m (393 feet) contour below Croaghskearda Mountain. From here there are great views down to the coast and across Dingle Bay; Ballymacadoyle Hill, enclosing the southern side of Dingle Harbour, can also be seen, but the town itself is hidden by a hill to its east.

A stream is traversed by stepping-stones, and the route crosses fields to reach another stretch of boreen. Be vigilant for way-markers along here; some consist of yellow arrows painted on stone walls. The route wanders quite a bit along this hillside and it is easy to go astray, particularly if signposts are missing; do not leave it too long before you ask directions. Your immediate goal, the Connor Pass road, is a couple of kilometres due west.

A farmyard with a beautiful stone-built farmhouse is reached and passed through, following a boreen to the right of the house, before the Way meanders uphill to reach eventually a rampart-like green road at Ballybowler, below the 490 m (1,607 foot) peak of Knockmoylemore.

In a deep valley to the left the River Garfinn thunders down from the Connor Pass as the route swings out onto open heathland and round the hillside towards the north-west. There are fine views down to the left across a hillside scattered with lichen-dappled boulders, each with a thatch of turf or gorse, and to the north the 625 m (2,050 foot) Ballysitteragh looms above Knockmoylemore on the far side of the Connor Pass.

The roaring of the Garfinn below grows until the green road draws level with it, and the Way crosses the cataract over a concrete bridge. At the far side a rough track is followed through a chevaux-de-frise of scattered erratics to a green road. This was the old road to Dingle up to the time of the Great Famine, when the present Connor Pass road was constructed on a famine relief scheme. Soon the main road is crossed and the route follows the tarred side-road steeply downhill into Dingle town.

The pre-Norman Irish name for Dingle was Daingean Uí Chúis, the Fortress of Ó Cúis, the chieftain who ruled the area. Its marvellously sheltered harbour was an ideal location for a trading port from very early times, and in the sixteenth century, when trade with Spain was at its height, it would have provided safe mooring for the Spanish galleons. It has been said that many of the old Dingle families have Spanish blood from those days.

STAGE 4: DINGLE TO DUNQUIN

DISTANCE: 22 KM (13.5 MILES). AGGREGATE CLIMB: 350 M (1,150 FEET). WALKING
TIME: 6.5 HOURS.

*About 13 km (8 miles) of this stage is on tarred roads, with the balance over
boreens, the beach at Ventry, and a magnificent track along the southern
slopes of Mount Eagle. If the weather is good the unfolding landscape and
spectacular vistas should more than relieve the length of the day's walk.
The last few kilometres of this stage introduce the walker to the unique
ruggedness of the Dingle Peninsula's Atlantic coast, and the scenery
becomes more dramatic and breathtaking with each step.*

*Dunquin has a number of houses offering bed-and-breakfast, in addition
to a hostel. There are no restaurants, so arrangements should be made in
advance for an evening meal. There is a twice-daily bus service in
summertime (the table no. 276 Dingle–Dunquin bus) connecting to Ventry,
Slea Head and Ballyferriter; details should be checked in advance with the
local Bus Éireann office.*

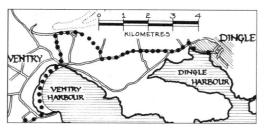

The Way leaves Dingle by
the road along the harbour
front, crossing the
Milltown River by a stone
bridge. An astonishing
sight can be seen a little
further on. In the typical
suburban front garden of a
new two-storey house stands a massive 3 m (10 foot) gallán. It is called the
'Milestone', because it is apparently a mile from the centre of Dingle, but it
has probably been here since two thousand years before Dingle came into
being. In the fields around are more ancient ceremonial stones, some with
patterns of circles and lines carved on them; indeed over seventy of these
prehistoric monuments have been counted within 3 km (1.8 miles) of
Dingle.

Soon the Way turns off the main road and winds through the countryside
towards the hill of Caherard, passing to the north of it by a grassy boreen
that was once the main route between Dunquin and Dingle. Reaching
tarmac again, the route passes a monastic site called Kilcolman before it
follows a road downhill towards Ventry Harbour and enters the village.

Ventry is a small seaside resort with a number of bed-and-breakfast
places and a small caravan park, a pub, a shop, and a pottery shop where you
can buy unique and colourful local pottery as well as having a snack or
coffee.

The Way takes to the shore at Ventry for the first of a number of beach
stretches on the circuit of the peninsula. It is a curving and flat beach where

the tide goes out quite far, busy in summer at the Ventry end but usually deserted at the far (southern) end. At the back of the southern end of the beach is a marsh where a variety of wildfowl can be seen, including in summertime the colourful shelduck.

Mount Eagle is now beginning to dominate the surroundings; it is not the simple dome-shaped hill it seemed from further away but has a great hollow coomb gouged out of its centre, which contains a lake. At the southern end of the beach the Way turns inland to reach the main Slea Head road, and almost immediately turns up a grassy boreen between two houses. A great panorama of Ventry and Dingle Harbours opens up behind, and as the thick fuchsia hedges lining the boreen recede, the entire western coastline of the Iveragh Peninsula, terminating in Valencia Island and Bray Head, comes into view to the south. Beyond, if visibility is reasonable, two spire-like shapes, the Skelligs, can be seen projecting sharply from the horizon.

The boreen being followed soon peters out and the Way continues along its line to the right of a stone wall. As the gradient levels out, Inishvickillane, the southernmost of the Blasket Islands, comes into view across a patchwork of stone-walled fields. The island is owned by former Taoiseach Charles Haughey, who has built a summer house there and imported a herd of red deer to colonise the fertile if windswept land.

Soon a thickly overgrown green road is joined, and as the Way descends slightly the Iron Age promontory fort of Dunbeg can be seen below on the cliff edge. Passing a group of cottages and a short section of tarmac, the route climbs again, up a rocky green road beside a stream tinkling under an umbrella of fuchsia. Heather, thyme, gorse and cornflowers decorate the Way here in summer, and red admiral butterflies can be abundant on warm days.

Dingle comes into view behind, across that narrow neck of land that divides Dingle Harbour from Ventry Harbour. Choughs and ravens coast along the heights above, their calls echoing off rock faces and boulders. Nearly a kilometre below, the main road in summer can be a continuous procession of tour buses and cars, while up here one feels remote from it all, as if on a personal tour.

Soon another of the Blaskets comes into view as the first of a number of beehive huts along this stretch can be seen beyond the stone wall on the left. These circular structures date from the Early Christian period and are thought to have been used as religious hermitages. They were built entirely of stone, even the roof being cleverly corbelled from the tops of the walls. Some are today fulfilling new uses as sheds or hen-houses, while others, overgrown with hats of gorse and heather and looking like Central American Mayan tombs, are shown to the tourists for a small charge.

The Way now drops into Glanfahan, where it crosses a bridge over a picturesque mountain stream. After passing an old cottage, the route begins to rise again and to round towards the north-west as it skirts Slea Head. As the open Atlantic is faced for the first time, the surroundings become dramatically rugged: the hillside that the Way passes over now has a minimum of vegetation and is scattered with a confusion of rocks and boulders.

As the westernmost flanks of Slea Head are reached and the Great Blasket and Dunmore Head come into sight, it is well worth stopping for a while to enjoy the impressive view and the constantly changing patterns of light on the islands and the sea. John Millington Synge wrote of a visit to this place at the turn of the century that it 'seemed ten times more grey and wild and magnificent than anything I had kept in my memory'.

Even on calm days the sea seems to be agitated here: the Blasket Sound between the Great Blasket and Dunmore Head is rarely without a vicious rip tide, and interface where two opposing forces of billions of tonnes of water wrestle with one another. Creamy-white gannets put on a spectacular show of diving from a height of eighty metres, with wings folded, into the teeming waters, to surface seconds later swallowing fish. These great birds, whose wings can span up to nearly two metres, come here from the Skelligs about 40 km (25 miles) to the south, where twenty thousand of them breed every year. Dark cormorants crisscross the bay purposefully, centimetres above the water's surface, in rock-steady, straight-line flight. Fulmars revel in the updraughts from the cliffs and seem to spend their time performing beautiful aerobatics just for the fun of it.

Perched on the hillside below is Coomeenoole, a scatter of small houses, farms and ruins interlinked by stone walls and clocháns or beehive huts, some very ancient, some quite modern. The Way descends the hillside to meet the main Slea Head road, which seems to appear from under the cliffs, and follows it round the bay towards Dunmore Head. Drawing level with the little strand between the head and the mainland, the remains of a cargo ship are visible, tossed ashore here in 1982, now perched in the grip of evil-looking pointed rocks along the side of the head.

Many ships have been similarly wrecked in this area, the most famous being the *San Juan de Ragusa* and the *Santa María de la Rosa*, two great ships of the Spanish Armada. In the late summer of 1588 the invasion armada of Felipe II of Spain, having failed to make a landing in England, was swept north round the coast of Scotland, and what remained of its 130 warships and transports attempted to return to Spain by way of the west coast of Ireland. Atlantic storms, however, played havoc with the overloaded vessels, and Irish waters became the last resting-place of over twenty of the great ships. The *Santa María de la Rosa*, a Basque-built merchant ship, sought the shelter of the Blaskets. The raging eddying seas in the sound were bad enough, but when the tide changed it became a maelstrom, and the *Santa María*, its sails in shreds, foundered, all but one of the 250 on board drowning. Later the *San Juan*, another merchant ship, was driven onto the coast, but somehow it was found possible to transfer its crew to another Spanish vessel before it also sank. In the 1960s much of the remains of the cargo and effects of the *Santa María* were rediscovered and excavated in a complex and difficult underwater archaeological dig.

Passing by Dunmore Head, the northernmost Blasket Island, Inis Tuaisceart, comes into view beyond a fringe of spume-rimmed jagged rocks that must have been among the last things to be seen on earth by those Armada sailors. The whole coastline has now taken on a rugged harsh look, forged by the heavy seas that have hammered at the cliffs here for thousands of years. Clogher Head extends into the sea ahead, behind which the ragged Sybil Head reaches 152 m (499 feet) out of the sea. In from the coast Cruach Mhártain (406 m—1,332 feet) is a backdrop to the scattered village of Dunquin, called by an early tourist in 1845 'the wildest place in the whole world', where 'the women dress like men and the men like women'.

The Way drops to a small beach, passing a riot of thrift, thyme, cornflowers, montbretia and heather hanging over a vigorous cascading stream, the whole effect being one a classic landscape gardener would find difficult to equal. Leaving the beach, the Way ascends inland past a controversial Interpretative Centre built to commemorate the Blasket Island and its people, to reach Kruger's bar, the end of this stage. Nearby is the An Óige hostel and a number of houses offering bed-and-breakfast accommodation.

Kruger's, where accommodation may also be had, used to be owned by a larger-than-life Kerry character, Kruger Kavanagh. After some years in the United States, where he had show-business connections, he retired in the 1920s and bought the bar. He was so well liked in America that hardly a year went by for the rest of his life without some Broadway or Hollywood star making their way to west Kerry to spend time with him. This phenomenon in turn attracted more attention from writers, poets and artists, and Dunquin became a little cultural mecca, presided over by Kruger Kavanagh.

STAGE 5: DUNQUIN TO BALLYCURRANE

DISTANCE: 24 KM (15 MILES). AGGREGATE CLIMB: 200M (656 FEET). WALKING TIME: 6.5 HOURS.

This stage has 11 km (7 miles) on tarmac, 4 km (2.5 miles) on beaches, and the balance on clifftop tracks and boreens. It can be divided into two stages: 13 km (8 miles) to the village of Ballydavid and 11 km (7 miles) to Ballycurrane. At Ballydavid, TP's pub offers food, and at least four houses and a hostel provide overnight accommodation. At Ballycurrane you have reached almost as far as urban civilisation extends this side of Mount Brandon. Some overnight accommodation is available, and at An Bóthar pub on weekend nights you can hear and see the best traditional music and dancing I have chanced upon on the Dingle Peninsula. There are a couple of restaurants in nearby Ballyferriter and another in the Dún an Óir Golf Hotel—passed by the Way about 6.5 km (4 miles) out of Dunquin—but unless transport is available, arrangements will need to be made in advance for an evening meal.

The table no. 277 Dingle–Ballydavid regular bus service operates on Tuesdays and Fridays only. Cuas, near the end of this section at Ballycurrane, is also served by the table no. 277 bus.

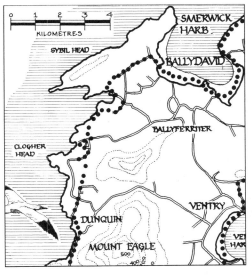

The Way follows the road northwards and uphill from the crossroads near the An Óige hostel and before long leaves the road to head across open moorland under the Minnaunmore Rock. Here in the 1960s an entire village was built for the filming of *Ryan's Daughter*, one of the first films to cash in on the unique and dramatic scenery of the Dingle area. As the highest point of the plateau is reached, a panorama unfolds of the coast that this stage of the Way will follow. A hillocked arm of land called the Three Sisters, looking like three great tidal waves frozen in time, encloses Smerwick Harbour, with the bulk of Ballydavid Head beyond.

Dropping to the tarmac again, the Way passes the studios and showrooms of the potter Louis Mulcahy, who is well known for his vast full-bodied urns and vases, pieces that are very difficult to make and fire successfully. Further on, the main road is left behind again as the Way drops to Clogher Beach beside a tinkling brook. More film must be exposed to the light in this place than in any other spot in the Dingle area. The combination of the changing skyscape, dramatic light patterns on the sea and rocks and the often violent and thunderous sea makes it very difficult to take a bad photograph here. For those with an interest in geology, Clogher Beach and its little headland have lots of fossils to offer.

Leaving the beach, the Way follows the road uphill and soon turns onto a stony boreen to reach the shore again. A path is followed north-eastwards along the edge of a low cliff, with Ballydavid Head looming ahead on the horizon, looking from this angle like a big brother to the Three Sisters. The cliffs have a stark, ragged and primordial look here, as if the cataclysmic volcanic event that bore them from the depths of the earth finished only hours before. The path wends its way between clumps of thrift and thyme, while offshore, gannets put on an entertaining show as they dive constantly for food. Choughs, oystercatchers and curlews cry indignantly and take to the air when their grazing along the path is disturbed.

As the Way comes parallel to a pair of bungalows it turns inland to wander through the hamlet of Ballincolla which, judging from the number of ruined botháns and outhouses, was once a populous village. The road loops round between hedges of montbretia, meadowsweet and, curiously, a species of bamboo, until it reaches the shore again near the Dún an Óir Hotel.

Passing the hotel, the Way follows a track north-eastwards along the golf links to meet a boreen on the far side. The lush and fragrant growth of wildflowers and herbs along here contrasts dramatically with the harshness of the rocky shoreline recently passed. In 2 sq. m of dry-stone wall, deeply invaded by plant life, I counted twenty-two separate species of plants, not including grasses.

After passing a little hamlet of stone-built houses and outhouses, the road descends towards Smerwick Harbour, passing a strange stockade-like structure that protects a tomato nursery.

Before reaching the beach it is worth taking a detour to visit the site of the siege of Dún an Óir of 1580. At the end of a track can be found the eroded remains of an Iron Age promontory fort. Here in 1579 a small force of Spanish soldiers established themselves to assist in an Irish revolt, reinforced the following year by six hundred Italians under the command of Sebastiano di San Giuseppe of Bologna. Lord Winton de Grey, the Lord Deputy appointed by Queen Elizabeth I with a brief to destroy all rebellion in Ireland, arrived at Smerwick in November 1580 and laid siege to the expeditionary force. He was still smarting over his ignominious defeat two months before by Fiach Mac Hugh O'Byrne in the Battle of Glenmalure, and was anxious to vindicate his queen's trust. Included in his army was the young Walter Raleigh, while the Lord Deputy's secretary was Edmund Spenser, later to become one of the finest poets of the sixteenth century.

It is clear today that the promontory would have been difficult to defend against a serious attack from the higher ground inland, but it was probably the sight of Admiral Winter's fleet sailing into the harbour that was the last straw: San Giuseppe decided to surrender, on condition that his garrison be spared. No sooner had they laid down their arms than de Grey sent in 'certeyn bandes who streight fell to execution . . . there were 600 slayne'. There is a local field called Gort na gCrann (Field of the Heads) where, it is said, the heads of the unfortunate foreigners were buried after the massacre. Only the Italian commander and some of the officers were spared.

On reaching the beach the Way follows it round the broad sweep of the bay to the village of Ballydavid. The name Smerwick is not Irish but Scandinavian, from the Norse *Smjör-Vík* (Butter Harbour). Ballydavid was originally a Viking trading-post, from which they shipped butter and other foodstuffs to the Vikings of Limerick.

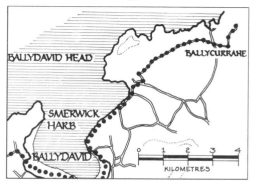

The Way passes the pier and leaves the village to follow a grassy cliffside track, passing by a World War II look-out post. Inland, the steel-framed transmitter mast of Raidió na Gaeltachta reaches into the sky. Outcrops of crystals and minerals in the rocks that make up the cliffs along here will delay those with an interest in geology—and probably weigh down their knapsacks, as they did mine!

The Way rejoins the public road just north of Ardamore and drops through Feohanagh, which must be the most remote community on the peninsula. Crossing the Feohanagh River the route turns towards the great massif of Brandon, now looming close; and unless it is very misty, the saddle over which the Way crosses the mountain, between Masatiompan and Brandon, should be visible. Above to the left can be seen the remains of a signalling tower dating from the Napoleonic wars, looking like just one more rocky crag on the skyline. If you have the time and energy, there is a marvellous cliff walk from the tower north-east to Brandon Creek.

At the next crossroads, where a sign indicates Brandon Creek to the left, this stage of the Way comes to an end. It is from Brandon Creek in the sixth century that St Brendan is said to have sailed out into the Atlantic to discover America a full nine-and-a-half centuries before Christopher Columbus made his voyage. St Brendan was born near Killarney about the year 489, and after studying under St Enda, was involved in the foundation of a number of monasteries in Ireland and Britain. His adventures crossing the Atlantic were set down in a Latin manuscript, 'Navigatio Sancti

Brendani Abbatis', reputed to have been written by Brendan himself and telling the story of reaching the Promised Land via the Isle of Sheep, the Paradise of Birds and the Isle of Smiths.

Whether the Navigatio is just a medieval thriller or a poetic description of a real journey will probably never be known, but in 1977 the latter-day explorer Tim Severin 'restaged' Brendan's voyage, using the same boat design and setting out from the same Brandon Creek, to see if it could be done. After fifty days, during which he and his crew experienced many adventures and incidents that had remarkable similarities to those set down in the Navigatio, they made land on the northern coast of Newfoundland.

An Bóthar pub and guesthouse is not far now to the right at the crossroads.

St Brendan's Voyage

STAGE 6: BALLYCURRANE TO CLOGHANE

DISTANCE: 22 KM (14 MILES). AGGREGATE CLIMB: 750 M (2,460 FEET). WALKING TIME: 7.5 HOURS.

This is the most mountainous stretch of the Dingle Way, ascending to a saddle between Brandon (953 m—3,126 feet) and Masatiompan (765 m—2,509 feet) at about 650 m (2,130 feet). If covered in good weather the stage should not present problems for most walkers, and the rewards are great. It is an area, however, that is prone to low clouds and mists, so if in any doubt about the weather or your ability to deal with it, do not take the chance. After the long descent on the east side, a stop for liquid refreshments can be made nearly 5 km (3 miles) short of Cloghane, at the picturesque fishing village of Brandon. Cloghane has accommodation, but arrangements should be made in advance for evening meals. At the time of writing there is no bus service to Cloghane.

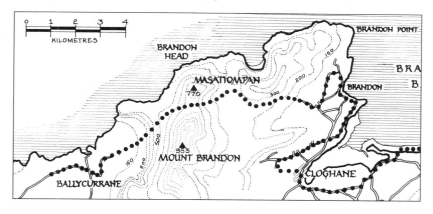

This stage sets out from the crossroads south of Brandon Creek and heads towards the wall of mountain that fills the eastern horizon. In clear weather Brandon Mountain, the second-highest in Ireland, dominates the scene. To its left Masatiompan plunges steeply and abruptly into the sea. The Way wanders gently uphill, passing some remote farms, until the tarred road comes to an end at Tiduff and the route ascends in earnest, up along a turf track following a fence. Part of the route to the pass, an overgrown military road to another signal tower of the Napoleonic wars, can be traced high up on the slope ahead.

As the Way rises, a panorama of the route that has been followed opens up behind, the cliffs of Ballydavid Head shelving dramatically into the sea, with Smerwick Harbour and the Three Sisters beyond extending to Sybil Head. When the fence runs out, widely spaced way-markers indicate the route ahead; be vigilant, however, if visibility is not good, and always try to keep one marker in sight, ahead or behind.

The track gets rougher as it rises through large patches of bare rock, stripped of their peat covering over the centuries by erosion and by cottagers seeking fuel to warm their winters. It is a steep and steady climb, but the gradually widening views give plenty of excuses to stop for breath. The gradient eases off near the cliffs of Beennamon, where in rough weather the waves on the rocks below send a thick salty mist in over the land, and there is often a rainbow arching over the cliffs. The signal tower that was built here was soon abandoned when it was discovered that it was almost always mistbound.

Ahead now rises the spectacular rocky western façade of Masatiompan, and the sea to the north comes into view again over high cliffs. A last climb brings the Way up onto the saddle, an area stripped almost bare of any grass or turf, scattered with grey slabs of sandstone and patrolled by soaring ravens. To the left are the grey ramparts of Masatiompan, and up to the right are the conical domes of Brandon Mountain. A slender ogham stone called the Monument stands in the middle of this desolate place, with a Greek cross inscribed on it.

To the east a fabulous view unfolds: beach-ringed Brandon Bay sweeps round to the low-lying Magharees, overlooked by the bulk of Stradbally Mountain and Beenoskee, while beyond, Tralee Bay stretches inland. Below to the left is the northernmost spur of Brandon Mountain, deeply bitten into by Sauce Creek, where Slieveglas drops over 300 m (984 feet) into the sea. This is a magnificent viewpoint, possibly the finest on the Dingle Way, and it is worth while lingering over it with a map to find and identify far-off features.

The Way now drops steeply into a valley east of the scree and boulder-strewn slopes of Masatiompan. The path can sometimes be hard to discern, but frequent way-markers indicate the route. At the valley bottom, stone-walled fields with ancient patterns of cultivation are passed before a couple of ruined cottages at Arraglen are reached. This is all that remains of a community of thirteen families who established themselves here in the eighteenth century after quarrelling with their neighbours at Murrirrigane on the far side of the hill. Note how one of the tiny, narrow stone cottages seems to grow out of the ground, its gable and chimney built up off the bedrock.

Slieveglas is the crash site of one of the four aircraft to come down on Brandon during World War II, when a giant Sunderland seaplane, en route from Lisbon to Foynes (precursor of Shannon Airport), hit the hillside in 1943, killing eleven of its crew and destroying 27,000 poignant letters from prisoners of war in Japanese camps to their relatives in England. The other aircraft to come to grief on Brandon were a Luftwaffe Condor in 1940, another Sunderland in 1943, and an RAF Wellington bomber a month later.

Now the Way turns from the sea again, following a rough roadway round the southern side of Brandon Point. The tarred road is eventually joined, and the route continues to descend towards the cluster of grey roofs that is the village of Brandon, with its small pier extending into the bay. The hydrangea-decorated hamlets of Teer and Lisnakealwee are passed—the latter renowned on the peninsula for its high-kicking Gaelic football players —before the route, after a tantalising loop round to the north, reaches Brandon.

Brandon has a shop, a post office and a few pubs, the most picturesque of which is Nora Murphy's little bar overlooking the pier. In the last century this was a vigorous fishing village, with as many as a hundred Dingle currachs and a number of sailing hookers operating from the old pier.

The Way leaves Brandon, heading south along the shore to cross a footbridge and, a short distance after, reaching tarmac again. The road winds through farmland and, crossing the main road, heads up into the townland of Cloonsharragh. The wide, sandy estuary of the Owenmore River can be seen below to the left, where some years ago a large school of sixty-three pilot whales stranded themselves on the beach.

Turning off the tarred road, the Way crosses a stream and, joining a pleasant green road like an overgrown garden pathway, drops down towards Cloghane. A ruined church, surrounded by a typical Dingle cemetery, is passed, described by the writer Richard Hayward as 'the ugliest huddle of tombs I have ever seen in my life'. When I passed by, some of the tombs were damaged, exposing to view their grisly contents.

Close by are the remains of a thirteenth-century church, the trabeated doorway of which faces the green road. An effigy of the pagan god Crom Dubh can be seen on the inside of one of its walls, an example of the practice in Early Christian times of legitimising such gods and converting them into Christian saints. Until early this century the feast-day of this ancient god, Domhnach Chrom Dubh—the last Sunday in July—was celebrated in Cloghane by people who came from all over the Dingle area.

The Way suddenly enters the village of Cloghane opposite T. Moriarty's pub and turns right onto a pleasant narrow street of stone-built houses. On the front of O'Connor and O'Dowd's pub a plaque commemorates the war-time air crashes on Brandon, while in the yard of the pub the remains of an engine from the Condor that crashed on Slieveglas stand on a little pedestal surrounded by geraniums. In 1989 another of the plane's engines was presented to the German Air Force museum and was received on its behalf by the original pilot, on a return visit to Ireland after nearly fifty years.

STAGE 7: CLOGHANE TO CASTLEGREGORY

DISTANCE: 22 KM (13.5 MILES). WALKING TIME: 5.5 HOURS.

This stage can be broken into two very easy days by walking nearly 13 km (8 miles) to Castlegregory the first day and covering the 14.5 km (9 mile) circuit of the peninsula the following day. The stage includes 6.5 km (4 miles) on tarred roads, but is mostly along broad sandy beaches, best walked at low tide. There are a number of bed-and-breakfast prospects in Castlegregory, in addition to two camping parks. On reaching Castlegregory you are again connecting with the table no. 273 bus route to Tralee (limited service only).

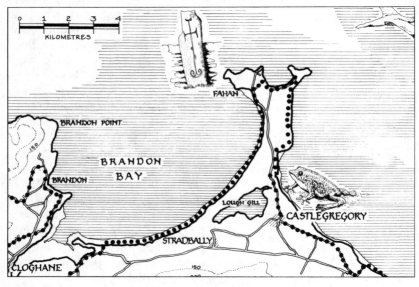

The Way leaves Cloghane heading south, leaving in the background Brandon Mountain, with Stradbally Mountain and Beenoskee now looming ahead. Off to the right as the road bears round to the east a new range of high peaks appears, the mountain wall over which the Connor Pass road climbs to reach Dingle. Soon the road is heading north-east, over a series of humped-back bridges, until the extensive lagoon at the back of Brandon Bay, a haunt of herons, ducks and waders, is passed.

The Way turns off the main road below Fermoyle House and, crossing a narrow three-arched bridge, follows a track through marram grass, ablaze when I passed with fragrant lady's bedstraw. In minutes the track reaches the beach and heads eastwards, out towards the sandy peninsula that divides Tralee Bay from Dingle Bay. The breakers can be most impressive along here, especially when the tide is high, with thundering wave after wave racing in from the bay to explode on the sands and then to draw back, sucking and rustling the shingle. Ahead now on the horizon, hardly higher than the beach itself, the thin, undulating line of the Magharees stretches northwards. Off to the left the mountainous landmass of the north-western Dingle Peninsula comes to an abrupt and bulbous end at Brandon Head.

If the tide is not too high, a brisk pace can be maintained on the level sands, the only interruptions being the frequent streams emptying mountain waters into the sea. If you are dividing this stage into two and heading for Castlegregory, take the third exit from the beach, which leads up to Stradbally village. Castlegregory is almost 3 km (1.75 miles) further on.

Continuing along the beach, the individual houses in the village of Fahamore at the end of the peninsula soon become clearly distinguishable. To the east now, behind marram-covered dunes, lies Lough Gill, an important wildfowl reserve. Whooper, Bewick's and mute swans can be seen together here in season, and the relatively uncommon gadwall duck can also be spotted. One extremely rare inhabitant of the lough area you are unlikely to see is the natterjack toad, Ireland's only native toad, which is confined to a small number of coastal areas in Kerry.

If the tide is high when you walk this stretch, you may find it more comfortable to cut inland and follow the edge of the dunes through an abundance of fragrant wildflowers, of which wild thyme, pyramidal orchids, clover and lady's bedstraw were blooming when I passed.

The northern part of the Magharees is a populous and prosperous-looking place, where the sandy soil, the climate and the underlying limestone combine to produce good carrots, potatoes and onions, in addition to a newer crop, daffodils. When Arthur Young passed this way two hundred years ago he reported the place 'all under the plough' and 'famous for the best wheat in Kerry'.

The Way turns off the beach at Spillane's bar, where a good meal can be had, and continues past the old national school between stone-walled fields to reach Scraggane Bay. Fahamore Pier, where the local fishing boats moor, extends from the left shore into the bay. The Way follows the rocky shore round the bay, at the eastern portal of which is another little village, gathered close to the ruined church of Kilshannig and its graveyard. Standing propped against the north wall of the church is a cross-inscribed stone slab that is an example of the merging of the Christian and pre-Christian traditions. What looks like a crescent shape at the top of the stone is the remnant of a chi-rho symbol, the Greek initials for 'Christ', while the divergent spiral at the bottom is a powerful pre-Christian symbol.

Some of the contemporary grave decorations here are remarkable and unusual; note the colourful and almost surrealist pictures painted on some sea-polished stones marking graves.

Out to sea now the Magharee Islands or Seven Hogs can be seen, the rugged limestone plateaux of the furthest islands looking like a small fleet of aircraft carriers.

The Way now turns back towards the mainland again, passing through an informal scatter of cottages and crossing a common of cropped grass and clover to reach the shore. If the weather is clear the views inland from here are good. To the east the windmill at Blennerville will locate Tralee, to the south-east the craggy massif of Caherconree rises above the village of Camp; and to the south rises the bulk of Stradbally Mountain.

After about 1.5 km (1 mile) the tiny Lough Naparka is passed just inland; nearby, an ancient village has disappeared beneath the wind-blown sand. Rounding a promontory, pass Sandy Bay before the route crosses Trench Bridge, which controls the flow of water from Lough Gill, and follows the road into the village of Castlegregory.

This is the only village on the north shore of the Dingle Peninsula that survived through the Great Famine. It takes its name from a sixteenth-century castle built here by Gregory Hoare. The castle has long disappeared but some stones from it can be found, built into the walls of the older houses. The simple Catholic church has a fine stained-glass window from the Harry Clarke studio.

Old Churchyard, Cloghane

STAGE 8: CASTLEGREGORY TO TRALEE

DISTANCE: 23 KM (14 MILES). AGGREGATE CLIMB: 275 M (900 FEET). WALKING TIME: 6 HOURS.

After 10.5 km (6.5 miles) of this stage, the outgoing route at Killelton is rejoined. If you do not wish to retrace the route along the mountain flanks to Blennerville and Tralee described in Stage 1 (page 98) you can wait nearby on the main road for the table no. 275 Tralee–Dingle bus, or alternatively go back about 2.5 km (1.5 miles) to Camp and wait for the bus in the comfort of Ashe's pub. All but about 6.5 km (4 miles) of this last stage to Tralee is on tarred roads.

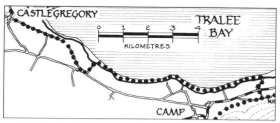

Leave Castlegregory by the long straight road leading east, through open country and salt marshes. Approximately 1.75 km (1 mile) from the village the road fords a stream, which is crossed by a picturesque footbridge. From here a sandy track heads towards the dunes lining the shore, where pyramidal orchids and bursts of lady's bedstraw decorated the grassy slopes when I passed. Nearby is a commemorative cross erected for a Volunteer who died here in a gun battle in 1921, just beyond which there is an opening to the beach, but the Way follows the sandy road inland. Soon tarmac replaces the sand, and the main Tralee–Castlegregory road is met just opposite the Tralee Bay Hotel.

Turning left, follow the main road for a short distance before the route drops towards the shore again to reach Aughacasla Strand and follows it eastwards. The low-lying Magharees to the north-west are already receding below the horizon, while nearly 12 km (7.5 miles) away to the north, Illaunabarnagh, a dramatic Skellig-like crag, rises abruptly from the sea off the north Kerry coast.

The Way now follows the beach for nearly 5 km (3 miles), bringing us closer to the base of the Slieve Mish Mountains until, rounding a point, an elegant spire of combined limestone and sandstone can be seen rising from behind the cliffs ahead. This is Kilgobbin Church, surrounded by an extensive graveyard, and worth a brief visit.

A little more than 2.5 km (1.5 miles) after passing the church, the Way turns up a track that takes the route back to the main Tralee road. If you want to rejoin the outgoing route, turn left along the road for a few hundred metres and then right, up a narrow side-road, which takes you back to the outgoing Way 0.75 km (0.5 mile) west of Killelton (see page 100).

7

THE GRAND CANAL WAY

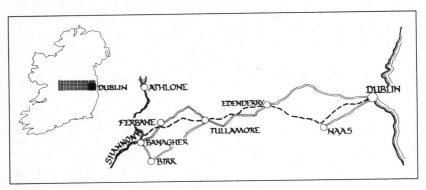

Work on the construction of the Grand Canal began in 1751, to link the east coast of Ireland with the west, and to open up the midlands. It was a difficult and expensive venture; it took thirty-two years to complete the first 42 km (26 miles) and the Shannon was not reached until 1805. It did indeed open the midlands to trade, and towns such as Tullamore benefited enormously from the canal up to the time that rail and road transport finally made it redundant in the 1950s.

As part of the Office of Public Works' great efforts to renovate Ireland's canals for amenity use, the towpaths have also been renovated as walking routes. Along the Grand Canal there exists today an informal linear park, a unique and rich habitat for flora and fauna that have been all but banished from the surrounding countryside by modern agriculture. The canal bank is also a living industrial museum, where fine examples of eighteenth- and nineteenth-century engineering works and architecture, still in use, can be enjoyed. Towpaths vary from grassy paths to gravel and tarmac side-roads, and of course, with the highest point 85 m (280 feet) above sea level, the route is, to all intents and purposes, flat.

The Grand Canal Way stretches 130 km (81 miles) from its beginning in Dublin's docks to the River Shannon. The first ten miles or so are through the city and suburbs, a few areas of which, between Portobello and Clondalkin, were decidedly un-scenic and unpleasant when I walked them. You can avoid these by taking a bus to Clondalkin. At the Shannon end, you need to walk a further 5 km (3 miles) to access accommodation and services at Banagher.

How to Get There
The route begins in Ringsend in central Dublin, and ends at Shannon Harbour on the River Shannon, which is about 138 km (86 miles) by road from Dublin.

Maps and Guides

The route is covered by the Ordnance Survey 1:127,000 (0.5 inch to 1 mile) map nos 15 and 16. The excellent *Guide to the Grand Canal*, published by the Office of Public Works, intended for cruising the waterway, is also worthwhile for walkers.

Enquiries

Office of Public Works—Canals Section, 51 St Stephen's Green, Dublin 2; telephone 01 6613111

Ethel Power, Offaly Tourism, Bury Quay, Tullamore, Co. Offaly; telephone 0506 52566

STAGE 1: RINGSEND TO CLONDALKIN

DISTANCE: 12 KM (7.5 MILES). WALKING TIME: 3 HOURS.

This first stage begins in the docks of Dublin city, and climbs westwards through the Georgian quarter of Dublin, to eventually reach the suburbs and the sometimes less pleasant surroundings of the city perimeter, before ending at Clondalkin, at one time a monastic settlement. While the dormitory town has some bed-and-breakfast accommodation, any part of the city can be accessed by bus from here.

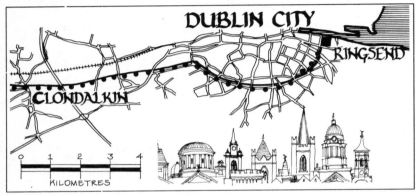

The Grand Canal begins at Ringsend Basin, a broad expanse of water adjoining the River Liffey, surrounded by old mills and warehouse buildings. A high-tech modern building, seemingly floating in the water of the basin, and called by locals the 'Box in the Docks', houses the Inland Waterways Interpretative Centre, where you can enjoy learning some of the fascinating lore of Ireland's rivers and canals.

There is a lot of rebuilding and refurbishment going on around here making inroads into the jungles of buddleia, that purple-flowered butterfly shrub that colonises urban decay. The canal is followed up a limestone-cobbled street and under a very low bridge to Pearse Street, named after Padraig Pearse, one of the executed 1916 Rebellion leaders. Here the towpath is joined, the beginning of a green linear oasis.

At Huband Bridge, signified by a delicately sculpted limestone centrepiece giving a date of 1791, you can see down past the 'Pepperpot' church, framed by row upon row of Georgian window reveals, and Dáil Éireann, the Irish Parliament. Beyond Baggot Street Bridge on the canal bank there are a couple of enthusiastic monuments to the poet Patrick Kavanagh, who lived just around the corner. Some of his lines, carved on the gable of a canal-side seat, are brought alive here:

> Brother, commemorate me thus beautifully,
> Where by a lock,

Niagarously roars the falls for those who sit
in the tremendous silence of mid-July . . .

A little further on, a bronze of the poet reclines greenly on a tree-shaded seat.

Soon after, the great green dome of Rathmines Church can be seen dominating the skyline on the south-side of the canal, and it is clear that the 'better' parts of town are being left behind. The next canal lock is at Portobello, opposite a one-time Grand Canal Hotel.

To cater for tourists and travelling merchants, the Grand Canal Company established a series of canal hotels, the first here at Portobello, in what was then the outskirts of Dublin, and others at Sallins, Robertstown, Tullamore Harbour and Shannon Harbour. The Portobello Hotel, now beautifully restored as part of a private college, was described in an 1821 guide-book which added '. . . the beauty and salubrity of the situation, enlivened by the daily arrival and departure of the canal boats, render it a truly delightful summer residence'. The hotels at Sallins and Tullamore are long since demolished, and Shannon Harbour Hotel is an ivy-covered ruin while that at Robertstown still stands, awaiting a boom in canal usage.

Looking north at Bloomfield Avenue the spire of St Patrick's Cathedral, where Jonathan Swift was Dean, can be seen. The canal, having started in Georgian surroundings, has progressed westwards through late Georgian, Victorian and Edwardian layers to reach twentieth-century nondescript surroundings. The scale of dwelling-houses passed has gone from elegant Georgian town houses to tiny cottages, and then to brave-new-world blocks of flats, standing in deserts of short, herbless grass. As the delapidation increases, so does the density of billboards, and the rash of unsightly flashing signs. Soon the towpath runs out and the canal is followed on the south bank beside a busy road. On the north side now are back gardens, allotments and sheds. Few trees now line the canal; many stumps, however, show the high level of vandalism.

In the distance, before Suir Bridge is reached, the towering Victorian buildings of the Guinness Brewery can be seen to the north. At the bridge the canal turns westwards and climbs comparatively steeply to the next lock; looking back after Inchicore one can see how steeply the land drops towards the city; in the distance is the Hill of Howth, the northern portal of Dublin Bay.

The canal now passes through a cordon of high-tension cables, pylons and unsightly industrialisation, a visual blight that seems to girdle all cities. In spite of these surroundings, however, there are early signs of drawing near to the countryside: the water is fringed by banks of tall reeds, and coots, water-hens and even the odd kingfisher are taking the place of the tamer swans and mallards of the lower reaches.

At the 7th lock is a great red-brick pub and the surroundings beyond there are like that of a battlefield long after the war has passed by; not an area to walk at evening time. A tarmac track leads south from the Ballyfermot bridge and uphill towards the 8th lock. On Christmas Day 1792, just below the lock, a passenger boat, on which the season was being celebrated 'riotously', sank with the loss of eleven lives. Howth is beginning to disappear behind a veil of high-tension pylons, as the canal passes through an area of green fields apparently forgotten, at least for the moment, by the industrial and housing developers. When I passed, these pastures were being enjoyed by a large number of Travellers' piebald horses, over thirty in the herd. I found the wildlife increased dramatically along here, with rabbits, mallards, willow warblers, magpies, and the ubiquitous swan and wood pigeon.

Beyond the 8th lock, on the north side of the canal, can be seen the old Guinness filter beds, where water was drawn off the canal for use in the stout-making process, although I'm told the real water comes from near Milltown in Co. Kildare, and that this is only used for the washing-up!

Soon the roar of traffic fills the air as the canal approaches and passes under the south Dublin motorway; the messages contained in the graffiti-adorned undercroft to the bridge suggest that it is a kind of low-life gathering-place outside of daylight hours, so avoid walking here in other than broad daylight.

After the motorway the reed-lined canal is followed up towards Clondalkin, the medieval round tower of which can be seen to the south beyond a taller red-brick tower-chimney. At the bridge that takes the road into Clondalkin is the Lough and Quay pub; the centre of Clondalkin and its round tower are less than 0.8 km (0.5 mile) to the left at the pub.

Clondalkin, not so long ago a quiet village, is now a burgeoning, blooming, bustling centre of a dormitory town, with old streets and buildings unsuccessfully trying to cope with the changes. The main street passes through the site of a seventh-century monastic settlement, the only survivor of which is a grand round tower.

Waterhen

STAGE 2: CLONDALKIN TO SALLINS

DISTANCE: 21 KM (13 MILES). AGGREGATE CLIMB: 23 M (75 FEET). WALKING TIME: 5.5 HOURS.

During this stage the canal finally leaves Dublin's suburbia behind and entering Co. Kildare, takes to the open country.

Clondalkin is well served by Dublin Bus; if you wish to commence the route here, the nos 51B and 210 buses will drop you at the western edge of the town. Sallins is served by the table no. 123 Dublin–Naas bus, but has no registered accommodation.

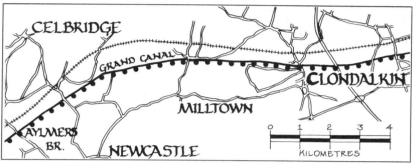

The canal is followed from the 9th lock along a pleasant path lined in summertime with high creamy froth of cow-parsley. Soon a vista to the south opens up and the gentle curves of the Dublin Mountains can be seen on the horizon, dominated by the rounded summit of Seahan, one of the many legendary seats of the hero Finn McCool. On the left, the municipal grass of the 'public open space' merges with the traditional meadow grasses of the canal side, and one wonders which will eventually dominate. Here the canal still holds its own, displaying when I passed, pretty stands of cowslips, and all along the pathside the sky-blue eyes of speedwell speckled the thick sedges.

Beyond the next lock, on the far side of the canal, the ruins of one of the characteristic lock-houses built about 1760 by the original Grand Canal engineer, Thomas Omer, can be seen. As the path winds its way around clumps of remaining hedge spared by the open space-makers, look out for the sad remains of a row of crack willows. They are probably as old as the canal, and mark the original canal reservation; in spite of attempted felling, burning and general abuse, they are still putting out leafy sprouts. (The Dublin Bus nos 51B and 210 will drop you near here.)

The towpath soon reduces to a narrow track through high grass and nettles. The clarity of the canal water allows one to see clearly the astonishing range of supermarket trollies, old washing machines and other detritus that cover the canal bottom.

It is about here that you feel for the first time that the city is being left behind, and the countryside is taking over. The fields are no longer just left-over, forgotten pockets of land grazed by gypsy horses, but carefully cultivated tracts of land growing crops. Birdlife is on the increase too, with plenty of reed-buntings, chiff-chaffs and willow-warblers singing out their distinctive songs from the bushes and the little linear marsh beside the canal.

After passing Lucan Road Bridge the towpath continues on the north side of the canal, here thick with Canadian pondweed, the tips of its stalks protruding from the water like a plantation of miniature pine trees. Beyond the buildings clustered about the bridge, the towpath reduces to a narrow grassy track bordered with banks of meadowsweet, bird's-foot trefoil and speedwell overhung with hawthorns and willows. Through gaps in the bushes to the south the Dublin Mountains can be seen stepping down in gentle undulating slopes towards the west. Soon the canal enters a cutting through a low hill at Gollierstown, and passes through the remains of a disused limestone quarry. It is a landscape of trees and ponds, low cliffs, and overgrown grassy hummocks, a natural garden teeming with wildlife that is sure to attract your attention and slow your progress.

Emerging from the cutting, the ruin of another of Omer's lock-houses is passed before the towpath seems to pass through someone's garden, complete with clothes-line to reach Hazelhatch Bridge. Here McEvoy's public house provides refeshments, a good place to take an early lunchstop; the village of Newcastle is less than 3 kilometres away to the east. At the bridge the towpath reverts to the south side of the canal, where a row of strange canal craft, many of which look decidedly uncanal-worthy, are moored.

A good gravel towpath extends straight on into the distance now with few distractions, allowing a steady pace and good progress to ivy-clad Aylmers Bridge. The surroundings have undergone a subtle change since Hazelhatch Bridge; on the far side of the canal now are stands of great beeches and other parkland trees, and to the left is the wall of Lyons House demesne. Lyons House was built by Lord Cloncurry, a notable patriot who included among his friends Theobald Wolfe Tone and Henry Grattan. His political activities led to his spending two separate periods in the Tower of London without trial. If you did not stop for lunch at Hazelhatch, the pleasant grassy banks of the 13th lock, looking back steeply down towards Aylmers Bridge and beyond, provide a pleasant alternative.

After Henry Bridge the towpath becomes a tarmac road separated from the canal by a fringe of ash trees. In a field just beyond some luxurious bungalows can be seen the remains of a stone-built chimney, all that remains of an extensive nineteenth-century limestone quarry, which used a miniature tramway to take the stone to the canal for barging away. Beyond, on a hillside, can be seen the ruins of a round tower in the Oughterard churchyard, where the original Arthur Guinness is buried. Further on is the disused church which used to serve the now long-gone quarry village of Ardclough.

At Ponsonby Bridge it is a relief to get back to a grassy towpath, which takes you to Devonshire Bridge and the Morell Aquaduct beyond, which takes the canal over the Morell River. The canal now runs along the top of a substantial embankment, from where the Dublin Mountains fill the horizon to the south and east, while to the north-east the Hill of Lyons comes into view, with the shape of a prehistoric earthworks on its summit clearly visible.

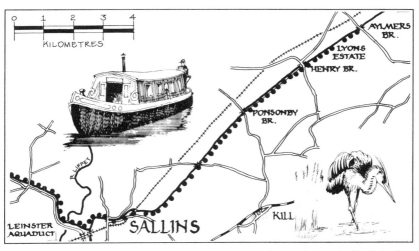

The canal now curves gently towards a wooded area, beyond which is the village of Sallins. Herons, pheasants and the ubiquitous wood-pigeon frequent the canal-side here, and in winter the open grasslands on both sides attract fieldfares, redwings and lapwings, while the marshy stretches beside the canal shelter snipe.

Passing under a railway bridge, the canal winds around to reach Sallins.

Fresh-water Crayfish

STAGE 3: SALLINS TO ROBERTSTOWN

DISTANCE: 11.2 KM (7 MILES). WALKING TIME: 2.8 HOURS.

This stage takes the canal westwards across the flatlands of Kildare to Robertstown, a village that grew up around the canal hotel and the coal-yards associated with the canal. Robertstown has no bed-and-breakfast accommodation; the table no. 120 Dublin–Edenderry bus can be accessed at Brockagh Cross, 1.6 km (1 mile) north of Robertstown.

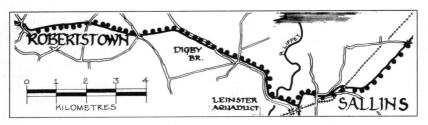

Sallins has a pleasant quay, decorated by flower-beds rimmed by white-painted tractor tyres. Dainty, yellow wagtails sport at the water's edge, and families of swans loiter about the boats hoping to be fed titbits.

Within a couple of hundred yards the towpath has left the village behind. It bends and curves westwards, passing the junction with the old Corbally extension to Naas, where there is a tiny island called Soldiers Island, since it was garrisoned during the 1798 Rebellion. The waters of the canal along this stretch were very clear and healthy looking when I passed, with stands of green aquatic plants growing thickly on the undulating gravel bottom. Fresh-water crayfish, or their cast-off shells which are easy to mistake for the crayfish themselves, can often be seen on the bottom. Like their much larger, salt-sea cousins, they were once actively fished for eating, attracted into basket traps using raw meat as bait. The fresh-water crayfish is also a favourite of the otter, and where they are to be found otters will often be seen.

At the Leinster Aqueduct the Liffey is reached and crossed, 34 km (21 miles) after the canal parted company with the river at Ringsend. A five-arch stone construction, the aqueduct was built in 1785 and is an excellent example of the engineering works of the time. The canal is followed now into open countryside; a little more than 1.6 km (1 mile) beyond the aqueduct, look out on the right for another example of Georgian engineering, an intricate overflow valve consisting of a series of concentric stone-built rings, the largest about four metres across.

Further on Sandymount House, a late eighteenth-century villa, can be seen to the right near Digby Bridge. When I walked here, the house was owned by one of the Rolling Stones, and the locals told me he had installed a complete pub as part of the renovations.

At Digby Bridge cross to the south bank of the canal and soon a copse of beech trees, where squirrels played when I passed, provide a welcome bit of variety along the waterside. An elaborate set of gates, and two neat doll's house gate lodges, mark the entrance to Landenstown House demesne further on.

At the 18th lock the Grand Canal reaches its summit at 67 m (219 feet) above sea level and follows a cutting through a low eminence called the Hill of Downings. The next lock, over 8 kilometres on, is the first of eighteen that gradually lowers the canal levels again until the River Shannon is reached. After the next bridge the much overgrown, quarry-like areas on both sides of the water are where the dense pottery-like clays which used to line the bottom of the canal were excavated. Here the water seems stiller and even clearer than before, and from the towpath, raised a metre above the surface, thick patches of Canadian pondweed rising vertically from the bottom look like miniature coniferous forests.

Emerging from the cutting, the low hills of Kildare come into view to the south-west, while the unmistakable shape of the power station cooling-tower at Allenwood appears ahead. The surrounding country drops away as the canal follows a rampart across a broad marshy area called the Bog of Moods, towards the picturesque village of Robertstown, dominated by the terracotta pile of the old canal hotel. This is the highest village on the Grand Canal; it is said the top step of the hotel's front door was at the same level as the top of Nelson's Column in Dublin's O'Connell Street. Although rather dilapidated today, the place is still unspoiled by subsequent development, and one can easily imagine it as it was in the heyday of the Grand Canal.

Robertstown

131

STAGE 4: ROBERTSTOWN TO EDENDERRY

DISTANCE: 21 KM (13 MILES). WALKING TIME: 5.25 HOURS.

This stage passes by the old canal harbour at Lowtown before heading north-westwards across the desolate Bog of Allen to the market town of Edenderry. Bed-and-breakfast accommodation is available in Edenderry, and the town is served by the table no. 120 bus from Dublin.

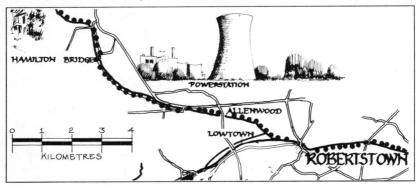

Walking westwards out of Robertstown, follow the road over Binns Bridge and along the north side of the canal. In the distance to the west, the cooling-tower of the turf-burning Electricity Generating Station at Allenwood dominates the horizon, looking incongruous in this rural setting. After nearly 1 km (0.6 mile), Lowtown Junction is reached, and our route follows the right branch towards Edenderry. A beautifully restored lock-keeper's cottage introduces Lowtown Marina, where the old stables for the barge horses have been converted into workshops serving today's leisure boats. The place rings with vigorous industry at weekends in springtime when enthusiasts gather to ready their craft for the coming boating season.

Just past the buildings on the south bank the Barrow branch line joins the canal, on which it is possible to cruise south via Rathangan, Athy and Carlow to the old monastery town of Graiguenamanagh 96 km (60 miles) away, and from there down to Waterford Harbour and the south coast. (See The Barrow Way, page 33.)

After the marina the towpath becomes a grassy track, and the canal reaches out westwards on an embankment, crossing the deep Slate River by an aquaduct. The power station cooling-tower is looming closer now, dominating the church at Allenwood. Away to the left can be seen the Hill of Allen, legendary home of Finn McCool and the Fianna. After Bond Bridge the towpath is reduced to a rough, almost non-existent track through grass, scrub and brambles. To the right is the village of Allenwood, a scatter of bungalows along the roadside; the main product of this area, besides electricity, is turf, and almost every house has its own dark rick to keep the winter wind and cold at bay.

At the next canal bridge, called locally the Skew Bridge because it is the only bridge crossing the canal at an angle, the route crosses to the south bank. To the right the 88 m (289 foot) high power station cooling-tower looms; when the 40 megawatt peat-burning station was built in 1952, its contribution to the national grid was significant, but this is no longer so, and it will soon be closed down.

After Skew Bridge the canal-side becomes quieter, as the road on the far side veers away towards the village of Carbury. The surrounding land drops gently away as the canal flows along a rampart and passes by a flimsy lifting-bridge. The next bridge is humped-back Hamilton Bridge, over which the route crosses to rejoin the north bank; this stretch is said to be good for coarse fishing, and is often lined with patient anglers.

Before long, the tubes and chimneys of a derelict peat-briquette factory is passed on the south bank, and after a long straight stretch the canal bears around to the left again to reach Ticknevin Bridge. This little gathering of houses is the last you will see for nearly 7 km (4.5 miles), as the canal crosses a bogland wilderness before reaching the outskirts of Edenderry.

At the beautifully landscaped Ticknevin Lock the first glimpse of Edenderry can be seen, a high concrete water tower that just extends above the tree-lined horizon. The round green hill with the little bump on top that can be seen to the right is Carbury Hill, where the River Boyne rises. Ticknevin is the last lock on the canal for over 29 km (18 miles), which did not help when a breach occurred in the stretch in 1989, emptying sixty million gallons into the surrounding countryside.

Soon the landscape takes on a very different flavour. A grassy path wends its way along the canal between gorse bushes, sometimes separated from the water by a veil of reeds. Bogland scattered with scrub and birch trees stretches away on both sides, and there is a very remote and isolated feeling about the surroundings. Snipe dart and jink away to cover as they are disturbed, and teal taken unawares at the canal-edge flap their wings in a panic-stricken escape to the safety of the far bank.

Before reaching the coniferous wood that has been the horizon since leaving Ticknevin Lock, the canal veers left and stretches silver into the distance to the west for as far as the eye can see. This is a real wilderness section, with the wood which parallels the canal blocking any long views that might include evidence of man's presence. I was told by a local man when I passed here that the place is teeming with wildlife in spring and summer when pheasants, duck and other marsh birds are mating and nesting, preyed upon by foxes and stoats.

At the western edge of the wood, Edenderry comes into view again, with the ruins of Blundells Castle and a church tower joining the water tower on the skyline. Looking behind, the cooling-tower at Allenwood, passed nearly 10 km (6 miles) further back, is also in view again.

The Grand Canal here continues westwards along the top of a massive 8 m (26 foot) high rampart, which must have involved an enormous amount of material in its making. More than double the volume of the visible rampart was required, however, to fill the bog beneath, which continued to swallow material for ten long years, nearly bringing the whole canal project to a premature end, before the ground stabilised.

The canal now passes out of Co. Kildare and into Co. Offaly, and crosses the Rathangan/Edenderry road by way of the Blundell Aqueduct. The town of Edenderry is just 1.6 km (1 mile) away by this road, but our route, following the canal into the town, has another 3.2 km (2 miles) to go. Beyond the aqueduct is where the breach in the canal occurred in 1989, and the banks on both sides have been completely and expensively rebuilt.

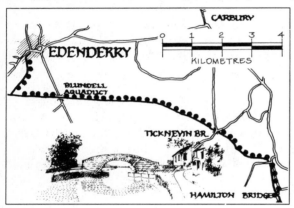

Edenderry was an outpost of the English Pale, and there are many castles and Norman mottes in this area. The distinctive mound of one of the local mottes occupies a nearby hilltop to the left, built in the centre of a much older tree-planted earthen ring-fort, its shape clearly visible in wintertime when the surrounding trees are leafless.

The little white house at the end of this long straight stretch of canal never seems to get nearer, but eventually the feeder canal to Edenderry is reached, crossed by a very quaint four-foot-wide horse bridge. Turning north, the canal is followed towards the town, overlooked by Blundells Castle. The castle was built in the sixteenth century by the Cooley family, who founded the town, and was sacked by King James's army in 1691. Soon the canal veers around to the right and arrives at Edenderry Harbour, a pleasant pool on the south side of the town.

Edenderry town and its castle and churches are worth exploring. The main street is lined with terraces of sturdy Victorian houses and shops, pierced by archways which give surprise views of open countryside beyond. There are plenty of good pubs and restaurants here; Kavanagh's public house opposite the early nineteenth-century Market-house has pitch-pine panelling behind the bar that in a previous life was used as the choir stalls in a monastery in Cork!

STAGE 5: EDENDERRY TO DAINGEAN

DISTANCE: 19 KM (12 MILES). WALKING TIME: 5 HOURS.

This stage follows the canal out into a deserted, desolate countryside. The remoteness of the area is enjoyed by animals and birds rarely to be seen in more populated areas; I enjoyed sightings of otters and buzzards when I walked here. There is a pub at Rhode, but availing of its pleasures will add 3.2 km (2 miles) to your journey to Daingean.

Bed-and-breakfast accommodation is available overlooking the canal at Daingean, and the friendly staff at the Sportsman's Inn provide good country lunches at very reasonable prices, and might be persuaded to provide an evening meal.

Daingean is served by the table no. 121 Tullamore–Dublin bus.

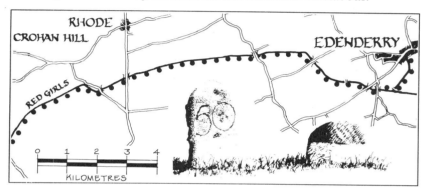

Leaving Edenderry, follow the branch canal to rejoin the Grand Canal, and crossing the horse bridge, follow the north bank to Colgan Bridge before crossing to the south bank. The towpath is a pleasant and easy grassy path which can be a little overgrown in summertime. George's Bridge is passed after a few minutes, and soon after, the redundant, grass-covered Rathmore Bridge.

Further along, look out for a well-rubbed canal milestone, covered with yellow, grey and green lichens. After Cartland Bridge the canal passes through open countryside and, as Trimblestown Bridge is reached, the first high ground to be seen for some time, Crohan Hill, comes into view ahead. In the context of the surrounding flatlands, it is an impressive eminence with a pronounced prehistoric summit cairn. The hill was the site of the main stronghold of the ancient chiefs of Offaly, the O'Conor Faly, who ruled these lands from the fourteenth to the eighteenth century, battling with their neighbours and the English alike to hold them. It is referred to in Spenser's epic *Fairie Queen*, and on its slopes are the remains of a graveyard, two churches and several holy wells. In one of the churches local tradition holds that St Bridget, Ireland's female patron saint, received her veil.

The canal now stretches silver and straight into the far distance. It is fine open country here, the only interruptions being copses of conifers to the south of the canal, and the sky the dominant feature. Soon after, the two great cooling-towers at Rhode Power Station come into view to the north, and Rhode Bridge is reached, where a sign advertises Mulvin's pub in the village. Under the bridge look out for the polished and shiny grooves worn in the quoin stones by a century and a half of canal horse's tow ropes.

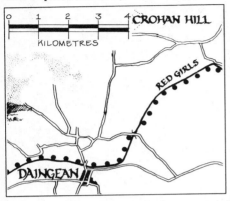

After Toberdaly Bridge, where the ruins of a castle can be seen to the north, the canal passes through a surrealist landscape of peat bog, acres of which are wrapped in plastic sheeting which reflects the sunlight like a dark undulating sea. When a wine-glass shaped water tower appears ahead and the canal mounts a high embankment, Daingean is not far off. A stretch of the canal along here was named the Red Girls by the bargemen of the nineteenth century, and it is still called this today. Apparently a family of red-haired beauties once lived in a canal-side cottage here who shortened the journey for the bargemen sufficiently for them to be immortalised in a placename.

Soon after Kileen Bridge the canal takes a tight turn to the right, and runs the last 1.6 km (1 mile) into Daingean parallel with the road.

In the sixteenth century this place was called Ballyroy, or the town of the King, and the poet Spenser spoke highly of its 'good store of people and trade'. A great fort was located here when Offaly was planted by Mary Tudor, and the town was renamed Philipstown, after Mary's husband, Philip II of Spain, who is said to have stayed here. Nothing remains of the fort today but a few bramble-covered mounds in the fields south of the old courthouse, which was designed by the architect Gandon. More noticeable are the buildings near the bridge surrounded by a high wall. These were built in the nineteenth century as a reformatory, and on closure in the 1950s, were taken over by the National Museum of Ireland to store some of the many artifacts it does not have space to display. In the graveyard at Daingean is buried Bishop Dodgeson, grandfather of Sir Walter Scott.

STAGE 6: DAINGEAN TO TULLAMORE

DISTANCE: 15 KM (9.4 MILES). WALKING TIME: 4 HOURS.

This stage follows the canal through a sparsely populated countryside towards Tullamore, once an important canal terminus. Tullamore has a range of accommodation and some good restaurants. The Bridge House, a marvellous rambling lounge bar which attracts a colourful collection of customers of all ages and backgrounds, provides excellent bar food at all times of the day, and for those who prefer a more formal evening meal, there is also a well-appointed restaurant.

Tullamore is served by the table no. 121 Dublin–Tullamore bus, the table no. 19 Dublin–Portumna Expressway bus, and the table no. 77 Waterford–Longford Expressway bus. Tullamore is also served by train.

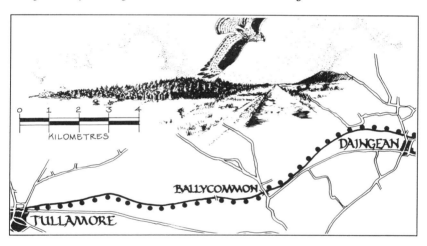

Leaving Daingean follow the towpath along the north side of the canal, first along a pleasant grassy canal bank, and then along a road which stretches into the distance. On the right are the severe grey walls of the old Reformatory, over which can be seen cypresses and monkey-puzzle trees. St Conleth's Reformatory School was opened in 1870 and once imprisoned up to 350 boys under 16 years of age. In recent years it has become a repository for the National Museum, storing artifacts such as Daniel O'Connell's coach.

Not long out of Daingean the canal flows into open countryside with Crohan Hill still visible behind, and beyond the flatlands to the south the low silhouette of the Slieve Bloom Mountains can be seen.

When I walked this way in March, I found that daffodils grew wild in the hedgerows round about, giving the greyness of the countryside a colourful lift. They were, possibly, all that remained of country cottages that have long since returned their mud walls to the ground. Some of the cottages that remain in this poor land, scattered with copses of birch and ash, are still thatched, and in every haggard there are one or two vintage cars serving out their years as hen-houses.

At Ballycommon Bridge, the gable of a pub signals a welcome and refreshment, but I found it closed when I passed. Beyond the bridge, the black-and-white timbers of Ballycommon Lock, the first since Ticknevin, over 29 kilometres back, are a welcome sight, and almost a relief, as the frequency of locks in the earlier stages develops a reassuring rhythm for walkers. A few minutes later the disused canal branch going north to Kilbeggan, designed by the railway engineer William Dargan, is passed.

Reed-buntings seem to become increasingly common along the water margins as the canal edges westwards. In winter and spring great flocks of lapwings and fieldfares graze in the fields beside the canal; when I passed a flock of about a thousand fieldfares flowed from field to field like an animated grey cloud, while a great gathering of lapwings wheeled squealing through the sky.

After Ballycommon the canal seems to descend relatively steeply towards Tullamore. The modest Offaly Rowing Club boathouse is followed by a long pleasant grassy stretch, after which a cluster of blue-and-white moored canal barges signal the headquarters of the Celtic Canal Cruisers at the 24th lock. Soon after, the sight of a church tower and a steeple ahead suggest the town of Tullamore is close.

A long, straight, pleasant stretch brings the towpath towards the towers and spires of Tullamore. After a long period in what seems to be an uninhabited countryside, houses and farm buildings become more frequent in the landscape around. The lock house at the 26th lock, fronted by bright green topiared bushes, is a period beauty. It was built by the canal contractor of the time, Michael Hayes, to his own design and cost £42 more than the standard lock house of the time!

The square-towered, pinnacled church to the south, which has the lines of an ancient English cathedral, is St Catherine's Church, designed in 1815 by Francis Johnston. The extensive canal harbour is passed as you enter the town, where once another hotel building, like those at Robertstown and Portobello, stood.

Tullamore is an energetically bustling and prosperous country town which still has, in spite of recent 'redevelopment', a rich heritage of excellent period buildings. Strangely, it owes much of what it is today to an early aviation disaster. In 1785, during the course of one of the earliest balloon ascents to be witnessed in Ireland, the craft caught fire, and flying out of control fell into the town, causing a conflagration which was soon out of control. Over a hundred houses, a third of the town, were destroyed before the fire was brought under control. The Bury family, landlords of the town, were enabled by the destruction to develop the town on an improved plan. Over the ensuing sixty years new streets were laid out, and a town hall, courthouse and churches were built, while the population trebled.

STAGE 7: TULLAMORE TO FERBANE

DISTANCE: 29 KM (18 MILES). WALKING TIME: 7.25 HOURS.

This is a long stage but not too onerous if the weather is good. It can be reduced by breaking the journey at Rahan, 8 km (5 miles) from Tullamore, where the considerable remains of a monastic settlement founded by St Cartach in 580 can be explored. Rahan has a pub and bed-and-breakfast accommodation with evening meals available. Ferbane, which is 1.7 km (1 mile) from the canal, has bed-and-breakfast accommodation, and Hine's pub can provide simple meals at any time. Ferbane is served by the table no. 71 Cork–Athlone Expressway bus and table no. 122 Dublin–Birr bus (limited service only).

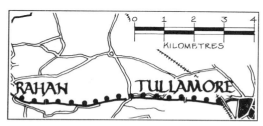

Leaving Tullamore on the north bank, a ruined tower-house with a grand corner machicolation is passed. It is called Shra Castle, and was built in 1588 by John Briscoe, an officer in the army of Elizabeth I. Soon the dramatic and gothic silhouette of another ruin, Ballycowan Castle, can be seen some distance ahead. Watch out for the crude craft consisting of a few boards tied to plastic bottles moored along the canal here; farmers use them to pole across to their lands on the far side. Beyond the ruins of a pre-penal church surrounded by tombstones, the towpath reaches Ballycowan Bridge, and the castle, spectacular in its size and in the number and height of its chimneys, is straight ahead. It is a good example of an early Irish fortified house, built in 1626 by a Jasper Herbert, who settled here in the reign of Elizabeth.

The canal crosses over the Tullamore River beyond the castle, and soon after, the Clodiagh River, which flows from here in a meandering course westwards to swell the Brosna and enter the Shannon. Less than 1.6 km (1 mile) from where the Clodiagh rises in the Slieve Bloom Mountains, another initially modest stream comes to the surface and flows on to become the Barrow, second only to the Shannon, draining with the Suir and Nore most of the south-east corner of Ireland.

On the south bank before Corcoran's Bridge there is a guesthouse called Canal View, which advertises evening meals and snacks and non-residents welcome, and when I walked here, saturated by heavy rain, it looked good enough to swim across to! Not much further on is a pub with a slated roof which for some strange reason is called the Thatch.

The village of Rahan is a short distance to the north, a prosperous place with well-built bungalows and farmhouses. The remains of St Cartach's great monastic settlement include the ruins of two twelfth-century churches, and a third dating from the same period which is still in use as the local Church of Ireland parish church.

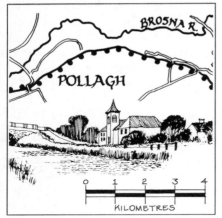

After Rahan, the canal meanders through pleasant countryside and past a place called Goldsmithslot, where I saw two otters crossing the towpath in that sinuous way of theirs when I passed. Spanking new bungalows display in their front gardens reminders of a former life such as old iron pots, open fire cranes and other artifacts of the cottage era.

Pollagh is not really a village, but more the centre of a scattering of houses spread across a few square miles of broad, flat, raised bog. A graceful bridge complements the church, a modest but unique structure with a pointed tower and a mixture of gothic and romanesque windows. It was built in 1907, and the bricks used in its construction were donated by the parishioners. While the main industry in the area is based on the peat bogs, the clay found under the peat here makes very good bricks, and many locals still remember when the area was scattered with small brick kilns, and practically every man worked at least part-time in brick manufacture. Each man made an extra hundred bricks a week until they had enough for the building. Bricks are no longer made locally, but are salvaged carefully as they are worth £1 each.

The church has an unusual plan shape, but as soon as you enter your eye is drawn to the sanctuary, with its Harry Clarke windows and furnishings by Michael Casey made from bog yew. The medusa-like, surrealist tangled roots of yew trees which grew in the area nearly five thousand years ago have been tamed, varnished to a rich deep brown, and incorporated into the altar, tabernacle surround and other elements of the sanctuary in a most effective way.

Beyond Pollagh, the Brosna River can be seen as silvery patches between a series of green grassy mounds a few hundred yards to the north. It will remain close all the way to the Shannon. Thomas Omar, the canal engineer, planned originally to save money by using the river for navigation, but the canal option was found to be more practical.

The canal now passes through the Turraun Peat Works, an extensive sea of peat in the process of being harvested. A light railway line crosses the water over a swing bridge before the ground drops away as the canal flows along a rampart high above surroundings that were very bleak when I passed here during heavy rain. The canal crosses the broad and slow-flowing Silver River by way of Macartney's Aqueduct, named after Sir James Macartney, a chairman of the Canal company who was knighted at the Ringsend Docks during the canal-opening ceremony.

After the viaduct the towpath takes on a tarmac surface, and a few minutes later a glimpse can be had of the ruins of Coole Castle in the trees to the north. As the canal bears around to the left, Armstrong Bridge 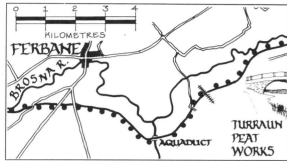 comes into view at the end of a long straight, and here you can turn right and head up the road into Ferbane.

Clononey Castle

STAGE 8: FERBANE TO SHANNON HARBOUR

DISTANCE: 10 KM (6.25 MILES). WALKING TIME: 2.5 HOURS.

This last stage to the Shannon is short and pleasant, passing through picturesque Belmont and by historic Clononey Castle. Shannon Harbour has two pubs and a shop, but no accommodation or public transport. For these you will have to travel on a further 4.8 km (3 miles) to Banagher, which has good restaurants, a good range of accommodation, and is served by the table no. 122 Birr–Dublin bus (limited service only).

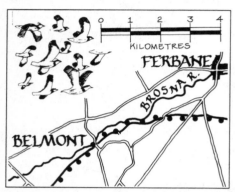

Coming from Ferbane, you can rejoin the canal at Armstrong Bridge or save 1.2 km (0.75 mile) by keeping right on the road to meet the canal at Glyn Bridge below the deep, chasm-like 32nd lock. After the long stretches of bogland that the canal passed through in the previous stage, it is a relief now to follow this stretch of towpath on the north bank, enclosed by trees and hedges ringing with birdsong. The banks have such an informal look about them that it seems more like a slow-moving river than a canal.

Herons, absent for the last 16 or more kilometres, are now back in force, each patrolling his-half mile of canal. The Brosna can be seen again to the north, somewhat lower than the canal and flowing more briskly. When I walked, it was the centrepiece of a Constable-like scene, with old ivy-covered oaks overhanging a ruined mill, and cattle bowing down to drink from the river. At Judges Bridge, the road which once crossed it is no more, only its ghost lined by hedges runs north past a ruined house with tall gables and slender windows.

The village of Belmont is 1 km (0.6 mile) north of Belmont Bridge; it is a place of fine trees, where landlords were probably responsible for the great variety of species, including grand old yews, Scots pines and beeches. Its ruined mills and pleasant harbour with moored canal craft make a picturesque scene; it is no surprise that it won an award in the Tidy Towns competition in 1990.

I changed over here to the comfortable carpet of grass on the south bank as the north bank was very boggy when I passed. Shortly after sighting the next bridge ahead, L'Estrange Bridge, look to its north for the shape of a tower-house. This is the early sixteenth-century Clononey Castle, located beside the road a little more than a kilometre from the bridge, and well worth a visit.

Clononey was built by the MacCoughlans, who were once the princes of this area, and was only one of the dozen 'fair castles of the MacCoughlans' that once existed in Offaly. It is said that from the ramparts of Clononey the first recorded killing by a firearm in Ireland took place in 1519, when a James MacCoughlan, Prior of Delvin, was shot during a power struggle. A German by the name of de Renzi took over Clononey about 1608 and persuaded the Crown to colonise the area, which was the beginning of the end for the MacCoughlans. Since that time the castle had been occupied on and off until the early 1900s, which accounts for its good if ruined condition, complete with three of its bawn walls and a fine gateway. I was told that dances were held in the building in the 1940s, up to which time the stairs were intact, but the local parish priest had them demolished to prevent young people sneaking upstairs to 'take the air'! Near the entrance to the castle is a large slab of limestone with a barely legible inscription indicating that two sisters named Boleyn, cousins of Elizabeth I, lie buried there.

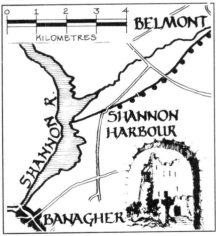

After Clononey Bridge there is less than a mile to go to reach the village of Shannon Harbour, which grew up in the early 1800s around the meeting of the canal and the Shannon. In the summertime it is a colourful and busy place, bustling with pleasure craft and their crews coming or going or mooring here a while, and you do not seem to notice the extent of decay in the place. In the winter, however, when the great river has flooded its banks and become a vast inland lake, its brightness contrasts with the sombre, ivy-shrouded ruins of what must have been a place of considerable extent. The great canal hotel here had a busy but short life, and is now the centrepiece of a cluster of Georgian ruins which include the Canal Agent's house, and an old police barracks.

The last bridge on the Grand Canal is Griffith Bridge, which like many of the others bears the grooves in its stone quoins left by a century and a half of straining, rubbing tow ropes as countless horses, having passed under the bridge, moved back out onto the towpath. At Griffith Bridge you have completed the Grand Canal Way; an extra 2.4 km (1.5 mile) jaunt will take you out to the point where the canal meets the mighty Shannon.

8
THE KERRY WAY

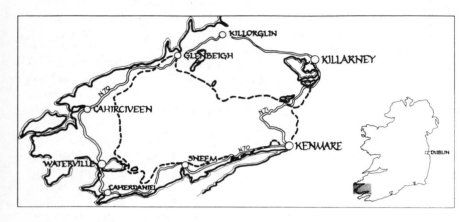

The Kerry Way circumnavigates the broadest of the county's rugged and mountainous peninsulas, the Iveragh Peninsula, passing through places such as Killarney and Glenbeigh that have been renowned for their scenic beauty since interest in such things began to capture the imagination in the eighteenth century. At 215 km (134 miles) it is Ireland's longest way-marked trail, but its circular layout allows it to be handily covered in part or parts from one base.

The scarcity of overnight accommodation along parts of the route may make some of the stages I have set out a little long for the unseasoned walker to enjoy, but with imaginative planning and careful arrangement of transport it should be possible to shorten these, for instance, by omitting sections on tarred roads.

How to get there
Killarney, the starting-point of the Kerry Way, is 302 km (188 miles) from Dublin, 275 km (171 miles) from Rosslare Harbour, and 135 km (84 miles) from Shannon Airport. The town is well served by bus routes and by train.

Maps and guides
The route is covered by the 1:50,000 Discovery Series map nos 78, 83 and 84. The 1:50,000 *Kerry Way Map*, produced by Kerry Regional Tourism Organisation in association with Cospóir, shows the entire route; but for someone unfamiliar with the area it is helpful to read it in conjunction with the Discovery maps. The route is included in *Walk Guide—Southwest of Ireland* by Seán Ó Súilleabháin, published by Gill & Macmillan. Bord Fáilte

information sheet no. 26C also describes the route.

Enquiries
Cork Kerry Tourism, Tourist House, Grand Parade, Cork; telephone 021 273251

The Bridle Path

STAGE 1: KILLARNEY TO BLACK VALLEY

DISTANCE: 21 KM (13 MILES). AGGREGATE CLIMB: 375 M (1,230 FEET). WALKING TIME: 6.25 HOURS.

Passing through the Muckross House demesne, this first stage of the Kerry Way rises past the spectacular Torc Cascade under the flanks of Mangerton Mountain to follow the old Kenmare coach road before dropping along the shore of the Upper Lake to reach Gearhameen at the eastern end of Black Valley. Nearly 8 km (5 miles) of this stage is on tarmac and the rest on forestry roads, paths, and the old Kenmare road, which varies from good gravel road sections to moorland pathways.

The Way officially starts at the River Flesk, 0.75 km (0.5 mile) from the centre of Killarney, which means the first 1.75 km (1 mile) is on a pavement beside a busy road, with little to see other than an endless parade of bed-and-breakfast signs. I recommend starting at the Muckross demesne, thus reducing the distance to be walked to 19.5 km (12 miles). The distance back to Killarney by car from Gearhameen Youth Hostel is 19.5 km (12 miles) by the Gap of Dunloe or 29 km (18 miles) by the main Kenmare road. In season it is also possible to return to Ross Castle, just outside Killarney, by boat from Lord Brandon's Cottage near Gearhameen.

In addition to the youth hostel there is at the time of writing one registered guesthouse at Gearhameen, close to the Way, where an evening meal can be had if required. There is a small grocery shop and a church next to the youth hostel. There is no regular bus service at Black Valley.

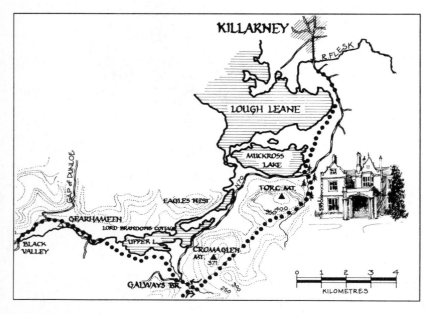

The Kerry Way begins at the bridge over the River Flesk and follows the road southwards past an avenue of bed-and-breakfast signs with fascinating names. After these come the hotels, one of which, the Lake Hotel in the trees to the right, has been welcoming visitors to Killarney for nearly two hundred years. In the distance, over the trees of Muckross demesne, the mountains fill the horizon.

Soon the Way turns in the main gates of Muckross House, where you have your first real view of Killarney's famous lakes, scattered with tree-covered islands. In the background Shehy Mountain looks, like most of the mountains in the area, taller than it really is, because of the steepness of its sides. As the Way follows the tarred avenue through the demesne, the gaunt and roofless ruins of Muckross Friary can be seen to the left, surrounded by a graveyard. Founded by the Franciscan friars in the middle of the fifteenth century, it was first suppressed in the sixteenth century and then again during the Cromwellian wars a century later. The friary surroundings and interior have been in constant use over the centuries as a cemetery, and many of the local chieftains were buried here, including Dónall Mac Cárthaigh, Prince of Desmond, who provided the land and resources for the construction of the friary. Here also are buried three of Kerry's most famous poets, Séafra Ó Donnchú an Ghleanna, Aogán Ó Raithile and Eoghan Rua Ó Súilleabháin. Enclosed by the cloisters is a great yew tree, reputed to have been there since the foundation of the friary.

Soon the avenue winds south and heads directly towards the Scottish-baronial façade of Muckross House. Built for the Herbert family in 1843, it was presented to the nation with its 40 sq. km (15.5 sq. miles) of land in 1932 by the then owners, Mr and Mrs Bourn, and their son-in-law, Senator Vincent. Today it is the centre of the Bourn-Vincent Memorial Park—itself now incorporated in the 105 sq. km (41 sq. mile) Killarney National Park—and houses a valuable collection of antique furniture, and exhibitions on the wildlife and folklore of the Killarney area.

The Way passes to the right of the house to reach Muckross Lake, with the eastern peaks of Macgillycuddy's Reeks towering to the right ahead and the bulk of Mangerton Mountain filling the horizon to the left. In the foreground the old boathouse at the lake's edge, almost hidden in the undergrowth, completes a splendid scene.

The Way comes out into the open almost at the foot of Torc Mountain, a majestic peak with a primordial, unfinished look, layered with coniferous and deciduous trees for two-thirds of its height.

Leaving the demesne and passing through a tunnel under the main public road, the Way follows a stepped pathway up to the Torc Cascade. The woodland clinging to the side of Torc Mountain through which the pathway climbs contrasts dramatically with the carefully laid-out parkland below. It is a wild forest of larch, birch, oak and holly, growing from a forest floor scattered with boulders and clothed with mosses, a confusion of species from saplings to ancient and gnarled trees. The mountainside is so thickly covered that the Owengarrif River seems to appear like magic out of the treetop branches to create the Torc Cascade, crashing thunderously down 12 m (39 feet) to a rock bed only a few metres from the pathway.

The route now climbs away from the waterfall to a viewpoint that provides an almost aerial panorama of the Lakes of Killarney beyond which, in the distance, the mountains of the Dingle Peninsula make an undulating horizon.

After the path levels out and reaches a forestry road, the thinning trees reveal the twin summits of Torc Mountain to the right and to the left the rising outliers of Mangerton Mountain. The Way now heads south-west on which was once the old Kenmare road, which before the Great Famine was the main coach road from Killarney across the peninsula to Kenmare. In the early nineteenth century the landowner, H. A. Herbert, closed off the road and the area between Mangerton Mountain and the lakes, evicting those who lived there, to create a deer park, which he stocked with red deer, whose descendants still roam these lonely hills and valleys. A little further on the remains of the old bridge, demolished by Herbert to dissuade continuing users of the road, can be seen on the right, before the Way crosses a modern bridge and begins a steep climb.

Levelling out, the road continues through the moss-covered woodland with the Owengarrif River now far below on the left, until a sign proclaims that you are entering the main deer range of Killarney National Park. Soon the trees are left behind and the Way follows the gravel road out onto bleak, open, boulder-strewn moorland, overlooked by the great ridge of Mangerton. Arthur Young rode this way from Kenmare in 1776 and described it aptly as 'the wildest and most romantic country'.

As the southern slopes of Torc Mountain are passed on the right, the massed peaks of Macgillycuddy's Reeks, now less than 10 km (6 miles) away, are revealed. The old road is washed away in places, while in others the large cobbles that form its surface are as level and even as the day they were laid down. Red deer can frequently be seen here, and their hoofprints are recorded in the mud of the old road.

Crossing a low ridge, the strange moonscape valley of the River Crinnagh, backed by the ragged ridge of Cromaglen Mountain and Stumpacommeen, appears ahead. The flat bottom of the valley was probably once a lake, and the large glacial erratics that protrude from it would have been islands. The old coach road disappears into the bog at the valley bottom, and the Way follows a path southwards, crossing the River Crinnagh by a footbridge. To the left there is a fine waterfall, called Core's Cascade, as the Way, crossing some old undulating cultivation ridges and the ruins of a cottage, rejoins the coach road at the bottom of Eskamucky Glen. This is a magical rock ravine overhung with ancient oaks, birches and hollies, growing from crevices in great canted slabs of sandstone, and one cannot help wondering how horse-drawn coaches ever made it to the top of its stony staircase.

After the glen the Way crosses a rough plateau before it drops to cross the Galways River and pass through a stretch of old oakwood into the next valley. Here a gravel road is met; at this point the final stage of the Kerry Way comes from the left from Kenmare and returns by the old Kenmare road to Killarney. The outgoing Way turns right to reach the main Killarney–Kenmare road at picturesque Derricunnihy Church.

A short distance after passing the church the route turns right into the woods and drops downhill. This typical Killarney woodland must be the nearest thing left in Ireland to the ancient wild woods that developed after the last Ice Age but which had almost all been cleared by early agricultural practices before the end of the Bronze Age. Most of the rhododendrons that had begun to get out of control in Killarney in recent years have been cleared from this wood, allowing the mossy forest floor to breathe again and red squirrels to browse in the wildflowers between the trees.

Down to the right is the Derricunnihy Cascade, where the Galways River takes a last tumble before dropping to flow into the Upper Lake. The Way switchbacks up and down as it bears round to the left, giving tantalising glimpses of the Upper Lake through the trees, its islands thickly covered with the strawberry tree or arbutus.

Less than half an hour after entering the forest the Way comes into the open with the lake below, its margin and its islands lushly wooded. The Upper Lake is considerably smaller than Killarney's main lake, Lough Leane, and, being more remote, has a very different character. On its shores thrives a wide variety of lush flora, including a number of species not common so far beyond the shores of the Mediterranean. The bulk of Macgillycuddy's Reeks fills the horizon ahead as the path wanders westwards, a cluster of tiny cottages at their foot.

Soon the white-painted tea-house near Lord Brandon's Cottage and its tall castellated round tower come into view ahead. Lord Brandon was a wealthy clergyman who built the cottage as a retreat early in the last century. The original cottage no longer exists, and the name is now attached to a modest house that used to contain stables. The tea-house serves refreshments, and in season, it is a terminus for boats to and from Killarney.

Passing between the tower and the tea-house, the Way crosses a five-arched stone bridge spanning the Gearhameen River, and follows the broad, slow-flowing stream through lush sheep pastures, punctuated by groves of oak, birch and holly, towards the eastern peaks of Macgillycuddy's Reeks.

A little more than 0.75 km (0.5 mile) after crossing the Gearhameen River a junction to the right will bring you to Hillcrest farmhouse, where Mrs Tangney provides bed-and-breakfast and an evening meal for travellers; booking, of course, is essential in the busy season.

The route climbs away from the river past the Gearhameen school, reaching the Black Valley youth hostel and the end of this stage 1.75 km (1 mile) further on.

STAGE 2: GEARHAMEEN TO GLENCAR

DISTANCE: 20 KM (12.5 MILES). AGGREGATE CLIMB: 500 M (1,640 FEET). WALKING TIME: 7 HOURS.

This stage passes up Black Valley into a dramatic wilderness of mountains and lakes, with the 1,039 m (3,415 foot) Carrauntoohil, Ireland's highest mountain, looming to the north. The Way then crosses two mountain passes and drops to reach the hamlet of Glencar. Except for nearly 5 km (3 miles) on tarmac, this stage is mainly green roads, forestry roads and mountain paths. There are two steep ascents to slow your progress, the first over the bridle path between Broaghnabinna and the main reeks, and the other up the steep Lack road and over the saddle into Derrynafeana Glen. In spite of the proximity of so many high peaks, the maximum height attained is about 375 m (1,230 feet). Inexperienced walkers should, however, plan this stage carefully, identifying possible escape routes, and should not attempt it in doubtful weather.

Glencar is a scattered hamlet, with no particular centre. Hostel accommodation is offered at the Climbers' Inn, the end of this stage, and limited hotel and bed-and-breakfast accommodation is also available in the area. There is no regular bus service at Glencar.

Leaving Gearhameen and following the road uphill into open country, the towering peaks of Macgillycuddy's Reeks promise that the stage ahead will offer some dramatic scenery. After about five minutes the road to the spectacular Gap of Dunloe is passed on the right, and the Way continues into the Black Valley, past bungalows that look strangely out of place against the backdrop of the ageless crags behind them. Below is the first of the three lakes strung along the valley bottom drained by the Gearhameen River.

About 3 km (1.75 miles) after passing the hostel the tarmac comes to an end and the route follows a green road out onto the hillside. After passing a small coniferous wood, the Way enters another wood and follows a very rough pathway to the open ground beyond. On the far side of the valley, at the foot of steep craggy mountains, Lough Reagh can be seen, fed by the infant Gearhameen River, which comes cascading down from a higher plateau. The scale of the mountains is beginning to build up now; the few houses beautifully sited at this end of the valley are diminished to mere specks in the landscape, which culminates in the gargantuan bulk of Broaghnabinna, looking much higher than its 745 m (2,444 feet). The Way continues westwards to meet a green road and then a tarred road that comes winding up from the valley. Following the road uphill, the route enters the upper Black Valley, with immense scree-strewn slopes reaching skywards on both sides. The tarmac is soon left behind and a green road is followed through a landscape of lush and fertile sheep pastures divided by a network of great stone walls. The stupendous, silent slopes all around make one feel a most insignificant part of nature.

Half way up the valley a cluster of gaily painted but abandoned old cottages is passed before the ground begins to rise towards the saddle between Broaghnabinna and Curraghmore, the needle-like silhouette of a gallán or standing stone on the skyline pinpointing where the Way will cross, following an old route called the Bridle Path, into the next valley. When the track runs out, a series of way-marker posts and yellow arrows painted on rocks identifies the route uphill.

Thackeray said of the mountains of Connemara, 'I won't attempt to pile up big words in place of these wild mountains.' It is a great temptation to try to describe the scene laid out below and beyond now, but it is better to say, as Thackeray did, 'Come and see!'

Choughs and ravens are common in this area, and the echoes of their distinctive calls rebound around the slopes. Red deer can also be seen by the careful observer, almost perfectly camouflaged against their background and discernible only when they move.

Use the gallán on the skyline as your target until you get within 200 m (656 feet) of it, then bear away from it to the right, following the way-markers across the saddle's flat top. If you miss the posts, look for a stile on the fence that crosses the saddle from north to south. Over the stile, the track passes between two great erratics that have been sculpted by aeons of wind and rain into fantastic shapes.

A new vista now opens up to the west, down an emerald-green valley through which the Caragh River, collecting silver tributaries from both sides, lazily meanders on its journey to Lough Caragh, 14 km (9 miles) away. The Way drops steeply down the mountainside between boulders and crags, heading for a cottage on the right-hand side of the valley, beyond which a winding road heading west can be seen. A stream and a couple of fields have to be crossed, until a track running through the farmyard is met and followed up to the tarred road.

After about 1.5 km (1 mile) on the road the Way turns right and climbs to join the Lack road, a grassy continuation of the ancient route the Way has been following since it left the tarmac at Black Valley. To escape now before the second climb of the stage, continue to follow the road, which will bring you to Glencar after about 8 km (5 miles).

As the Lack road rises, the landscape to the west is gradually revealed, and Cloon Lake with its wooded island comes into view nearly 8 km (5 miles) away. Across the valley Lough Namweela can be seen nestling at the base of Knockaunathin, sending a tributary cascading down to join the Caragh River.

The route dwindles to a track as the Lack road zigzags to the top of the pass. Here the full impact of the cluster of peaks that are the 'roof of Ireland' is felt when the summits of Caher (975 m—3,199 feet) and Curraghmore (822 m—2,697 feet), with a deep ravine between, framing the further-off Carrauntoohil, come into sight.

To the north, another new vista appears: in the foreground, against the wall of the Reeks, is the Glen of Derrynafeana, with the Gearhanagour stream wandering northwards to empty into Lough Acoose. Beyond the hills that back the lough, Dingle Bay can be seen, and the horizon is made up of the mountains of the Dingle Peninsula, with Mount Brandon prominent to the left in good visibility.

In minutes the route begins to zigzag steeply down again into Derrynafeana Glen. Keep an eye out for the way-marker posts, but if you lose them, descend carefully into the glen to reach the west bank of the Gearhanagour, the mountain stream that descends from a deep ravine in the Reeks, and follow it to meet a stone-walled green road.

The green road passes a farmyard, and then a group of old cottages, after the last of which the Way turns left and follows a rough track round the hillside. This path disappears frequently and you will need to be vigilant in watching out for way-markers: the goal is a green road running along the hillside north-west of Lough Beg, Lough Acoose's smaller neighbour. On the slopes of this hill and above the river that links the two lakes, the remains of a prehistoric settlement were unearthed in 1990, beneath the peat that has covered the area for about three thousand years. The green road, dropping down to lake level, passes Lough Acoose to reach the public road.

Turning west again, the Way follows the road down past the wood of Gortmaloon and out into open flatlands. (Turning right at a fork in the road will take you after less than 1.5 km (1 mile) to the hamlet of Shanacashel, where there is a pub and a shop, and a little further on to the exclusive Glencar Hotel.) A new range of Kerry mountains now lines the horizon to the right ahead, the main peaks of which, Coomacarrea and Teermoyle, reach 775 m (2,542 feet) and 760 m (2,493 feet), respectively.

The Climbers' Inn at Glencar is reached 3.25 km (2 miles) after reaching the tarmac. In addition to bed-and-breakfast accommodation there is a shop, a pub and a post office here. Farmhouse bed-and-breakfast is also available nearby.

STAGE 3: GLENCAR TO GLENBEIGH

DISTANCE: 17.5 KM (11 MILES). AGGREGATE CLIMB: 300 M (984 FEET). WALKING TIME: 5 HOURS.

This stage brings the Way into the lush valley of the Caragh River and then up to circle Seefin Mountain before descending to scenic Glenbeigh and the Atlantic coast. The stage can be reduced to 13.5 km (8.5 miles) if the alternative route round the west of Seefin is chosen. Of this stage 4.75 km (3 miles) is on tarmac and the balance on forestry roads, paths and green boreens.

Glenbeigh has plenty of bed-and-breakfast accommodation, but booking may be necessary in the holiday season. The Old Glenbeigh Hotel is a rambling old establishment where no two rooms are the same; there are fireplaces everywhere, and the food and service are excellent. Out of season you can enjoy all the comforts they have to offer for a little more than you will pay in a guesthouse. Glenbeigh is served by the table no. 279 Tralee–Killarney–Cahersiveen bus, and the table no. 280 Ring of Kerry service (summer only).

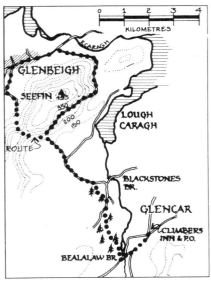

Opposite the Climbers' Inn the Kerry Way follows a green road for less than 1 km (0.5 mile) to reach Bealalaw Bridge over the Caragh River. Crossing the bridge, the route follows a fisherman's track along the western bank of the river until, drawing level with wooded Bealalaw Island, it turns left to follow a drainage channel. After a few minutes a young spruce plantation is entered, and the route emerges a few minutes later, turning right to meet and follow a forestry road.

After about 1.5 km (1 mile) the picturesque little Drombane Lough can be seen through the trees to the right. The public road is joined for about five minutes before the Way turns left onto an old mossy forestry road, carpeted with wood sorrel and lined with foxgloves in summer, and climbs steadily. When the road comes to an end, the Way follows a track uphill through the trees until after a few minutes an open pathway along the top of this little rocky outcrop is reached. Here a viewpoint reveals a new vista over yet another lake, Lough Caragh this time, with a backdrop of the mountains of the Dingle Peninsula. To the left is the ridge of Seefin, and to the right, Macgillycuddy's Reeks are seen from a new angle.

The Kerry Way

The Way now descends flights of rustic steps through a rock garden of colourful heathers, lichens and mosses, sheltered by holly and birch. Passing through a cleft in a miniature cliff of sheer rock, the path rises and falls as it rounds this beautiful wooded hilltop, with, when I passed, red squirrels scurrying across the forest floor and up to the safety of the treetops. It is one of the most pleasant coniferous woods I have ever been in.

Before long the pathway reaches a green forestry road and, turning right, the route follows it downhill to the public road. Turning left, follow the tarred road through patches of woodland until after nearly 1 km (0.5 mile) it begins to climb gently towards the bare ridge of Seefin, now filling the horizon ahead. Going left past Bunglash national school, the road climbs towards Windy Gap, the pass to the west of the summit of Seefin, and meets a green road.

The main Kerry Way turns right, circling east of Seefin to reach Glenbeigh in less than 8 km (5 miles). A more enjoyable alternative in my opinion is to turn left, and reach Glenbeigh by way of the Windy Gap in less than 5 km (3 miles). Turning right, however, the Way follows a good gravel road high above Lough Caragh, with good views beyond as far as the Reeks.

The scenic peninsula extending into the lough and almost dividing it in two is called Madame O'Donoghue's Island, which conceals in its trees the remains of a cillín—a graveyard for unbaptised children—where many burials took place during the Great Famine.

Passing a couple of very isolated farmhouses, the road bears round to the left, revealing Castlemaine Harbour and the Slieve Mish Mountains behind, dominated by the massif of Caherconree. Soon the road slips down between Seefin and the ragged escarpment of Commaun, with the panorama ahead broadening all the time. The Caragh River, first seen as a mountain stream from the Bridle Path west of Black Valley, now reappears below, swollen to a deep and fast-flowing river with foaming rapids, entering the sea at Rossbeigh Creek. The Caragh is mentioned in one of the old Celtic sagas, which relates how the runaway lovers Diarmaid and Gráinne were carried across the river by a friendly giant named Modán. As Inch Strand and Dingle Harbour appear across the bay, the route winds down to meet the main road from Killorglin, and follows it into Glenbeigh.

The alternative route into Glenbeigh follows the green road, an old coach route, to the left above Bunglash national school, circling the southern flank of Seefin and passing over the Windy Gap. There is a marvellous sense of arrival when the gap is reached: one moment the Reeks to the east dominate the view, the next moment they are left behind and a new scene appears to the west, centred on the expanse of Dingle Bay. Straight ahead is the half-forested Rossbeigh Hill, and at its foot the village of Glenbeigh. Beyond, the pale sands of Rossbeigh Strand stretch into the blue of the Atlantic, echoed by Inch Strand extending from the far shore.

As the route descends towards Glenbeigh, the furthest extremes of the

Dingle Peninsula come into view: the entrance to Dingle Harbour, Ventry, Mount Eagle, and finally the unmistakable shapes of the Blasket Islands. Soon tarmac takes over from grass, and when the main road is met it is followed into Glenbeigh, passing the gaunt walls of a ruined mansion called Wynn's Folly. This was built early in the nineteenth century by Lord Headley of Aghadoe, a notorious landlord who attempted, not very successfully, to establish himself here as a feudal baron. His son became a Muslim and took the name Al-Hadji, which did not help the baronial image.

Glenbeigh has been a popular 'watering-place' for the last hundred and fifty years, since Lady Headley had some 'sun-bathing lodges' and cottages built to attract visitors to what was, before the roads were built about the same time, one of the most remote corners of Ireland.

At Drung Hill

155

STAGE 4: GLENBEIGH TO FOILMORE

DISTANCE: 20 KM (12.5 MILES). AGGREGATE CLIMB: 650 M (2,100 FEET). WALKING
TIME: 7 HOURS.

*This stage begins with an exceptionally fine hill walk along the shores of
Dingle Bay, and then drops and turns inland into the valley of the River
Ferta, which drains into Valencia Harbour. Fransel House provides good
accommodation at Foilmore; Cahersiveen, 6.5 km (4 miles) further on, has
a good range of accommodation. If the total distance is a problem, the
stage can be divided into two sections by leaving the Way west of Been Hill
and turning north to overnight at the picturesque seaside village of Kells,
12.75 km (8 miles) from Glenbeigh, and covering the 16 km (10 miles) to
Cahersiveen via Foilmore the next day.*

*Cahersiveen is served by the table no. 279 bus which provides a regular
service to Tralee, Killarney and Killorglin, and table no. 280 Ring of Kerry
service (summer only). Accommodation and evening meals are also
available at Kells, which is served by the same buses.*

Leaving Glenbeigh, take
the right fork at the southern end of the village,
cross the River Behy, and
turn right. A short dis-
tance on, the route turns
into the woods and as-
cends a pathway through
the trees. I understand
there have been some
problems about disap-

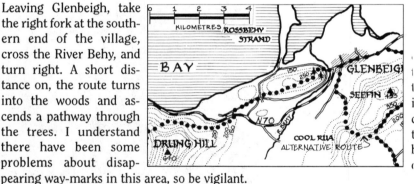

pearing way-marks in this area, so be vigilant.

As the path heads south-east, watch out for the second brief opening
through the trees to your left, one that gives a view almost straight up the
main street of Glenbeigh village. Opposite this, turn directly uphill on a
rough, narrow pathway, which eventually leads to the forest edge, where a
fence has to be crossed to gain the open hillside. (If there are any difficulties
finding this, you can follow the forest path as it contours around the south
side of the hill to meet up with the way-marked route again.)

Continue uphill through heather, moss and fraughans, keeping the fence
on your left, while a great panorama unfolds behind. In the immediate foreground is the village of Glenbeigh, at once remote and yet so close that you
clearly see and hear all the activities going on. Beyond the village the Caragh
River runs through a mosaic of gorse-bounded fields into Dingle Bay.

Within a few minutes the first summit along the Rossbeigh ridge is
passed, and ahead, the conical peak of Drung Hill appears from behind

rounded Rossbeigh Hill. The Dingle Peninsula forms the horizon to the north, stretching out into the Atlantic and terminating in the Blasket Islands, which can be clearly seen in good weather.

Near here, according to the sagas, in a cave overlooking Rossbeigh Strand the fugitive lovers Diarmaid and Gráinne took shelter while their giant protector, Modán, went off and caught three salmon in the Behy River, using a holly berry for bait. Having fed on these fish, Diarmaid is said to have defeated three sea warriors from the North Sea, together with their venomous hounds, in an epic contest of arms.

Reaching the top of Rossbeigh Hill, the Way continues west and then drops steeply down a scree-strewn slope to meet and follow a rough track. To the left is the lush valley of the Behy River, sheltered by a ring of mountains. Girdling the northern flanks of Drung Hill, the old coach road that the Kerry Way follows can be seen.

Soon the track passes a bungalow and, reaching tarmac, follows a narrow road towards Drung Hill for nearly 1 km (0.5 mile) before turning left to cross a bridge over the main Cahersiveen road. This bridge once crossed the former Great Southern and Western Railway line until it was closed down in the 1950s and became a road.

The road at the far side is followed westwards for nearly 1 km (0.5 mile) before turning left up an old boreen, once the 'high road to Iveragh and Cahersiveen', the only coach road along this coast for more than a century. The rough paving rises steadily, passing ruins of old cottages and fields bearing the marks of ancient cultivation, with stiles taking the Way over more recent boundary hedges that cross the old road. For a while the going is wet and quite rough, but the reward is great when the route navigates the steep northern slopes of Drung Hill, where the stone wall built to prevent wayward coaches from plummeting 150 m (492 feet) down to Dingle Bay has long since disappeared. The drop to the sea is spectacular, down a heather-clad hillside so steep that the coast road below is out of sight. This is a rare promenade, giving unique views up and down the coast. Daniel O'Connell, the 'Liberator', passed this way many times and is said to have once been thrown out of his coach here when one of the horses lost its footing.

Soon the old road rises to the pass west of the summit of Drung. The historian Charles Smith wrote in the late eighteenth century: 'There is a custom among the country people to enjoin everyone that passes this mountain, to make some verses to its honour, otherwise . . . they must meet some mischance . . .' This should not create too much of a problem, however: the most unlyrical walker could not fail to be inspired to poetry by the magnificence of these surroundings.

The northern slopes of Knocknadobar rise ahead now; to their left the broad estuary of the Valencia River glints, while to their right the Blasket Islands can be seen strung out into the Atlantic. The route descends towards a coniferous wood, giving a glimpse between hills to the right of the gracefully curved Gleensk railway viaduct. Passing through the wood, the old road crosses open heathland with a great mountainous amphitheatre formed by the steep flanks of Beenmore (671 m—2,201 feet) and Been Hill (626 m—2,054 feet) off to the left.

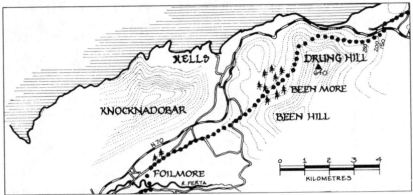

Past a sad group of ruined cottages—one of which, when I passed, still contained a large wooden bedstead—a tarred side-road is met; the Way continues straight on, but if you are heading for Kells it is a little more than 3 km (1.75 miles) to the right. Kells Bay is a quiet and picturesque inlet, steeply backed by the rugged hills of Mount Foley and Knocknadobar. Holiday bungalows and houses step up along the hillside behind the beach and small harbour, overlooking Dingle Bay and the peninsula beyond. John Millington Synge, author of *The Playboy of the Western World*, said of this area nearly a hundred years ago: 'One wonders in this place why anyone is left in Dublin or London or Paris when it would be better, one would think, to live in a tent or hut with this magnificent sea and sky, and to breathe this wonderful air which is like wine in one's teeth.'

Continuing on the Kerry Way, follow the road for a few minutes until the route leaves the tarmac again, dropping down a boreen to the right, a continuation of the old coach road. The main Cahersiveen road is below to the right, beyond which are the long, steep flanks of Knocknadobar, used for millenniums for grazing cattle in summertime.

Reaching tarmac again after a little more than 0.75 km (0.5 mile), the Way follows it south-westwards towards Valencia Harbour, now coming into view ahead backed by the bulk of Valencia Island. Soon the fuchsia and montbretia-fringed road descends into a broad valley and the townland of Foilmore, and shortly after passing a wood, Foilmore Church comes into view, signalling the end of this stage. The town of Cahersiveen is 6.5 km (4 miles) straight on.

STAGE 5: FOILMORE TO DROMOD

DISTANCE: 17.25 KM (10.75 MILES). AGGREGATE CLIMB: 725 M (2,378 FEET). WALKING TIME: 7 HOURS.

This stage provides an exceptionally fine ridge walk to the valley of the Inny River, before crossing another ridge to reach the townland of Dromod, north of Lough Currane.

A spur of nearly 6.5 km (4 miles) on tarmac needs to be added to the distance mentioned to reach accommodation at Waterville, or 2.5 km (1.5 miles) to reach an isolated farm guesthouse called Beenmore at Oughtiv. The series of ascents and descents across the ridges can be tiring and will slow the pace; the terrain to Dromod includes 9.5 km (6 miles) on open heathland, over 3 km (2 miles) on tarmac, and the rest on green roads.

Waterville is a popular seaside resort in summertime, with a wide range of accommodation, but advance booking is recommended in the high season. The small town also has a variety of restaurants and pubs, among which I recommend the Sheelin for its seafood. Waterville is served by the table no. 279 bus which provides a regular service to Tralee, Killarney and Killorglin, and table no. 280 Ring of Kerry service (summer only).

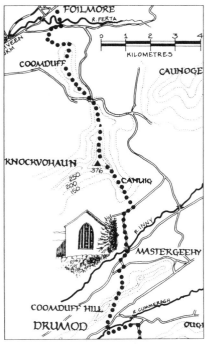

Almost opposite the turn leading a short distance to Foilmore Church, the Way turns off the road onto an old Mass path. Crossing a footbridge over a stream, pass over open fields and stiles to reach and cross another footbridge over the River Ferta. This area was formerly bogland, and the fields here were created in the nineteenth century using seaweed and sand brought up the river by boat from Valencia Harbour.

The road is followed westwards for a few minutes, then the Way turns up a boreen towards Coomduff Hill, and soon crosses a ladder stile into a pasture. Two more stiles are crossed to reach a gravel road, where the Way turns left. Cahersiveen and Valencia Island are in view now out at the coast, while behind us the great monolith of Knocknadobar, its ragged ridge giving it the look of a giant fossilised stegosaurus, fills the skyline.

The Kerry Way

A few minutes after passing a cottage the Way crosses a stile into pasture again, and shortly afterwards turns uphill through a gateway. The pathway soon peters out, but keep ascending, watching out for the next stile, of which there are many to be crossed on this stage. Gradually the green and fertile Foilmore Valley is left behind and a new valley presents itself to the east, remote and dark, boggy and flat, rising gradually directly east towards Teermoyle (745 m—2,444 feet) and Coomacarrea (775—2,543 feet).

Ladder stiles become way-markers guiding the Way up to the first peak on this ridge, 239 m (784 feet) above sea level, from where the first of a series of great long-range vistas to be had along this stage is to be seen, taking the sweep of flat moor and pasture to the Atlantic at Valencia Harbour, guarded by the twin portals of Killelan Mountain (281 m—922 feet) on the mainland and Geokaun (271 m—889 feet) on Valencia Island. In the foreground, to the left of the road towards Cahersiveen, an old ruined workhouse can be seen, built in the middle of the nineteenth century to provide shelter and sustenance for the destitute; the road itself used to be called the Paupers' Way.

The Way rises and falls as the ridge is followed southwards, each new high point revealing more of the landscape ahead. After about 3 km (2 miles) the Way drops and crosses a public road that passes through a dip in the ridge, and then it climbs uphill again, with more and more mountain peaks, layer on layer, coming into view towards the east.

From Knockavohaun, at 376 m (1,234 feet) the highest point of the ridge, a grand panorama presents itself. To the south-east the secluded mountain-bound Derriana and Cloonaghlin Loughs reflect the sky and contrast with their craggy surroundings. To the south-west Hog's Head, the eastern portal of broad Ballinskelligs Bay, reaches into the ocean, with Scarriff Island beyond. Mount Eagle and Slea Head on the Dingle Peninsula are visible to the north-west, with the necklace of the Blaskets stretching out from them. Although not a high summit, the grandstand location of Knockavohaun gives it views few higher peaks can better.

The Kerry Way bears left from the summit to descend along a spur to Canuig Hill and down towards the Inny Valley. Just before a ruined stone wall crosses your path downhill, the Way bears right onto a rough track that leads down through an abandoned hamlet of stone houses to reach the public road.

Turning right, the route descends to cross the wide, boggy valley of the Inny River. Rising from the flatness just beyond Knag Hill, on the south side of the valley, the spire of the church at New Chapel Cross, near Waterville, can be seen. The Inny River is crossed and, turning right, the hamlet of Mastergeehy appears shortly after. If you carry on straight here Waterville is 9 km (5.5 miles) away. The Way, however, turns uphill towards a Gothic-windowed church gable. Look out on the left for the old post office, which looks just like an ordinary house with a telephone box in the front garden.

After winding past the church, the Way turns right and, a short distance downhill, turns left up a boreen that follows the route of an old Mass path. Bluebells decorate the boreen walls here in early summer, while tall foxgloves take their place later. Over a stile the route deteriorates into a boggy track that ascends the flanks of this long, narrow ridge, passing a grove of trees that are what remain of an ancient forest that once covered the Inny Valley.

Shortly before the top, the track becomes a rough pathway through heather, but improves to a comfortable green road descending the far side. At the top the ridge can be followed south-westwards to Waterville, about 7.25 km (4.5 miles) away.

As the Way descends, Lough Currane and its backdrop of mountains fill the horizon ahead. Legend has it that the lake came into being during the great battle between Ireland's ancient inhabitants, the spell-weaving Tuatha Dé Danann and the sea-borne Milesian invaders. A cataclysmic storm, conjured up to swamp the invasion fleet before they could establish a beachhead, scattered the Milesians to the winds. One of their princes, Donn, perished with his crew when his ship foundered on the Bull Rock off Dursey Head, and Fial, modest daughter of King Milesius, swam to shore, having escaped drowning only to die of embarrassment on being seen by her husband coming ashore naked! A megalithic monument at Baslikane near Waterville is said to mark her grave. During the storm the torrential rains are said to have inundated the low ground between Cahernageeha and Knag Hill, forming Lough Currane.

As the green road levels off near the valley bottom, two of the many galláns in this area can be seen in a field below, near a couple of bungalows. Shortly after, the route crosses a stile to the left to connect with another section of boreen that bears right and left and down to the public road at Dromod. Waterville is now about 6.5 km (4 miles) to the right, while Beenmore farmhouse, about 2.5 km (1.5 miles) away to the left, offers accommodation.

The Reeks from Knockavohaun

STAGE 6: DROMOD TO KILCROHANE

DISTANCE: 17 KM (10.5 MILES). AGGREGATE CLIMB: 525 M (1,722 FEET). WALKING TIME: 6.25 HOURS.

This stage crosses a rocky spur to the lonely north side of Lough Currane and, passing between the lake and its smaller neighbour, Isknagahiny, rises through the Windy Gap at 385 m (1,263 feet) above sea level for a spectacular arrival at the southern side of the Iveragh Peninsula. If there is any doubt about the weather it would be well for inexperienced walkers to leave this stage for another time. Apart from 3.5 km (2.25 miles) on tarmac, most of the route is on forestry roads, boreens and mountain tracks. For overnight accommodation it is a further 1 km (0.5 mile) to Castlecove or 3.25 km (2 miles) to Caherdaniel, together with a distance back to the Way from your previous overnight accommodation.

A good range of accommodation is available at Caherdaniel, including an approved caravan park and camping park, and a number of houses in Castlecove offer bed-and-breakfast. Caherdaniel is served by table no. 280 Ring of Kerry service (summer only).

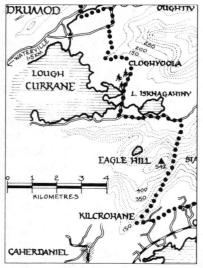

Leaving the tarred road at Dromod, opposite where the Way joined it after dropping from Coomduff, the route crosses fields, scrubland and a wooden bridge over the picturesque Cummeragh River, which drains the beautiful Derriana, Namona and Cloonaghlin Loughs, secluded in the mountains 8 km (5 miles) to the north-east. Meeting tarmac again, the Way continues south towards a craggy spur called Mullach Leice, extending from Beenmore.

Shortly after bearing round to the right the route turns left down a boreen past a whitewashed cottage. When the boreen comes to an end the Way carries on out into rough, rocky sheep pastures. When I passed here there were not enough way-markers and I lost my way temporarily. If this happens to you, just keep heading in a southerly direction until you reach a fence; follow the fence uphill, and when it reaches a cliff face the Way will be found again, passing through a little gate onto a track that was once a cattle road to Cloghvoola. Follow the track up to the erratic-strewn top of the spur, and keep the fence on the right as you turn through 180 degrees and start down the other side.

This damp, rocky habitat is host to the large-flowered butterwort, which produces a beautiful deep-purple violet-like flower on a long stem, between May and July.

The route heads eastwards now along a barely discernible track, aiming for a small grove of conifers and, after them, another stand of trees, where a derelict farmhouse is passed. As the Way descends into lonely Cloghvoola, the conical Eagle's Hill (542 m—1,778 feet) is the most dominant feature on the horizon ahead. In Cromwellian times the inhabitants of this place are said to have driven off a force of troops by stoning them from higher ground, giving the name Garraí Catha (Battle Garden) to the area. Other empty houses are passed on the way down as the track improves to a narrow roadway winding into a leafy valley, where the walls lining it are festooned with bluebells, foxgloves, London pride and honeysuckle. At the valley bottom the road turns towards Lough Currane and keeps a coniferous wood to the right for nearly 0.75 km (0.5 mile) until an inlet of the lough is reached, giving fine views to the west. Lough Currane is 13 km (8 miles) in circumference, and its shores are fretted with many inlets such as this, where anglers can find a sheltered 'stand' to spend a day fishing.

Less than ten minutes later the river linking Lough Isknagahiny and Lough Currane is crossed, and the Way turns left on meeting the main road. Note on the left here a great split glacial erratic, with a holly tree growing out of it, like a chicken hatching from an egg.

At the junction Waterville is 6.5 km (4 miles) away to the right, and the nearest bed-and-breakfast a little over 4.75 km (3 miles) in the same direction. The route continues eastwards past Lough Isknagahiny, while off to the left is the marvellous and strange layer-cake-gone-wrong southern face of Cloghvoola. Winding up and down through birch, oak and holly trees and soon leaving the lake behind, the old Glenmore national school, which is now a heritage centre, is passed. Just over 2.5 km (1.75 miles) after reaching the main road the Way turns right through a gateway and ascends a rough road past a little cottage.

Crossing a stile, the route follows way-markers out across open mountainside towards Eagle's Hill. The Windy Gap, over which the Way goes, is to the right of the summit. It is a boggy landscape of mountain streams and boulders, some of which sport yellow arrows indicating the route. Ravens and choughs are common here, their contrasting calls echoing off the bare rock faces.

Within moments of arrival at the Windy Gap, views of the loughs and of Coomcallee are left behind and a wider vista replaces them, taking in the broad inlet called the Kenmare River, with the Slieve Miskish and Caha Mountains of west Cork on the far side. Below, sandy inlets studded with rocky islets surround Castlecove Bay, while on the opposite coast Kilcatherine Point reaches out with Inishfarnard at its tip. Beyond these, in clear weather, Cod's Head and Dursey Island can be seen extending into the

Atlantic towards the Skellig-like Cow and Bull Islands.

Near the gap is a holy well dedicated to St Cróchán, which was regarded highly as a cure for complaints of the eyes. A contemporary of St Patrick, he went as a missionary to Cornwall after spending years in Ireland. Not far away there is a cave called St Crohaun's Hermitage, the stalactites from which were sold for large sums in the last century because of their supposed curative powers. The Holy Well, the Hermitage and the Church of Kilcrohane on the far side of the Windy Gap were the three stations of the 'pattern' that used to be held on the saint's day, 30 July, during which fifteen decades of the rosary were recited at each station.

The route now follows a track that becomes a green road as it descends, imperceptibly at first, round the flank of Coad Mountain, revealing more glorious views of the Kerry coastline. Do not be put off by an occasional fence crossing the green road; carry on downhill until it draws level with a rounded dome of rock rising between the main coast road and the sea, where a rough east-west track is joined. Following it westwards will bring you after 3 km (1.75 miles) to the village of Caherdaniel. The Kerry Way, however, turns left and follows the track eastwards and downhill. This, and much of the Way ahead, is what remains of the old coach road to Kenmare.

A few minutes after turning left, the track drops to meet a tarred road. Carry on straight until the tarmac bears round to the right, leaving a grassy track continuing eastwards past the ruins of Kilcrohane Church, where this stage of the Kerry Way ends; the main coast road is nearly 1 km (0.5 mile) away downhill, and the hamlet of Castlecove with bed-and-breakfast accommodation is a little further on.

The Beara from Windy Gap

STAGE 7: KILCROHANE TO TAHILLA

DISTANCE: 22 KM (13.5 MILES). AGGREGATE CLIMB: 325 M (1,066 FEET). WALKING
TIME: 6.5 HOURS.

*The Way now follows the old coach road along foothills almost parallel to
the coast, dropping to pass through the town of Sneem before reaching the
hamlet of Tahilla, overlooking Coongar Harbour. To the distance given
above you will have to add the journey rejoining the Way after the previous
night's accommodation. About 9.5 km (6 miles) of this stage is on tarmac
and the rest on boreens and forestry roads.*

*Limited overnight accommodation is available at Tahilla, but Sneem,
nearly 7 km (4.5 miles) short of Tahilla, has plenty of accommodation, so
an opportunity could be taken here to pause a while and explore the lush,
almost tropical landscape of Parknasilla. Sneem is served by the table no.
280 Ring of Kerry bus and by the table no. 270 Kenmare–Sneem bus, which
passes through Tahilla. Both are summertime services only.*

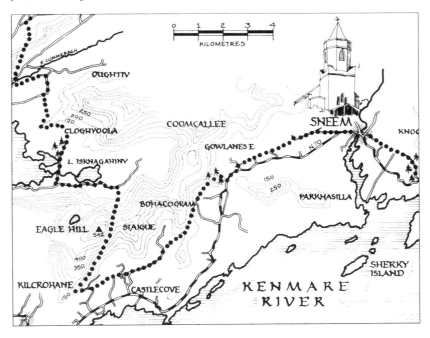

Leaving the tarmac, the Way follows a grassy green road eastwards, passing
below the ruins in Kilcrohane churchyard. The church is the larger, high-
gabled building, which may originally have been two-storey, while the
smaller building was possibly a presbytery. Although they have been much
added to, there are indications that the original structures may date back
further than the twelfth century.

As the narrow green road ascends between stone walls, the track that the Way followed from the Windy Gap can be seen to the left, slicing gently down the mountainside.

The route rises and falls as it follows the ghost of the old coach road, sometimes dwindling to a boreen or track, sometimes tarred to ensure longevity. Passing in front of a farmyard, a tarred stretch leading to the stone fort at Staigue is met and followed. Turning right here will bring you to Castlecove in less than 1 km (0.5 mile). Continuing on the Way, the road begins to descend gently, and nearly 1 km (0.5 mile) on, the route turns onto a green road, crossing a stream by a two-arched bridge. The impressive Staigue Fort, a massive circular stone caher, is sited in a bleak valley about 1.5 km (1 mile) further along on the tarred road. Only the extraordinary Dún Aonghasa on the Aran Islands is more massive and, like it, the precise age and purpose of Staigue still elude the archaeologists.

As the old coach road begins to climb it deteriorates and becomes quite boggy in places. Looking directly back as height is gained, the bay of Castlecove with its little beach can be seen, while across the Kenmare River, Cod's Head and Kilcatherine Point, with Inishfarnard offshore, can be identified.

Soon the fences lining the old road peter out, and you must keep a sharp look-out for way-marker posts and the occasional yellow arrow painted on a convenient rock to direct you. Careful examination of the terrain ahead, however, will reveal faint signs of the old road as you continue straight on through rugged, lonely surroundings, with only sheep and ravens for company.

Eventually, as a pass through a craggy ridge is reached, a new view of layer after layer of high mountains comes up ahead, across the plain of Bohercogram. The next ridge ahead runs down to the coast in a series of peaks to terminate at the island of Garinish and is one of a protective ring of hills that gives the island and the area of Parknasilla their unusual semi-tropical micro-climate.

The route of the old road is clear ahead now, dropping into the plain along a line of fences and uphill onto the next ridge, where it enters the just-visible coniferous wood. Follow it downhill to meet a tarred stretch through the scattered cottages of Bohercogram, before continuing north-eastwards and ascending again. The final couple of hundred metres is up a grassy ravine, speckled with daisies and with butterwort when I passed.

At the boggy top of the ridge the route enters the forest and follows an even boggier road downhill to intersect a forestry road. To avoid another muddy stretch turn right onto this and follow it out of the wood. Another fertile plain is laid out now to the north-east, below the massif of Coomcallee, named after a legendary witch who ruled these mountains.

The public road is met after a few minutes, and after following it eastwards for 0.5 km (0.25 mile) turn down a side-road to reconnect with the line of the old coach road. Past a small stand of coniferous trees, the road takes on a good surface again and continues dead straight as the two church spires of Sneem come into sight, a little to the right, ahead.

As an area of turf cuttings is passed, look out for the silvery, gnarled remains of ancient tree roots that have been exposed. These are what remain of a thick forest that existed here before the bog was formed, possibly as long as four thousand years ago. Bog-deal, as it is called, is dense and heavy and was once much in demand for fuel and for building.

Soon the track, decorated with bog asphodel, becomes enclosed by hedges of holly, ash and willow and, passing by the remains of an old oakwood, drops through a field to cross a tall and elegant footbridge over a stream. The old bridge taking the coach road over the stream was still there when I passed, but was in a dangerous condition.

Within a few metres a gravel road is met and followed eastwards. Past a birch and conifer wood, the village of Sneem comes into sight again, and a little over 2 km (1.25 miles) after crossing the bridge join the main road to enter the village.

Sneem, originally a fishing settlement, is a neat award-winning village of considerable character, divided by the Sneem River into two distinct areas, each with its own central green surrounded by houses and shops of a 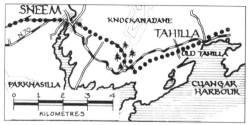 comfortable scale, painted in bright colours. Large pieces of modern sculpture placed in the main greens seem completely redundant amid such visual richness.

The Way leaves the village following a lane leading off the triangular green on the eastern side of the village, to the left of a pharmacist's shop. The lane soon becomes a pleasant pathway bordered with abundant rhododendrons and wild roses before it emerges into the open, with the rooftops of Sneem visible behind. The Way continues eastwards on pathways and tarmac towards a striped ridge called Knockanamadane, until it ascends onto a rocky hill with great views all around, particularly down towards the wooded shore and islands near Parknasilla.

Soon tarmac is reached again and the Brushwood Art Studios are passed as the road meanders downhill through a thick tangle of holly, birch and oak, all interwoven with rhododendron; and about ten minutes after passing the studios the main road is seen ahead. Perversely, however, the Way turns off, along a very muddy and grassy pathway going uphill again. After less than ten minutes, it drops steeply again to rejoin the road opposite a picturesque duck-pond. I understand that this detour, which one instinctively feels is unnecessary, will be omitted if it is found possible to run the route through the beautiful grounds of Clashnacree House.

Cross the road and follow the side-road past the duck-pond a short distance to the gates of Clashnacree House, where the old coach road is rejoined and followed eastwards. After fifteen minutes the ruined village of Old Tahilla is reached, a cluster of substantial but derelict houses. In the middle of the nineteenth century Old Tahilla was a thriving fishing community, and a nearby landmark called Cnocán na Líonta (Hill of the Nets) recalls those days.

Beyond the old village the coach road continues through bracken and fields, and soon a stile is crossed onto a side-road a few metres from the main road at Tahilla.

At Blackwater Bridge

STAGE 8: TAHILLA TO KENMARE

DISTANCE: 21 KM (13 MILES). AGGREGATE CLIMB: 350 M (1,150 FEET). WALKING TIME: 6.25 HOURS.

This stage closely parallels the coast and the Ring of Kerry road, passing through the Dromore Castle demesne before briefly returning to the high ground and descending into the town of Kenmare. Apart from a little over 3.25 km (2 miles) on the main road, the terrain mostly consists of boreens, forestry roads and open hillside. I understand that parts of this stage are in the process of being rerouted, so give priority to the signs rather than to the description here.

There is a wide range of accommodation in Kenmare, which is served by the table no. 44 Cork–Killarney bus (summertime only) and the table no. 270 bus, which provides a regular service to Killarney and a summer-only connection to Sneem.

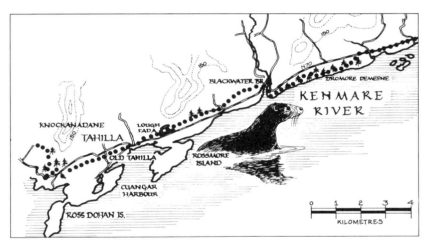

Cross the hedge on the other side of the road from Tahilla post office and head through bracken and gorse for about 50 m (164 feet) to reach a line of telegraph poles. The poles indicate the line of the old coach road and the Kerry Way at this point. Follow the rough and sometimes muddy path through bracken and bushes, never straying far from the telegraph poles, and soon the smaller lakes inland of Lough Fada are reached. These lakes, their dark waters brightened by displays of water lilies in summertime, lie in troughs between great rounded ridges of sandstone. If you climb the little ridge on the right you can walk overlooking Lough Fada, with views back along the coast past Coongar Harbour to Drongawn Lough on the headland beyond.

Past the lakes, traces of the old road seem to disappear and reappear sporadically before it ascends to cross a knoll. The terrain here was very

169

boggy when I walked, particularly between the rounded ridges of sandstone, which are a feature of this area. Derrenamacken Wood is now met, and after following its edge for a few minutes the Way passes through it, following a boggy track to reach tarmac on the other side. Ahead, across the Kenmare River and at this distance silver and motionless, a massive cascade called Ishaghbuderlick on the old maps streaks the northern flanks of the Caha Mountains, which are now beginning to take on three-dimensional shapes.

In minutes a turn to the left is reached. At the time of writing the route is being revised to turn left here and shortly after right again, to head over the hill for Blackwater Bridge, avoiding the extremely boggy and difficult to follow lower route that existed when I passed. The new section brings you down to meet a tarmac side-road and, passing a beautiful post office, the picturesque bridge and inlet are reached. You can descend to Blackwater Pier by way of a tunnel under the main road. It is nice to take a break and maybe some refreshments here in this peaceful place; while I did so I was entertained by a sea otter that came ashore nearby and spent a long time preening at the water's edge before slipping in again without a splash.

On the eastern side of the Blackwater inlet the Way turns down a forestry road, with the river glistening silver through the trees below. After a few minutes the route drops to the wooded and rocky shore of the Kenmare River, to follow a pathway strewn with pine needles, running eastwards.

After passing a tiny inlet the route follows a partially ruined stone wall steeply uphill and away from the shore to meet a forestry road. Continuing eastwards, pass through a woodland of conifers, ash, cedar and eucalyptus, alive with bird life. Joining another road the garden wall of Dromore Castle, subject of the traditional song 'The Castle of Dromore' and now a private residence, is passed.

After a stretch through recently harvested forest, where new young conifers compete with wildflowers, bracken and ferns, the Way drops downhill again to join the tarred avenue. The avenue is followed out into the open again, with a wall of cypresses to the left and the Kenmare River to the right, before the route turns onto a forestry road that ascends through a newly planted coniferous wood. Shortly before reaching the main road, the gaunt ruins of Cappanacush Castle come into view on a height to the right. This appears to have been a substantial structure in its time, built from sandstone with massive limestone quoins. Cappanacush was an O'Sullivan stronghold and the birthplace of many notable members of that clan, including a John O'Sullivan who was Adjutant-General to the pretender Charles Stuart.

Reaching the main Kenmare road, the Way follows it eastwards past an old church which turns a windowless façade to the road. Further on is a popular pub belonging to one of Kerry's sporting legends, Pat Spillane, who in his brief career (he retired at the age of thirty-four) represented Kerry in nine All-Ireland Gaelic football finals and won four All-Star Awards.

Five minutes from this sporting mecca, Templenoe post office is passed, then on the left the new Templenoe Church, before reaching a crossroads with a signpost indicating Templenoe Pier to the right. The Kerry Way originally turned left at this cross, but at the time of writing some right-of-way problems have meant it has had to be diverted further along the main Kenmare road. It is hoped that these problems can be resolved, but in the meantime the route continues along the main road, passing now a number of inviting-looking guesthouses, which will be tempting if you are beginning to tire; Kenmare is still 6.5 km (4 miles) away.

At the next crossroads, at Reen, the altered Way turns left, following a sign for the Ring of Kerry Camping Park. A few minutes beyond the caravan park, after a new bungalow on the right, the Way crosses a stile into a field dotted with gorse bushes. Further stiles and way-marker posts take the route out onto Gortamullin Hill, much frequented by pheasants and hooded crows. Out to the south-west now the views along the Kenmare River are very fine, from the slender wooded Dunkerron and Greenane Islands a few kilometres away to the Bull Rock, which can be seen in clear weather standing Skellig-like on the horizon off Dursey Head.

The Way crosses Gortamullin Hill south of the summit, and then begins to descend the south-eastern flanks, with the dramatic summits of Peakeen Mountain and Knockanaguish, between which the Kerry Way returns to Killarney, coming into view to the north. Kenmare town can now be seen ahead, its grey-slated roofs rising from green fields against a backdrop of the wooded Sheen River Valley.

The Way descends, crossing a series of gorse-scattered banks and heading for a cluster of red-roofed barns, before crossing two more stiles to reach a short, narrow and leafy boreen leading to a tarred road. The tarmac is followed down to the main road, and turning left, we reach the town of Kenmare in less than 1 km (0.5 mile).

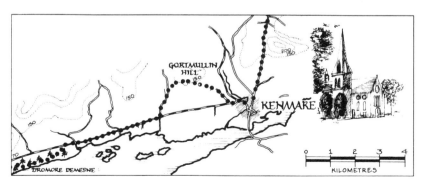

Kenmare's earliest inhabitants left evidence of their occupation in the remarkable Reenagoppul stone circle. The 4,000-year-old ritual site, fifteen standing stones surrounding a shallow chambered burial place covered by a massive capstone, stands on a prominence near the River Finnihy, within minutes of the centre of the town.

Kenmare was founded about 1670 by the Englishman Sir William Petty, who first came to Ireland in 1652 as Physician-General to the Cromwellian army and was responsible for the first comprehensive mapping of the country. At that time the Kerry countryside was possibly the least prosperous in Ireland, and Kenmare was regarded by the settlers as more isolated than the Indian Territories of New England. Attempts by them to 'civilise' the natives who, they were shocked to report, could not even speak English, were tolerated patiently at first, but after a number of years the Irish rebelled, placed all the English on a ship and sent them home!

In spite of this early disenchantment with foreigners, Kenmare is a welcoming place for tourists today, and in the high season German can be heard along with French, English and Dutch in the town's colourful streets.

Kenmare

STAGE 9: KENMARE TO KILLARNEY

DISTANCE: 24 KM (15 MILES). AGGREGATE CLIMB: 600 M (1,968 FEET). WALKING
TIME: 8 HOURS.

*This final stage brings the Way across the mountains and yet another
Windy Gap on the old road to Killarney, at the central point of which the
Lakes of Killarney and the coast south of Kenmare are visible in good
conditions. About 9.5 km (6 miles) of the stage is on tarmac, with the rest
on boreens and mountain tracks. The outgoing Kerry Way is rejoined 10
km (6.25 miles) out, near Galways Bridge.*

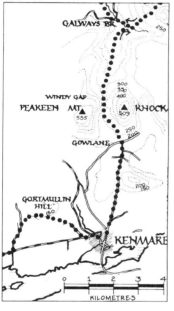

The Kerry Way leaves Kenmare passing St
Mary's Cathedral and follows a road that
narrows as it rises, giving fine views of the
town below. Soon the trees are left behind
and the road comes out on the open
hillside, with the dramatic profile of
Peakeen Mountain and its neighbour,
Knockanaguish, between which the route
will pass on its way to Killarney, coming
into view ahead. After one brief steep
descent into a valley, the road begins to
climb in earnest and passes through
Gowlane Cross.

The tarmac is now left behind as the
Way follows the old Killarney coach road, a
rough and rocky track so steep it is difficult
to imagine how horse-drawn coaches ever
managed even the first kilometre. There
was plenty of evidence when I passed that
even modern four-wheel-drive vehicles
become bogged down in quagmires along the route.

As the old road levels out, the Windy Gap is approached along the side of
a natural amphitheatre in the shelter of steep-sided Peakeen (556 m—
1,824 feet); outside the lambing season, when the wind is not blowing, this
is a strangely quiet and mystical place.

At the Windy Gap, the third and last pass on the Kerry Way so named,
there are great views in good weather to the north and to the south, taking
in both sides of the Iveragh Peninsula. Then the old road descends into the
desolate valley of the Derricunnihy River, which flows along nearby for a
while, cascading down towards its outfall in the Upper Lake of Killarney. As
the river bears away to the left, the route passes a group of ruined stone
houses to enter a beautiful and wild valley of scattered trees and rocks. A
little further on, a copse of rhododendrons hides a house that must have

been inhabited up to recently; now it is enveloped and consumed by the shrub, as nature, strong in this place, repossesses the land.

The Derricunnihy River meanders back and forth near the Way, having to fight its way downhill against layer after layer of the sandstone strata, tilted up like dams against it. Shortly after the first occupied house since Gowlane comes into view to the left ahead, the river is crossed by a series of giant stepping-stones. Passing the house, watch out for the point where the route connects with the outgoing Kerry Way: a track leading off to the right, up oak-covered slopes to return over Cromaglen Mountain to Killarney, as covered in stage 1.

At this point the main Killarney–Kenmare road is less than 1 km (0.5 mile) straight ahead.

Muckross House

9
THE LEITRIM WAY

Leitrim is a long narrow county that stretches over 80 km (50 miles) into the midlands of Ireland from a 4.8 km (3 mile) long sea coast on Donegal Bay. It is a scenic region of many beautiful hills, rivers and lakes, a wild terrain that allowed native Irish customs and laws to survive long after much of the rest of Ireland had been colonised by the Normans. The first of the great lakes of the Shannon River, Lough Allen, divides the county almost in two; north of the lake the landscape is made up of a series of flat-topped mountains, while to its south a patchwork of fields and hedgerows cover a typical post-glacial drumlin landscape.

The Leitrim Way is a 48 km (30 mile) route between Drumshanbo and Manorhamilton. Initially it wanders through drumlin country overlooking Lough Allen, and after crossing briefly into Co. Cavan near the village of Dowra, it ascends into the uplands of north Leitrim to reach marvellous viewpoints overlooking Counties Sligo, Fermanagh and Donegal, before finishing at Manorhamilton. It is a route very suited to those who enjoy a good rural roadwalk; other than a few hundred metres across moorland at Tullyskeherny, the route follows tarmac side-roads, forestry roads and old boreens. While the second stage of the route from Dowra to Manorhamilton is 32 km (20 miles) long, there are no taxing climbs involved. Little can be done, however, to shorten this stage without using two cars or arranged pick-ups.

How to get there
Drumshanbo is about 172 km (107 miles) from Dublin, served by the table no. 462 Carrigallen–Sligo bus and the table no. 469 Sligo–Longford bus. Carrick-on-Shannon, 11 km (7 miles) south of Drumshanbo, is well served by Bus Éireann, including the table no. 23 Dublin–Sligo bus.

Maps and Guides
The route is covered by the Ordnance Survey 1:127,000 (0.5 inches to 1 mile) map no. 7. Leitrim County Council, whom I found very helpful, produce a good 1:50,000 map/guide describing the route in English, German and French.

Enquiries
Leitrim County Council, Courthouse, Carrick-on-Shannon, Co. Leitrim; telephone 078 20005

Court Tomb at Tullyskeherny

STAGE 1: DRUMSHANBO TO DOWRA

DISTANCE: 16 KM (10 MILES). AGGREGATE CLIMB: 90 M (300 FEET). WALKING TIME: 4.5 HOURS.

This stage follows the line of an ancient boreen northwards along the lower slopes of Slieve Anierin, the southern spur of the Cuilcagh Mountains, with some great views out across Lough Allen. About 14 km (9 miles) are on tarmac, and the remainder follows short stretches of ancient narrow boreen, some stretches of which, when I walked, were somewhat overgrown. Drumshanbo has some bed-and-breakfast accommodation, and pub food can be obtained. Dowra has more limited accommodation and, similarly, pub food is available. Dowra is served by the table no. 462 Carrigallen–Sligo bus, which also serves Drumshanbo.

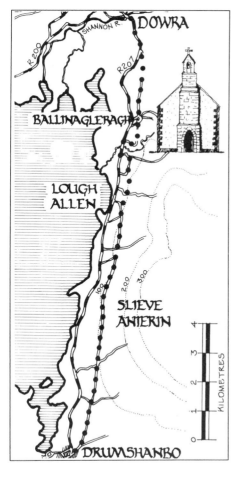

Drumshanbo is a village that grew up around iron-ore smelting works that served the considerable iron-mines in the area in the eighteenth century. Today mining again provides the principal employment, because of the proximity of the successful Arigna Mines. It is a village of gently curving, hilly streets of Victorian houses and shops, not to mention pubs, of which there seem to be a lot! There is an Interpretative Centre in the town that exhibits aspects of the Lough Allen area.

The route leaves the town passing the chapel of the Poor Clare Convent, with rounded Slieve Anierin (593 m—1,927 feet), the Mountain of Iron, filling the horizon ahead. Turning onto a narrower road, a grassy graveyard is passed in the valley of a meandering stream where a famous musician named Jack the Piper is buried among the many local people who died during the Great Famine.

The Way climbs gently

northwards along a pleasant, narrow and thickly hedged tarmac side-road. Soon the great expanse of Lough Allen comes into view stretching away to the north; the slender concrete chimney of the Arigna power station can be easily identified on the western shore, while the rising ground beyond it is scattered with farmsteads. Frequent grassy boreens lead up to the right towards the forest-clad flanks and bare ridge of Anierin, tempting walkers to take a diversion. Tradition has it that in a hidden enchanted cave on this mountain, Finn McCool and his Fianna lie spellbound, awaiting the appointed time to rise up and redeem Ireland from tyranny.

The road rises to drumlin tops and falls continuously, crossing over the valley's numerous mountain streams flowing towards the lough. Nearly 8 km (5 miles) north of Drumshanbo the tarmac runs out briefly as the route reverts to its original state as a narrow grassy boreen for a short distance, crossing a ford over the Stoney River. It may look like a harmless stream, but during a cloud-burst in 1930 it burst its banks and swept away seven houses.

A little less than a kilometre (0.6 mile) on at Cornamucklagh South, beyond a traditional cottage with a corrugated metal roof and in to the left of the road, can be found a megalithic monument dating from about 3000 BC called locally the Giants' Graves.

Soon the tarmac turns sharply downhill, while the route continues straight, entering a little field with picnic tables and descending to cross a stream. If you follow a path going upstream past the picnic tables, it will take you in a minute to a tiny magical valley under a canopy of foliage with a footbridge and waterfall, where a sweathouse can be found. These beehive-like structures, built from corbelled stone, were used in some of Ireland's northern counties from ancient times up to early this century as primitive steamrooms or saunas. Turf fires were burnt in the structures for a few days, after which green rushes were laid on the floor. The users of this unusual public facility, half a dozen at a time, removed their clothes and climbed inside, remaining as long as possible and sweating profusely, before cooling off in a nearby stream. The treatment was said to be good for rheumatism, 'the pains' and the grippe. Near here also, although I did not find it, is the holy well of St Beo-Aodh, who is said to have founded a school and monastery in the area in the fifth century.

The Way continues over a stile to reach and follow a narrow, high-walled boreen, wide enough for a single donkey with panniers. Soon the tarmac is rejoined again and the route continues between holly trees before continuing on straight and over a stile when the road turns left.

After a few minutes the route is back on the tarmac again and joins the main road to cross the broad Yellow River. Where the route turns downhill to meet the main road, there was in the nineteenth century a hamlet so busy and populated that it was known as 'The City'; today there are but three houses occupied in the area. A short distance after returning to the old line again, the hamlet of Ballinagleragh is reached. In addition to a couple of pubs, Ballinagleragh has a handsome church with a belfry built of locally quarried golden granite. The church is dedicated to St Hugh and was completed in 1842, with local men contributing their labour free of charge.

The Way continues past another holy well on a grassy stretch of boreen and just over 2 km (1.25 miles) further on joins the main road as it winds towards the strange mixture of derelict and colourfully painted houses that is Dowra, crossing the infant River Shannon to reach the village. Dowra is the southern terminal of the Cavan Way, a 25 km (16 mile) long walking route which goes north via the Shannon Pot to the village of Blacklion.

Dowra

STAGE 2: DOWRA TO MANORHAMILTON

DISTANCE: 32 KM (20 MILES). AGGREGATE CLIMB: 480 M (1,560 FEET). WALKING TIME: 10 HOURS.

This stage follows side-roads and forestry roads up onto a long flat-topped mountain known locally as the Glenfarne Plateau, after the glen that runs along its northern side. After descending briefly, the route rises again to cross the Burren-like limestone plateau of Tullyskeherny before descending to reach Manorhamilton. Except for a short distance across moorland at Tullyskeherny, the terrain is mainly tarmac and forestry roads.

Manorhamilton has hotel, hostel and bed-and-breakfast accommodation, and some restaurant facilities. The town is served by the table nos 65 and 66 Belfast–Galway buses, and table no. 470 Sligo–Glenfarne bus.

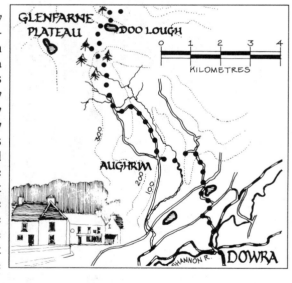

The Leitrim Way leaves Dowra following the Blacklion road, and after a short distance turns left to climb gently through a boggy countryside sparsely scattered with copses of poor trees and thorn bushes. To the north and north-east is the long, flat ridge of the Glenfarne Plateau, which the Way will cross over, at the head of the Barlear Valley.

About 7.2 km (4.5 miles) out of Dowra the route leaves tarmac and follows a green holly tree-margined road down into a flat marshy valley through which the Owennayle River meanders. Beyond a gateway the green road continues hedgeless to cross a narrow bridge over the river, where Co. Cavan, entered at Dowra, is left behind again. To the right as you cross the valley floor, look out nearby for a tiny sod-roofed building. Dwellings similar to this were the homes of the majority of people who lived in this area up to the end of the nineteenth century.

The valley crossed, the track rises to meet tarmac again at Coollegreane post office and turns right. The route follows tarmac up the side of a valley, passing through a small coniferous wood parallel to a deep ravine overhung with ash, hazel and thorn bushes. Down a pathway into the ravine a beautiful waterfall can be found, well worth a brief diversion from the route.

Turning right, the tarmac road becomes a forestry road which gently ascends along the western side of the desolate Barlear Valley, newly planted when I passed with many acres of new forestry. All around is a vast emptiness, the only sounds in still weather being the sound of your feet on the gravel road surface, and when I passed here, I heard the occasional cackle of a grouse, probably decrying the many acres of newly planted forestry that would soon drive the bird away from this valley.

Reaching the head of the valley the track winds upwards to reach a flat heather-covered plateau. To the south, 11.2 km (7 miles) away as the crow flies, and seeming much further, Lough Allen stretches into the distance, while rounded Slieve Anierin sweeps north to the rugged bluffs of Cuilcagh. When I passed, there was a mast here, testing the characteristics of the wind prior to the possible erection of electricity-generating windmills, which were proposed to take the place of the obsolete turf-burning station at Lough Allen.

To the right of the track a small cobble-girdled oval lake, called Doo Lough, reflects the bright sky and belies its dark name. Further on are old quarry workings which, to judge by the new survey poles in the ground when I passed, are exciting new interest. There were substantial iron foundries on the western side of this plateau in the nineteenth century using iron from local mines; the famous Halfpenny Bridge in Dublin was one of their more well-known productions.

The view to the north reveals itself slowly as the track begins to descend the northern side of the hill, but it is well worth waiting for. To the north-east are Lough Macnean Upper and Lough Macnean Lower, dividing Co. Fermanagh and Northern Ireland from Co. Cavan and the Republic. Dough Mountain and Thur Mountain, the latter of which will be constantly in view all the way to Manorhamilton, are directly to the north, and between them you can get a glimpse deep into the hills of Donegal.

The Way now descends gently into the western end of Glenfarne and passing through forestry, reaches tarmac again at Moneenlom. The road is followed towards the west, where King's Mountain, the rugged northern portal of Glencar, can be seen in clear weather on the horizon. Turning south again at Munnagashel, the route climbs a gravel road towards the high ground again. Soon grass takes the place of gravel and when the route comes out into the open there is a fabulous view off to the right, out along Glenade, with the Keelogue cliffs rising dramatically on the northern side. Up to the left rises the rugged western end of the Glenfarne Plateau, while to the north is dome-like Dough Mountain, whose flanks are riven with over sixty separate streams that radiate down from its top.

Soon the route enters forestry following a mossy path; take care here and be vigilant for the Way bearing right; I went astray here and it was some time before I was able to get back on track. The route heads in a south-westerly direction along an ancient boreen, and coming out into the open the summit of Benbo can be seen slightly to the right ahead, peering over Tullyskeherny.

This is a pleasant stretch of the route; the boreen is bounded in places by low mossy banks and completely overhung by foliage. It is wide enough to have been an old droving road, but whatever it was used for, it certainly gives the feeling of belonging to another time.

Crossing a gate, a forestry road is met and the route follows it downhill to cross the Scardan River, before rising in a loop to meet a public road. Turning right, look out for a derelict stone cottage on the right which has a diamond-pattern slated roof; it has the little projecting doorcase that is a local feature which can even be found on new houses. The road is followed for 1.3 km (0.8 mile), until the old Glenboy National School, now a residence and post office, is reached.

Here the route turns left up a gravelly road that rises quickly into the hills again, bordered with a palisade of silvery hazel and ash. As the route ascends, very good views open up as Belmore Mountain, north of Lough Macnean Lower, and the misty hills beyond, come into sight. At a bend in the road, the route carries on straight into a heavily forested area along a grassy boreen bounded by low moss-covered banks. (At time of writing, there is a possibility that in the future an alternative route to Manorhamilton may be established which will continue on straight to eventually cross the hill at O'Donnell's Rock.)

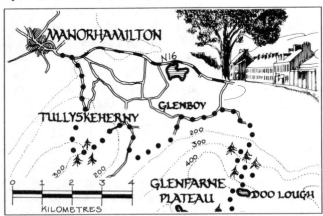

Soon the route turns into the forestry, but when I walked here the pathway was impassable due to fallen trees. Apparently the Way makes a short loop through the forest to rejoin the old boreen further on; if there are such problems when you pass here, continue along the boreen, crossing a fence if necessary, until you meet a stile where the Way comes out of the trees. The ground becomes extremely swampy in places, so keep to the raised bank at its side.

From the stile the route continues uphill for a short distance until another stile takes you out onto the open moorland plateau of Tullyskeherny where, when I walked, snipe were plentiful, darting and jinking away. After a short distance, a track is reached and followed northwards. It is a pleasant plateau this, a green place with patches of contrasting light-grey where the limestone bedrock bursts through. Here and there, lone wind-sculpted thorn trees that have weathered many winters provide meagre shelter for grazing sheep.

Some time in the past, probably millenniums ago, the people who farmed the area used the scattered limestone cobbles to build a number of broad cashels or circular-walled enclosures, either as animal pens or as protection for farmsteads. One of them in particular, to the left of the track, is still almost intact. Further on, to the right of the track, the box-like constructions formed with flat limestone slabs are what remain of a pair of court tombs, originally covered by earth, that could have been constructed as long as five thousand years ago.

The Leitrim Way reaches the public road by crossing a stile, and descends steeply with a great view of the valley running west to Manorhamilton laid out below. After 1.6 km (1 mile) the main Blacklion road is met, and the route turns left and follows it into Manorhamilton.

Manorhamilton (its Gaelic name is Cluanin, or 'little meadow') is situated on a hill surrounded by hills, roughly where an ancient O'Rourke stronghold was located, at the meeting point of five valleys. The castle, now an ivy-covered ruin, was built in the reign of Elizabeth by a Scottish planter named Hamilton, after whom the place is named. It was said to be the largest, strongest and most handsome castle in Co. Leitrim, and used to glitter in sunlight from the mica-rich stone from which it was built.

Red Grouse

10
THE MUNSTER WAY

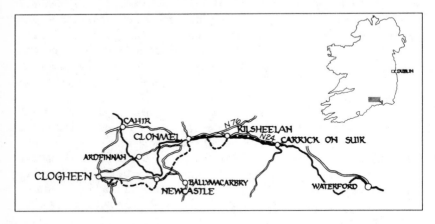

The Munster Way at the time of writing extends 80 km (50 miles) from Carrick-on-Suir, Co. Tipperary, in the lowlands of the Suir Valley, across the foothills of the Comeragh Mountains to finish, rather abruptly, on the northern slopes of the picturesque Knockmealdowns, near the town of Clogheen. At time of writing there are moves afoot to extend the route south from Kilsheelan into the beautiful valley of the Nier River before returning to Clonmel. It would be a great improvement to the Munster Way, but at present a route has not been approved. There are also plans to extend the route in the near future to Fermoy and ultimately to join up with the Kerry Way.

The route includes a rich variety of terrain, from river towpath and forestry roads to open mountain moorland and narrow by-roads, and passes through the award-winning village of Kilsheelan and the historic town of Clonmel.

I found the route to be well signposted in terms of the number of signs; in many places, however, particularly on the forestry stretches, summer growth had completely obscured signs that had probably been placed in winter or spring. If you come to what appears to be an unmarked junction, remember, the sign may be lurking in the high grass.

How to get there
The suggested starting-point at Carrick-on-Suir is about 160 km (100 miles) from Dublin and 112 km (70 miles) from Rosslare. The town is well served by bus from all main centres.

Maps and guides

The route is covered on the Discovery Series map no. 74 (1:50,000) and the Ordnance Survey 1:127,000 (0.5 inch to 1 mile) map no. 22. Bord Fáilte information sheet no. 26J also describes the route. East West Mapping, at time of writing, are preparing to publish a map guide to the route. The section between Kilsheelan and Ballymacarbry is covered in detail on an excellent 1:25,000 map and walks guide to the Comeragh Mountains and the Nire Valley, available from Eileen Ryan, Clonanav Farm Guesthouse, Ballymacarbry, Co. Waterford.

Enquiries

Tipperary (South Riding) County Council, County Hall, Clonmel; telephone 052 25399

Liam Lynch Memorial

STAGE 1: CARRICK TO CLONMEL

DISTANCE: 26 KM (16 MILES). AGGREGATE CLIMB: 250 M (820 FEET). WALKING TIME: 7 HOURS.

This first stage follows the River Suir to the village of Kilsheelan and, rising briefly into the foothills of the Comeragh Mountains, drops to the river again to reach Clonmel. The stage includes 14.5 km (9 miles) on the Suir towpath, nearly 8 km (5 miles) on tarred roads, and the balance on forestry roads. If the distance is daunting the stage can be split into two sections: Carrick to Kilsheelan, approximately 11.25 km (7 miles), and Kilsheelan to Clonmel, approximately 14.5 km (9 miles). Kilsheelan has limited bed-and-breakfast accommodation, but it is on the route of a number of regular bus services between Clonmel and Carrick, where there is a wide range of accommodation and restaurants.

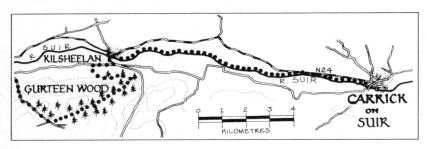

Carrick-on-Suir has been in existence since the thirteenth century when, known as Carrickmagriffin, it was granted royal assent to hold a fair. At that time it was probably a small settlement centred on a ford and an island in the Suir, and as such, had a significant strategic importance in controlling the use of the river for communications. At the time, the river was the only safe route for the Normans in and out of this rich hinterland, and for a long time their influence only extended a kilometre on either side of the river valley. By the early fourteenth century the place was in the ownership of the Butlers and had grown considerably, meriting the building of an enclosing wall, and later a bridge across the river. The Butlers, who acquired the title Earl of Ormond about this time, built a castle here on the site of the present Ormond Castle, and founded the Franciscan Monastery.

In the 1560s the 10th Earl of Ormond built, on the site of the older Ormond Castle, a fine Elizabethan manor-house which still survives. Here, for the first time in Ireland, stucco-work was used, and clay brick made an early appearance although used only in the chimneys.

The first bridge across the Suir at Carrick was built in the thirteenth century, and the present 'Old Bridge' was built around 1447. Carrick's prosperity was to some extent due to the fact that although almost 40 km (25 miles) from Waterford Harbour, it was the lowest bridged point on the

River Suir until the first bridge was built at Waterford in 1793. It was therefore able to reap the benefit of the tolls not only levied on river traffic, but on all trade which had to cross the bridge at Carrick to reach the port of Waterford.

The Munster Way begins at the west side of Carrick, where the main road comes to within fifty metres of the River Suir at a pleasant park. There is a good footpath along the river bank to start this stage, passing clusters of moored traditional fishing cots, tiny, shallow, flat-bottomed boats that I have seen only on the Suir and Barrow. It is an unusual sight to see one being poled down the river, the fisherman standing in the stern.

To the south a line of wooded hills, northern outliers of the Comeragh Mountains, stretches westwards parallel with the Suir. Tangles of river-water crowfoot lined the river bank when I walked, while the path edge was a riot of colour with pennyroyal, meadowsweet, chamomile, rose of sharon, vetch and wild carrot. Black-and-green-winged damselflies danced along the water's surface close to the bank.

After about ten minutes, pass the point to which the Suir is tidal, and shortly afterwards a small round tower on the far bank is passed. The Davin family, who ran a prosperous river transport business out of Carrick, owned the fishing rights here, and the tower was erected in the nineteenth century to guard a salmon weir. The Davins were a great sporting family. Pat Davin is said to have held six world athletic records at one time, and he was the first person to clear a 6 foot jump, while his brother Maurice was one of the founder-members of the GAA.

Half an hour out of Carrick the ruins of the first of a number of tower-houses, built in the fifteenth century to guard the Suir and its rich valley, can be seen on rising ground on the far side. For many centuries the river was the only means of communication between the port of Waterford and the hinterland, and in the early Norman period particularly it had to be well protected.

In less than an hour the formal riverside track disappears, and the bank is followed along a sometimes faint path through high grass and nettles, where a stick is handy for use as a machete. The abundance of nettles along the river ensures that if you walk in summertime you will be constantly entertained by clouds of colourful butterflies. When I walked here it was obvious from the state of the vegetation that at least some sections of the river bank were little frequented, the exceptions being good fishing stretches, where well-organised fishing clubs maintained the banks very well, sometimes transforming them into manicured lawns.

Soon the great rounded bulk of Slievenamon comes into view to the right.

O, sweet Slievenamon, you're my darling and pride,
With your soft swelling bosom and mien like a bride,

wrote Charles Kickham of this isolated mountain north of the Suir. The origin of the name (which means the Mountain of the Women) is lost in time.

A ruined church and graveyard on a prominence are passed next, and the grey square shape of another tower-house appears ahead. This is Poulakerry Castle, built in the late fifteenth century by a branch of the Butler family and from where, like other landowners along the river, they exacted tolls from the river traffic, earning them the protests of the merchants of Carrick, who called them 'common thieves and robbers'. Just below the tower-house, which is well maintained and seems to be occupied (judging from an incongruous television aerial sprouting from the roof), there are the remains of a small harbour. Yellow bursts of lady's bedstraw grew from the banks here when I passed. It is said that the soft stems and tiny flowers made it a popular bedding filler in Norman times; perhaps the ancestors of these plants gave the Butlers a comfortable night's sleep.

Around a sharp bend Landscape House, a pink, bow-fronted Georgian residence overlooking the river on the far side, is passed, and soon the bridge at Kilsheelan comes into sight ahead. Its elegant arches frame lush meadows on the far side of the Suir, beyond which can be seen the Scottish-baronial towers of Gurteen le Poer.

The grassy river bank beside the bridge is an ideal place to take a rest from walking, especially in summertime, when a swim in the cool waters of the Suir can be welcome. I was entertained here for some time by a young otter when I passed: after making a frenzied and unsuccessful foray against a flock of mallards on the water, he climbed the buttresses of the bridge and rolled on the sand there before swimming to the other bank and disappearing into the grass.

The picturesque and award-winning village of Kilsheelan is fifty metres to the right, well worth a visit for refreshments and a pause on the journey. Between the bridge and the village is a motte, constructed here by the Norman knight William de Burgo in the twelfth century. Originally there would have been a palisade of timber round the base of the mound and a wooden tower on the summit, and in this position it was probably built to guard a ford-crossing of the river. Today it has been converted into a Marian shrine, decorated with flowers and covered with tightly mown grass.

The cill of Kilsheelan is an ancient church, possibly eleventh century, with a north-facing Romanesque Transitional doorway, probably added in the thirteenth century, and badly mutilated in Cromwellian times.

The Way leaves the river bank and crosses the bridge into Co. Waterford and towards the foothills of the Comeragh Mountains. The gate lodge of Gurteen le Poer, standing opposite the main gates and modelled on a Greek temple, is worth attention before the Way starts uphill.

At the time of writing the route turns left at the junction just uphill, and enters Gurteen Wood. By the time this publication is on the shelves, however, I am informed that the route will be altered as follows. Turn right at the junction, which has a celtic cross le Poer memorial alluding to the claim the Gurteen branch of that family have held since the early eighteenth century over the extensive estates of Curraghmore to the east. After 1.2 km (0.75 miles) the route turns left into Gurteen Wood and zigzags uphill on a forestry track. Soon the route turns east and after descending for a short distance rejoins the original route again to follow the forestry road as it climbs steadily through the forest, giving fine views out to Slievenamon and over the south Tipperary countryside. Take care in this wood to continue in the right direction at junctions where, when I passed, way-markers were often hidden in the undergrowth at the roadside. The route curves round the eastern side of Gurteen Wood and then heads south-west along a long, straight forestry road crossing the southern flanks of the hill. Soon a pinnacle of bare rock, at 350 m (1,150 feet)—one of the summits of this particular hill—can be seen rising above the trees to the north. A few minutes later, across a clearing to the left, the dramatic peaks and ridges of the Comeragh Mountains come briefly into sight.

Eventually the forest thins out and the pyramidal shapes of the Knockanafrinn ridge in the craggy Comeraghs come into view again, with the Knockmealdown Mountains making an appearance in the south-west. When a nearby hill with a tall telecommunications mast on its summit can be seen, you are within ten minutes of the public road again.

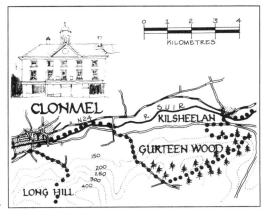

A massive gallán or standing stone called unimaginatively Cloghfaddagh (Long Rock) is passed before a clearing gives a view north-west to the town of Clonmel and the lush Golden Vale of Tipperary beyond. A few metres further on, the Way exits onto the public road near Harney's Cross and, turning right, winds down towards the River Suir again.

As the road descends, nearby Raven's Rock (318—1,043 feet) is passed on the right, while to the north-west the Galty Mountains, topped by the conical Galtymore Mountain (920 m—3,018 feet), come into view. Bearing left at the bottom of the hill the road passes the ivy-covered remains of a double-gabled manor-house, at one time the property of the Duchess of St Albans, to reach the Suir.

The Way crosses the river by a narrow humped-back bridge, built privately in the eighteenth century by Sir Thomas Osborne to give access to his lands on the south side of the river, and handed over to the public in the early 1800s. On the far side the Way heads west on the river bank towards Clonmel, now 3.25 km (2 miles) away, passing the extensive buildings of a special school run by the Rosminian Fathers. Past the Scheisser factory, the river comes close to the main Carrick–Clonmel road at a little park where, by the look of the great stones making up the river bank, there was once a busy harbour.

Soon the riverside path takes us over the county border into the Borough of Clonmel. For the last couple of kilometres into Clonmel the river is divided by a series of narrow, treed islands, and the far bank is thick with great silver-leaved willows overhanging the slow-flowing water. Frequently herons stand, still and sentinel-like, on low branches that extend over the river's surface. After a promenade under a row of fine old chestnut trees the first bridge of Clonmel is reached and, passing under it, the Way ascends steps to the street.

'Sweet Clonmel', as the poet Spenser called it, while a typical Irish market town, enjoys a beautiful situation at the foot of the Comeragh Mountains on the banks of the River Suir. Like most other river towns in Ireland it was founded by Norman pioneers, in this case probably Richard de Burgo early in the thirteenth century. Although a vibrant, modern place, Clonmel has managed to preserve buildings from almost every century since its founding. The earliest examples can be seen in Mary Street, where the nineteenth-century St Mary's Church shares an extensive site with remains of thirteenth, sixteenth and seventeenth-century churches and towers and a substantial section of the fifteenth-century town walls.

The Main Guard, fondly believed by local people to have been built to the designs of Sir Christopher Wren, dominates the eastern end of Sarsfield Street. Built in 1674 as the seat of the courts of the Palatinate of Ormonde, it has since served as a tholsel (custom house), barracks and shops, and is today much in need of refurbishment.

Comeragh Mountains

STAGE 2: CLONMEL TO NEWCASTLE

DISTANCE: 16 KM (10 MILES). AGGREGATE CLIMB: 375 M (1,230 FEET). WALKING TIME: 5.25 HOURS.

This stage climbs steeply into the hills south of Clonmel, to descend gradually and rejoin the Suir at the village of Newcastle. About 10 km (6 miles) of the route is on tarred side-roads and the remainder on boreens, forestry roads and the open hillside.

There are no registered bed-and-breakfast establishments in Newcastle, but the village is served by the table no. 386 Dungarvan–Clonmel bus and the table no. 388 bus to Clonmel (Fridays only). The village of Ballymacarbry, which has a good range of accommodation, is 1 km (0.5 mile) off the Way 6.5 km (4 miles) short of Newcastle.

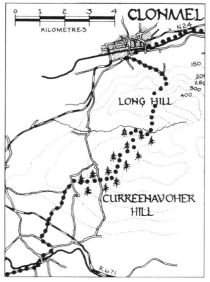

The Munster Way passes the town of Clonmel along the south bank of the Suir and, after reaching a picturesque weir at Old Bridge Street, heads through the outskirts of the town towards the hills. Passing a colourful memorial to Edel Quinn, an Irish missionary who died in East Africa in 1944, the Way goes to the right of a pub called the Emigrant's Rest and heads steeply up Roaring Spring Road. A magnificent panorama of the town of Clonmel and the lush Golden Vale opens up behind as the road climbs between ditches speckled with herb Robert, honeysuckle, vetch and speedwell. Soon altitude is gained and great clumps of rhododendron tower over the hedgerows, and foxgloves, ferns and fraughans take the place of the lowland wildflowers.

Near the top of the hill the Way turns right and passes through a remarkable tunnel of wild rhododendron ablaze with purple blossoms and loud with foraging bees in summertime. Emerging into the open, the route crosses the heather-covered slopes west of Long Hill, with the bulk of Slievenamon dominating the horizon to the north-east and the town of Clonmel spread out below.

Passing below a weather-beaten Holy Year calvary, the route heads towards the south-west. I found the way-markers missing in this area, and with few conspicuous features it is easy to go astray. From the summit of the hill, a short distance west of the Holy Year shrine, a fence running north-south can be seen to the west. Crossing a stile over this fence, continue west towards the next north-south hedgerow; behind this is an old boreen, the remains of an ancient road connecting Clonmel to Dungarvan. The Way takes this old road between hedges of ash, holly, gorse and bracken, downhill into the valley of the Glenealy River.

Past a tiny red-washed cottage with a sagging roof, the Way leaves the boreen when it turns sharply right, and keeps on straight, on a track that drops steeply between columns of foxgloves to a ford on the Glenealy River. Crossing by stepping-stones, the route ascends a stony track to meet a forestry road, which it follows up the side of a deep ravine. The forest here is very mixed, including oak, rowan and birch, as well as Monterey pine. Watch out for deer as you go: at least one herd of sika deer grazes on this hill.

Shortly after crossing a concrete bridge, the route hairpins off to the left and steeply climbs through young trees. Behind, there is a view back to Long Hill and the line of the ancient road that the Way followed down to the Glenealy stream. The road winds gently but steadily uphill, while brief clearings to the right give views out over Tipperary's Golden Vale. When I walked here in autumn the birch trees had yellow-gold leaves, and larches carpeted the forestry road with a fine coat of needles, through which the scaly brown heads of puffball mushrooms protruded.

I found that some way-markers had been spirited away during harvesting of the forest here; if this is the case when you walk the Way, keep heading westwards and you will eventually reach the public road, from where you can reconnect with the route.

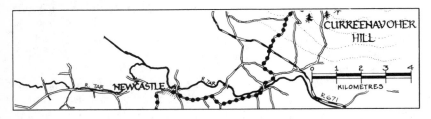

Soon the route begins to descend again, and a tarred public road is reached. Crossing the road, the Way enters another plantation and, following the forestry road westwards for less than fifteen minutes, meets another public road. Open moorland stretches ahead into the distance, with the gentle slopes of the Knockmealdown Mountains lining the horizon to the south-west.

The Way now heads downhill on the tarmac, while over to the east the main summits of the Comeragh range come into view, the highest of which, Fauscoum, reaches to 789 m (2,588 feet). Soon the main Clonmel–Dungarvan road is crossed and the route continues on a side-road, veering west to reach the tiny village of Four-Mile-Water, where Byrne's grocery and stationery shop can provide refreshments. The village of Ballymacarbry is 1 km (0.5 mile) straight on.

Turning right at Byrne's shop the route heads south again over a humped-back bridge crossing the Nire. At a ford near this bridge in 1637 the coach of the Earl of Cork, attempting to cross while the river was in flood, was turned over, and his seventh son, Robert, then aged ten, was swept downriver and nearly drowned. The earl subsequently paid to have a bridge built here. Robert Boyle went on to become a famous scientist and philosopher and a founder-member of the Royal Society and to give his name to a law of physics most schoolchildren know by heart, Boyle's Law.

Lonergan's pub is passed just beyond the bridge, and the Way enters Co. Tipperary again, looping round and climbing briefly to the south before dropping towards the village of Newcastle, shortly before which the appearance of a footpath at the roadside confirms that civilisation is nearby! Before entering the village, the ruins of Newcastle House, burnt in 1922, can be seen in the old demesne to the right.

Newcastle is a neat village, where three roads meet near the banks of the River Suir. This is a good farming area, with tractors always coming and going; the local forge, which no longer deals with horses, stands surrounded by a sea of mechanical agricultural implements.

Nugent's is a traditional pub worth a visit. On the western side of the village a large old ruined church with a Gothic doorway stands in a graveyard at the roadside. Beyond it, located picturesquely on the banks of the Suir and heavily camouflaged with an all-over mantle of ivy and elderberry, is the original New Castle, consisting of a small three-storey round tower and a series of other structures, one possibly a banqueting hall, surrounded by the remains of a bawn wall that appears to have a vaulted walkway on top.

Clonmel

STAGE 3: NEWCASTLE TO THE VEE (CLOGHEEN)

DISTANCE: 16 KM (10 MILES). AGGREGATE CLIMB: 425 M (1,400 FEET). WALKING
TIME: 5.5 HOURS.

*This stage ascends into the foothills of the Knockmealdown Mountains, and
drops again briefly before climbing through forest to reach the Vee, and
what is at the time of writing the end of the Munster Way. For those seeking
overnight accommodation at the end of the day there is an additional
4.75 km (3 miles) downhill by road to Clogheen. About 8 km (5 miles) of the
stage is on mountain tracks, forestry tracks and boreens and 13 km (8 miles)
on tarred roads, including the road to Clogheen.*

*There are two registered bed-and-breakfast establishments in Clogheen,
which is served by the table no. 7 bus to Clonmel and Kilkenny.*

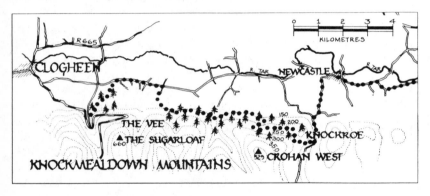

Heading west out of Newcastle, the Munster Way turns left off the main road
and follows a side-road south into the foothills of the Knockmealdowns.
Knockroe (312 m—1,023 feet) and Knocknageeragh (278 m—911 feet) are
the two peaks that can be seen ahead; the Way rises up the valley between
them.

A bridge over the Glenboy River is crossed and the route continues
uphill, with bracken-covered slopes reaching skywards on the right, while
the river cuts a deep ravine below to the left. Five minutes after passing two
large stone gate-piers on the left, about 5 km (3 miles) from Newcastle, the
Way turns off the road quite suddenly, over a low stone wall and onto what
was, when I walked here, an overgrown track.

You have to squeeze between brambles and gorse as the track ascends,
but soon the gorse lessens to reveal that you are following a stone-walled
boreen towards wooded Knockroe. Bearing left and passing the ruins of an
old shooting-lodge, pinnacled Crohan West (524 m—1,718 feet) rises ahead,
while more rounded peaks rise away from it towards the south-west.

Looping round three sides of a sheep pasture, the flat and fertile plains of Co. Tipperary come into view to the north, the Golden Vale more emerald than gold these days as cereal crops reduce and pasture increases. In the distance the River Suir can be seen winding its way south from Ardfinnan.

Before reaching the forest that sweeps down from Knockroe, the Way drops downhill through bracken and heather to reach a forestry road, and turns westwards along it. After nearly 1 km (0.5 mile) a strange round tower appears a hundred metres away to the left. It was erected in 1935 as an elaborate memorial to the revolutionary Liam Lynch, who was shot near here in April 1923 during a Civil War action with Free State government forces.

The Way continues to descend through the forest, keeping a westerly course, and less than 4 km (2.5 miles) from the round tower two massive water-tanks, providing the water supply for Clogheen, come into view ahead, nestled in the trees on a hillside. Within minutes a crossroads is reached as the Munster Way crosses a very ancient path, Rian Bó Phádraig (The Way of Patrick's Cow).

The turn to the right will bring you down to the village of Goatsbridge, a little more than 1.5 km (1 mile) away. The Way carries on straight to ford the Glengalla River and continue westwards on a forestry road on the far side. This section is a pleasant promenade through fragrant heather along the foot of the Knockmealdowns, giving very fine views over the trees out to the north. Although I saw none when I passed, the soft soil of the track displayed numerous prints of deer, so keep an eye out for a sighting of the animals. I did, however, see a pair of grouse, running along ahead of me before exploding into flight with a cackling call.

Soon the route winds its way downhill and, entering a mature wood, follows a rough path to reach the end of a forestry road. The Way takes the road westwards and, meeting a crossroads after some minutes, turns right to leave the trees onto the public road, nearly 6.5 km (4 miles) east of the village of Clogheen.

The northern peaks of the Knockmealdowns line the horizon to the left as the road is followed westwards, while the Galty Mountains are beginning to dominate the skyline ahead. Less than 1 km (0.5 mile) further on, refreshments can be had at Ryan's thatched pub, near which is Glenwood Farm, which provides bed-and-breakfast.

Two kilometres (1.25 miles) after meeting the tarmac, and after a bridge over a stream, the Way turns up a boreen and into the forest again. Forestry roads, lined with picturesque rhododendrons and conifers, are followed as they wind, southwards now, towards the Vee. When the rhododendrons are out of bloom in late summer, their colour is taken up by the rich heather margin of some stretches, as the route climbs a river valley deeply cut into the mountain.

Nearly 2.5 km (1.5 miles) after entering the trees the forestry road ends and the Way takes a path through the trees for a short distance to meet the public road, where a large signboard displaying a map of the Munster Way indicates that you have completed it. Although this is the end of the Munster Way, you are on the very threshold of great walking country. Not far above the road is Bay Lough, backed by high cliffs and ringed with pink-flowering rhododendrons in early summer. This beautiful place was, in the last century, a haunt of eagles.

The nearest town to the end of the Munster Way is Clogheen, nearly 4.75 km (3 miles) downhill. A town of stolid nineteenth-century terraced houses, it had great prosperity in that era when it was the centre of a vast wheat-growing and milling area.

Tomb overlooking the Vee

11

THE SLIEVE BLOOM WAY

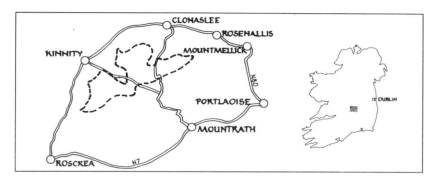

Lying astride the borders of Counties Offaly and Laois, the Slieve Bloom Mountains rise out of the flatlands of the Central Plain, from a distance a low, almost insignificant range of hills. Their seemingly featureless nature is deceptive, however, and as we draw near to the range we can see that the high ground is cleft by many deep and beautiful glens, hidden landscapes as full of character as they are of myths and legends.

The Slieve Bloom Way is a 77 km (48 mile) circuit around and through these mountains, taking in the higher ridges as well as the river valleys and foothills. The distances to the nearest villages from the Way, and the shortage of nearby overnight accommodation, suggest that for average walkers this is a route best tackled by a group with two cars, the extra mobility bringing the bigger towns around the area within range. Strong walkers will have little difficulty arranging their day's trekking to fit the available accommodation, while for more modest strollers there are plenty of very rewarding 'there-and-back' walks to suit.

How to get there
The nearest town to the Slieve Bloom Way with a regular bus service is Mountmellick, 87 km (54 miles) from Dublin and served by the table no. 124 Dublin–Mountmellick bus.

Maps and guides
The route is covered by the Ordnance Survey 1:127,000 (0.5 inch to 1 mile) map no. 15 and the Discovery Series map no. 54 (1:50,000). It is also indicated on a map-brochure titled 'Slieve Bloom Environment Park' prepared by An Foras Forbartha on behalf of Laois and Offaly County Councils. Bord Fáilte information sheet no. 26F also describes the route.

Enquiries
Ethel Power, Marketing and Development Officer, Offaly Tourist Council, Bury Quay, Tullamore, Co. Offaly; telephone 0506 52566

Tumulus at Forelacka

STAGE 1: GLENBARROW TO MONICKNEW

DISTANCE: 12 KM (7.5 MILES). AGGREGATE CLIMB: 175 M (574 FEET). WALKING TIME: 3.5 HOURS.

Rising to cross the heather-covered Ridge of Capard, with great views all around, this stage of the Way drops through forestry to meet the public road at Monicknew. The stage has nearly 8 km (5 miles) on forestry roads, 2.5 km (1.5 miles) on open heathland, and the rest on forest paths and fire-breaks. The stage ends at scenic Monicknew Bridge, a little more than 9.5 km (6 miles) from the town of Mountrath, where accommodation is available. For walkers who wish to spoil themselves, Roundwood House, a Palladian villa where exceptional food and accommodation are provided, is just over 4.75 km (3 miles) away.

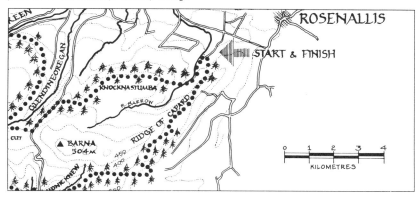

This first stage starts at the Glenbarrow car park, about 4 km (2.5 miles) from the village of Rosenallis. Leaving the car park, the Way follows a sign for the Ridge of Capard up a forestry road and into a coniferous wood. After 1.5 km (1 mile) a path through the trees takes the Way uphill, with a view westwards of the River Barrow Valley stretching deep into the mountains.

Soon a road is met, and the route turns right towards the Ridge of Capard. Crossing a tarred road and passing some picnic tables, follow a rough path through the heather, out along the ridge. The Way ahead now, a very indistinct path at times, is indicated by four tall, slender poles, the first of which should be clearly visible to the south-west.

After a few minutes a prospect across the flatlands to the east and south can be seen as the higher ground to the left drops away briefly. The town of Portlaoise should be easy to identify, and beyond it, the string of limestone hillocks—called 'hums' by geologists—on one of which the Castle of Dunamase stands. North of Portlaoise is the town of Mountmellick. If the weather is reasonably clear, the blue-grey undulations of the Wicklow Mountains will be seen lining the eastern horizon.

The heath here is the home of an abundance of meadow-pipits, among Ireland's most numerous birds. In spring and summer their song fills the air all around as they climb vertically to broadcast their song before parachuting slowly back to a heather perch. This is also a good place to see red grouse, often flushed out in front of you with an explosion of wing-beats, to skim away across the ridge just above the heather, cackling loudly. Some parts of the ridge stay very wet all year round, encouraging lichens so rich and healthy that in places they are like small shrubs.

After the third pole, on a little promontory to the left, a pair of stone cairns is passed. As the fourth pole is approached, another small cairn can be seen on another promontory to the left. These should not be confused with the next important feature to look out for, a much larger cairn further on past the fourth pole.

At this third cairn turn downhill in a south-easterly direction to reach the edge of the forest and, turning right, follow the forest edge to reach a gap. Follow this gap downhill over rough ground to reach a forestry road, and turn right. For the first time since reaching the eastern end of the Ridge of Capard it is now possible to stride out, the road rising and falling as it descends through thickly planted spruce trees.

The surroundings are just beginning to become monotonous when the road, climbing again, comes out onto the open hillside below one of the many summits of the Slieve Blooms, Baunreagcong. The relief is brief, however, and the road re-enters the trees a short distance on.

After a while the Way begins to descend south-west into the glen of Monicknew. About 1.5 km (1 mile) to the north now, on the heathery ridge above, the River Barrow rises in the Well of Slieve Bloom, a mystical well and one of the ancient wonders of Ireland, said to have the alarming property of bursting forth to flood the entire surrounding country if touched or even looked upon by a man.

The surroundings become more dramatic as the Way descends along the steep side of the glen, with a tributary of the Delour River flowing noisily below, to meet the public road at Monicknew Bridge.

Red Grouse

STAGE 2: MONICKNEW TO GLENDINE EAST

DISTANCE: 13 KM (8 MILES). AGGREGATE CLIMB: 225 M (740 FEET). WALKING TIME: 4.25 HOURS.

This stage crosses the Delour River to rise through forestry onto the remote south-facing slopes of Gorteenameale, and descends to the public road at Glendine East. Nearly 8 km (5 miles) is on forestry roads, 3.25 km (2 miles) on often trackless and sometimes rough heathland, and 3 km (1.75 miles) on the public road. The nearest village, Camross, 5.5 km (3.5 miles) south from where the public road is met at Glendine East, has no regular bus service. At the time of writing I could not find any overnight accommodation in the area around Camross.

The Way leaves Monicknew Bridge and, following the public road past a picnic area, climbs gently for nearly 1 km (0.5 mile) before turning left onto a tarred forestry road. Descending through mixed birch and spruce, the route levels out in the bottom of the valley and crosses concrete bridges over two cascading streams.

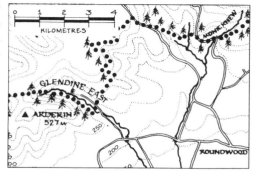

After the second bridge, a building with a decorative chimney and roof-tiles seen on higher ground to the left, is all that remains of Baunreagh House, a substantial nineteenth-century mansion demolished in 1938. Passing the building, now used as a forestry store, the Way turns up an old track. A rich and healthy coat of bright green moss grows on everthing here, and extends up the trunks of trees to a height of nearly three metres, hanging from the branches like surrealist decorations. This damp and sheltered habitat must provide succulent grazing, because I have seen both fallow deer and feral goats in small herds here among the trees.

Soon a forestry road is joined, and immediately after, the Way turns left and uphill through the trees to reach a magical mossy glade of beech trees, each one dressed in a green velvet coat. Just beyond, the public road is reached, and the Way turns right and uphill.

After ten minutes the Way turns left onto a forestry track leading up onto the hill of Gorteenameale, the ridge of which comes into view ahead. The track is really a 6 m (20 foot) wide channel fringed with lush heather and lichens, cut down through the dark peat surface of the hill and exposing the lighter-coloured boulder clay beneath. Frequent brooks, draining the high ground up to the right, cascade down beside the road and pass under it in culverts.

After looping round a few times, the forestry road comes gradually to an end, and the Way follows a rough pathway across a broad area of disturbed peat. The disturbance was caused in 1990 by a massive landslip, when an exceptional downpour of rain floated a wide section of peat off its boulder-clay foundation and it slid swiftly downhill, burying anything that stood in its way. At the end of the last century a similar landslip in Co. Wicklow entombed a cottage, together with its occupants, a married couple and their four daughters.

An impressive panorama of the mountains of the south-east can be seen from here in good weather. The long range of the Wicklow Mountains can be seen to the left, to the south of which are the twin humps of the Blackstairs and Mount Leinster; and further round the horizon the solitary mound of Slievenamon can be seen, behind which are the tops of the Comeragh Mountains.

The Way, now marked across the heather by black-and-yellow-striped poles at regular intervals, drops into a ravine to cross a stream that drains the plateau above Gorteenameale. Less than 1 km (0.5 mile) away, up on the ridge above, an almost perfectly circular lakelet can be found, a strange phenomenon that it is difficult to believe is a natural feature.

The Way—which would be almost impossible to follow at this stage without the striped poles—heads south-east and uphill now along the edge of a young spruce plantation. If you lose sight of the poles, keep following a 20 m (66 foot) fire-break between areas of young forestry as it loops round the hillside to meet the top of another forestry road coming from the south.

The rough road bears round to the right and then left until it is heading towards a wooded hill in the distance, partially harvested at the time of writing. Be vigilant for the point where the Way turns abruptly off the forestry road and up a set of rustic steps to meet a rough path. The path leads along a fire-break to the corner of an open area where turf cutting has been carried on. Keeping the trees to your right, go on to the next corner, where the Way turns right and runs along a fire-break to reach open ground.

A series of tall black-and-yellow posts are followed across the heath, descending gently towards the forest on the far side. In the distance the ridge dividing Glendine East and Glenamoon is in view, and beyond it the higher slopes of the Slieve Bloom's highest point, Arderin. In spite of being only 529 m (1,736 feet) above sea level, Alderin overlooks more territory than many a higher peak. Although not as remote as the heathland further north, this area is frequented by red grouse, and if you do not disturb one as you cross the heather, you may well hear their strange cackling call.

At the other side of the heath the Way passes through a gap in a fence, drops down to a forest road, and turns right. A couple of minutes later the route turns down a swampy track, and soon the steep sides of Glendine East come into view before the track reaches a forestry road, and the Way turns left. A few metres further on, the public road is reached. You are now at the southern end of the valley of Glendine East, and the village of Camross is 5.6 km (3.5 miles) away to the left.

St Finan Cam's Well

STAGE 3: GLENDINE EAST TO GLENREGAN

DISTANCE: 17 KM (10.5 MILES). AGGREGATE CLIMB: 350 M (1,150 FEET). WALKING TIME: 5.25 HOURS.

This stage follows an ancient route up and over the Glendine Gap, and wends its way through the western fringes of the Slieve Blooms to finish on another ancient Way, through Forelacka along the Camcor River. There are nearly 10 km (6.25 miles) on tarmac in this stage, through a constantly changing countryside littered with prehistoric tumuli and standing stones, 1.5 km (1 mile) along paths and tracks through Forelacka, and the rest is on forestry roads.

The village of Kinnitty is nearly 3.25 km (2 miles) off the Way at the end of this stage. It has two pubs, one selling simple hot snacks, and there is some accommodation available in the area, but there is no regular bus service.

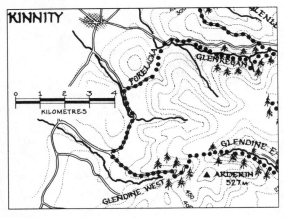

The Slieve Bloom Way leaves the public road and enters forestry again. Dropping downhill and crossing a stream, the route rises through mature trees to emerge into the open on the southern side of Glendine East. The name Glendine is from the Gaelic Gleann Doimhin, or 'deep glen', and as the Way ascends the place can be seen to be aptly named. Below to the right are fields patterned and striped with newly planted forestry, through which the upper reaches of the Killeen River meander.

A mile into Glendine East a number of 'hanging valleys' can be seen at the far side. While an active glacier was grinding and reducing the floor of the main valley, the floors of the tributary valleys, which probably contained little ice, remained at the same level. When the ice finally melted, the streams in the tributary valleys, whose floors 'hang' high above the level of the main valley floor, cascaded as waterfalls or rapids into the main stream.

The forestry road rises gently but persistently up the southern flanks of the valley, past impressive stands of slender and tall mature conifers, leaving the stream behind far below. As the route ascends, the glen takes on an almost tangible ambience of remoteness. For some reason, many of the great trees have cheated the forester's saw, and lie scattered in gargantuan tangled heaps, having been split and felled by the wind.

This valley is another likely place for seeing a herd of Slieve Blooms feral goats, big creatures with curving horns and long white or black-and-white coats, which are easy to spot against the dull forestry background. Most varieties of livestock would find it difficult to survive in the wild, but goats, among the first animals to be domesticated by man, have few problems. Voracious eaters, they can survive well on the poorest of herbage; the food must be good in the Slieve Blooms because these goats are the healthiest I have seen in Ireland. This remote valley is also a good place to spot some of the Slieve Bloom's fallow deer.

High up in Glendine East the forestry road is a comfortable surface to walk on, covered with grass, pine needles, mosses and wood sorrel. The trunks of long-dead trees lie scattered all about where they fell, a confusion of mossy poles like the remains of some gigantic Chinese matchstick puzzle. The road hairpins a couple of times near the top, and then runs out; the Way continues uphill along a pathway through the last of the trees, and out into the open, to cross the Glendine Gap. This is a pathway that has been in use for many centuries, and was shown on maps as early as 1623.

Before long, the end of a forestry road is met and followed downhill. Off to the left is the almost flat summit of Arderin, Ireland's Height, the highest point of the Slieve Blooms, marked by a tall thin mast. Ahead is the wide valley of Glendine West, falling away towards the flatlands, 8 km (5 miles) away, and a vast new Sitka spruce plantation. The conifers take the place of the potato crop that for a couple of centuries were coaxed by the people of Glendine from poor land reclaimed from heath. The glen had a large population up to the middle of the last century, as the numerous ruins in the glen indicate. The Great Famine, however, tipped the delicate balance of survival for most, so that within fifty years they were all gone.

About 4 km (2.5 miles) below the gap the first inhabited farmhouse on this side is passed. Not long after, a pair of stone-built piers with a cast-iron gate, slightly more elaborate than usual, is passed on the right. About 70 m (230 feet) into the field, to the left of an overgrown driveway, can be seen one of the Slieve Bloom area's many ring barrows. It consists of a mound of about 9 m (30 feet) in diameter, surrounded by a shallow fosse or ditch, which in turn is surrounded by a bank. Thought to date back to the Iron Age, these earthworks were built for ceremonial burials, and sometimes conceal a stone-slabbed cist.

About 0.75 km (0.5 mile) on, the Way turns to head north through the steep-sided Tulla Gap, where bluebells decorate the forest floor in early summer. Shortly before crossing a stream that falls down from Glenafelly, Fiddler's Rock can be seen in a field to the left. While not the usual columnar shape of a gallán or prehistoric standing stone, this cube-like boulder of quartzite, about 1 m (3 feet) high, has some long-lost ceremonial significance; a straight line drawn from it between two closely spaced galláns nearly 2 km (1.25 miles) away connects with the Forelacka tumulus further on.

Soon the Way follows the road as it turns towards the north-east, and rises gently between Knocknaman and Broom Hill, towards Forelacka. Beside the road on the right a holy well is passed, with a stone plaque proclaiming the well is dedicated to Finan Cam Naomha, or St Finan Cam. Cam means bent, crooked or dishonest in Gaelic; but in this case, it probably meant crooked in the sense that the man was lame or stooped. He was a sixth-century monk and a student of St Brendan; he founded monasteries in Kinnitty and at Rerymore near Clonaslee, the remains of which can still be seen.

The Way continues westwards, with Broom Hill now dominating the skyline to the right, with smooth pastures sweeping up its side to the forest-crowned summit. The road comes to an abrupt end at a gateway into a field, in the middle of which is a prominent tumulus, made to look most dramatic by the grove of larch trees growing on it. This is Forelacka Tumulus, thought to date from the Bronze Age, and part of the mysterious alignment that involves the Fiddlers' Rock, passed earlier.

Go through the gate and follow a track between the tumulus and a row of beech trees, leaving the tumulus on the left. Ford a little stream and go left where the track divides, to ford the same stream again. This leads to a short but most rewarding stretch of the Slieve Bloom Way, coming as a relieving contrast to the last few kilometres on tarmac. The Way follows an ancient route through the valley of Forelacka to the valley of the Camcor River. A local farmer told me this route was known as Hugh O'Neill's Road, after the Ulster prince who led his armies through the Slieve Blooms on his journey southwards to the disastrous Battle of Kinsale in 1601.

The track varies from a gravel road to a narrow pathway wending its way between thorn bushes from glade to glade, following a meandering stream. Dippers and grey wagtails frequent the rocks that the stream splashes past, and the indignant piping calls of wrens and the tinkling songs of robins mingle with the sound of rushing water. In early summer the sheltered air is fragrant with the perfume of may-blossom and primroses.

Soon the track passes out into open fields, and after passing through a gate, a tarred road is reached. The Way follows the road across the Camcor River, and climbs to meet the main road and the end of this stage. The Way continues to the right; the village of Kinnitty is 2.5 km (1.5 miles) to the left, and a house advertising bed-and-breakfast can be found just over 1 km (0.75 mile) away in the same direction.

Kinnitty is a picturesque little village with a stream flowing through a green in the village square. Bulfin, the cycling tourist, called it 'the most beautifully situated village I have ever seen . . . a sheltered Eden in the lap of her hills'. There are two public houses, one of which advertises hot snacks.

STAGE 4: GLENREGAN TO GLENKEEN

DISTANCE: 19.25 KM (12 MILES). AGGREGATE CLIMB: 350 M (1,150 FEET). WALKING
TIME: 6 HOURS.

*This stage rises up Glenregan to gain first glimpses of the land to the north
of the mountains, crosses the Silver River Valley and climbs to the Spink to
reach the western end of Glenkeen. About 13 km (8 miles) are on forestry
roads (which I found tended to become monotonous), 5.5 km (3.5 miles) on
public roads, and the rest on farm tracks. 12 km (7.5 miles) into this stage
the route passes within 1.5 km (1 mile) of the hamlet of Cadamstown. The
end of the stage is 2.5 km (1.5 miles) from the village of Clonaslee, where
some overnight accommodation is available, but there is no regular bus
service.*

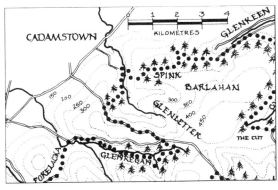

After turning right
onto the main road
north of the Camcor
River, the Slieve Bloom
Way heads towards the
uplands again, into the
woods of yet another of
the glens that cut deep
into these mountains,
Glenregan. After 1.5 km
(1 mile) the route turns
right, onto a forestry
road signposted 'Riverside Walk', and descending through a stand of mature,
tall spruce trees, the Camcor River is reached and crossed.

The Way climbs the southern side of Glenregan through a recently
harvested forest, leaving the Camcor behind in the valley, invisible but very
audible, rushing westwards. Siskins and blue jays were among the birds I
saw when I passed here, apart from the ubiquitous wrens, who are
enthusiastic colonisers of harvested forest.

Soon the Way drops down a grassy track to cross the Blackstairs River
and, rising again, reaches a forestry road and heads north. Yet again the
route crosses a river, this time the Blackcurragh, before ascending to
emerge from the forest after a short while to a dramatic change of
surroundings, a vast expanse of open moorland extending northwards to the
valleys of Glenletter and Barlahan, one of the most extensive stretches of
open highland left unforested in the Slieve Blooms.

The Way follows the road westwards and uphill past Glenletter Cross, and
continues uphill. For the first time since the Glendine Gap, the views from
the route stretch long into the distance, across the Central Plain, this time
to the north-west. In the near distance is the village of Cadamstown, while

the most easily identifiable features further off are the twin cooling-towers of the power station at Ferbane, 22.5 km (14 miles) away. This open hillside is a joy to walk on an early summer's morning, but its exposure means it can be miserable when the weather is bad.

To the north-west, deep in the valley, a meandering river glints. Appropriately named the Silver River, it has over the aeons sliced its way through the old red sandstone carapace of the Slieve Blooms to join the River Brosna and eventually the Shannon, 29 km (18 miles) away.

Nearly 2.5 km (1.5 miles) after leaving Glenletter Cross, open moorland is left behind as the road enters trees again and turns towards the north. Shortly after, the Way turns right off the road and, following a forestry road downhill through young trees, turns after five minutes onto a pathway. Soon a rutted track is joined, which takes the Way out of the trees and across a stile onto a muddy track. A few metres to the right is a picturesque ford on the Silver River, but the Way turns left and follows the track through scattered gorse and trees to open pastureland. Some way-markers were missing in this area when I passed here, so be vigilant. A number of fields have to be passed through here, so be careful to leave the gates as you find them.

After fifteen minutes the track turns sharply right and descends to the Silver River. A gate where the track turns right gives onto the public road leading to Cadamstown, about 1.5 km (1 mile) away. The Way, however, crosses the Silver River and rises up into the forestry again. After about 1.5 km (1 mile) of thick conifers, it is a considerable relief when the route crosses a stile onto open ground near a high point called the Spink (484 m —1,588 feet). From here there is a great vista out across the lowlands to the north-west, towards Kilcormac and beyond. After a few minutes, however, this welcome openness is left behind again as the forestry road passes through a gate and back into the trees.

The route now wanders through another vast area of coniferous forest, some of it in the process of being harvested when I passed. I found this stretch a bit monotonous, only the crossing of the County River and a tributary of the Clodagh River over forestry bridges providing relief until, about 4 km (2.5 miles) after passing the Spink, the Way abruptly leaves the forestry road, dropping down to the left along a tunnel-like muddy boreen, reaching the public road at the western end of the Glenkeen Valley.

Glenkeen is a very fertile-looking valley with a character all of its own. Now reduced to a few small farmsteads, there were as many as eighty homes in this rich and sheltered place before the Great Famine. Many of the farmers were Quakers, spreading out from the community founded in Rosenallis in the mid-seventeenth century.

After a couple of breaks in the trees to the right, the Way turns right onto a forestry road through thickly planted trees. This, however, is the end of this stage; the village of Clonaslee is straight ahead, 4 km (2.5 miles) further on.

STAGE 5: GLENKEEN TO GLENBARROW

DISTANCE: 16 KM (10 MILES). AGGREGATE CLIMB: 175 M (574 FEET). WALKING TIME: 4.5 HOURS.

This final stage explores the upper reaches of Glendineoregan and the forested Knocknastumba, before descending to seek out the young River Barrow, and follow it to the finishing-point. There are 12.8 km (8 miles) on forestry roads, 1 km (0.5 mile) on the public road, and the rest along paths through the beautiful and deep Barrow Valley, which more than makes up for the long forestry stretch.

The finishing-point, Glenbarrow car park, is a little more than 3.25 km (2 miles) from the village of Rosenallis, where self-catering accommodation is available. Rosenallis has no regular bus service.

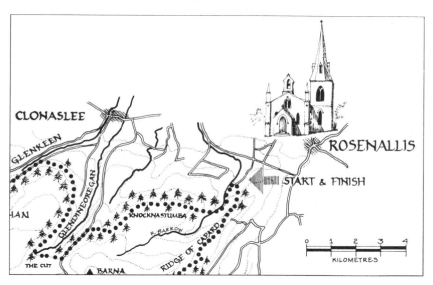

This stage begins where the Way re-enters the forest in Glenkeen, 4 km (2.5 miles) south-west of Clonaslee, and follows the forestry road south eastwards. Only an occasional glimpse of the outside world, relieving the hemmed-in feeling, is afforded by breaks in the densely planted trees as the forestry road wends its way along.

Nearly 2.5 km (1.5 miles) into the forest, after crossing a stream, the Way takes a fork uphill along a grassy forest road, and out into the open. To the right are the heather-clad slopes of Knockachorra Mountain, while to the left are scattered conifers descending the side of Glendineoregan, beyond which as the road rises, the long and almost flat ridge of Barna can be seen stretching off to the east. After a few minutes the road enters the forest again, but now the reservation is wide and the trees are comparatively young, so there is a feeling of openness that contrasts with the previous half-hour's walking.

There is a comfortable informality about this forest, with trees spreading untrained across the road and rogue seedlings of varying maturity growing anywhere and everywhere, breaking the long line of sight ahead. After less than fifteen minutes the grassy road deteriorates into a path through a rough cutting, swampy in places, and covered with the rich green coating of lush mosses, lichens and heather, a linear bog garden. The muddy ground shows up traces of all the creatures that have recently passed; apart from the expected deer-prints and those of well-shod walkers, I found signs of feral goats, foxes and stoats.

Nearly 2.5 km (1.5 miles) after reaching the grassy forest road, the route, on a good gravel surface now, bears around to the left to cross the infant Gorragh River and reach the public road. To the right can be seen the Cut where, during the building of this road to Clonaslee in the nineteenth century, a long cutting had to be excavated by hand out of solid rock.

The Way descends now with great views down Glendineoregan; 60 m (200 feet) below, the Gorragh River wanders along the bottom of the valley. After about twenty minutes' walking downhill, the Way turns onto a forestry road and heads uphill in a south-easterly direction. At the point of leaving the public road the village of Clonaslee is 4.75 km (3 miles) away downhill. Swinging round to the north-east, the forestry road passes within 0.75 km (0.5 mile) of Knocknastumba, the highest point of the north-east corner of the Slieve Blooms. Knocknastumba means the Hill of the Stumps, referring to the remains of the ancient pine trees still to be found under the blanket bog in this area, trees that flourished on these hills three-and-a-half thousand years ago.

About 3.2 km (2 miles) after leaving the public road, the village of Clonaslee comes into view below on the left, surrounded by a patchwork of fields, shortly before spruce trees enclose the forestry road again.

A little more than 2.5 km (1.5 miles) later, the Way leaves the forestry road and turns down a rough and swampy gully to reach and descend a narrow fire-break into Glenbarrow. On the far side of the valley a solitary ruined house stands in a grove of trees, a reminder that once this valley supported many families, the last of which left about fifty years ago. The Ridge of Capard, crossed by the Slieve Bloom Way on the first stage, forms the horizon ahead, while below the infant River Barrow is hidden by a cordon of birch and mountain ash trees.

The Elizabethan poet Edmund Spenser referred to this river as 'the goodly Barrow which doth hoord heapes of salmons in his deepe bosome'. It is one of the great rivers of Ireland, draining with the Nore and the Suir most of the south-east of the country, and is second in length only to the longest river in Ireland and Britain, the Shannon.

Descending into the trees, a muddy track along the river bank is joined, and the Way follows it downstream. This is an idyllic place, where the Barrow tumbles noisily over boulders and slides across flat slabs of sandstone, past banks speckled with primroses, wood anemones, wood sorrel and mosses of all kinds.

A few minutes after reaching the river the Way crosses it by a timber footbridge and, climbing the far bank, passes through a thick copse of coniferous trees, contrastingly hushed after the constant sound of the rushing water. Emerging from the trees high up on the southern side of the valley, where there is a bird's-eye view of the river and trees below, the path descends to meet the river again at a place called the Clamp Hole, where the water plunges down 12 m (40 feet) over a series of rock ledges into a pool.

Within minutes, the Barrow flows through a wide amphitheatre overhung to the north by high cliffs of glacial clays. Near where a promontory of rock extends out towards the river, a seldom-seen geological feature called cross-bedding—wide semi-circular swirl shapes on the surface of the flat sandstone bedrock—can be seen.

Soon the pathway leaves the river behind and ascends through trees to join a narrow, wildflower-lined boreen going uphill to the right. In a couple of minutes the Glenbarrow car park, where the Way begins and ends, is reached. The village of Rosenallis is a little more than 3.2 km (2 miles) away.

The Quaker Cemetery, Rosenallis

211

12
THE SLIEVE FELIM WAY

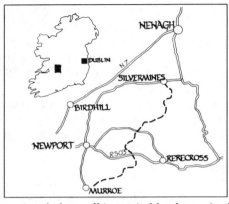

The Slieve Felim area consists of a series of partially wooded hills and valleys stretching east and west across south Limerick and north Tipperary. The Way is 10.8 km (18 miles) long, and although there was a shortage, when I walked, of overnight accommodation on the actual route, and no handy public transport, I found that arrangements could easily be made with bed-and-breakfasts for 'pick-ups' and 'drop-offs' at suitable places. As there are no restaurants along the route, arrangements should be made with your bed-and-breakfast for evening meals. If you have a car available Chaser O'Brien's in Pallas Grean, about 11.2 km (7 miles) from Murroe, provides excellent food at reasonable prices, while at the northern end of the route, Matt the Thresher's pub and restaurant at Birdhill, 14.4 km (9 miles) from Silvermines, provides similar fare. Murroe, at the southern end of the Way, is not on a bus route. Silvermines, at the northern end of the Way, is on the table no. 218 Limerick–Roscrea bus.

How to Get There
Murroe is 184 km (115 miles) from Dublin and 21 km (13 miles) from Limerick, and is served by the table no. 332 Limerick–Dundrum bus and by the table no. 341 Shannon–Cappaghmore bus.

Maps and Guides
The route is covered on the Ordnance Survey 1:127,000 (0.5 inch to 1 mile) map no. 18. Shannon Development provide a leaflet describing the route called the Slieve Felim Way.

Enquiries
Tipperary Slieve Felim Holiday Society Ltd, Main Street, Newport, Co. Tipperary; telephone 061 378599

STAGE 1: MURROE TO TOOR

DISTANCE: 16 KM (10 MILES). AGGREGATE CLIMB: 338 M (1,100 FEET). WALKING
TIME: 5 HOURS.

*This stage takes the walker up into the lonely wooded Slieve Felim Hills,
down across the valley of the Annagh River and up again over the
Mautherslieve Hills to reach the hamlet of Toor, where there is a public
house. 3.2 km (2 miles) of this stage are on tarmac, with the rest on forestry
tracks and paths. There is a pub at Toor, but no public transport or
accommodation. Rearcross, near the route, is served by the table no. 332
Limerick–Dundrum bus.*

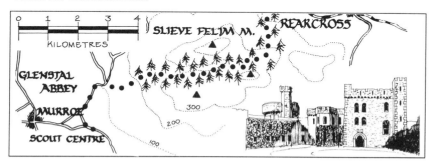

Before starting, it is worth your while visiting the village of Murroe which
has as a centrepiece an amazing high cross carved by Waterford sculptor
William Gaffney, and erected in 1923 to commemorate local War of
Independence heroes. The beautifully executed stone is richly decorated
with scenes from the life of Christ, with zoomorphic border decorations
drawn from the Book of Kells.

The Slieve Felim Way begins unceremoniously at Thomond Scout Centre
outside Murroe, and follows tarmac roads northwards and gently uphill past
the richly treed demesne of Glenstal. Glenstal Abbey is a Norman Revival
castle built by the Barrington family in the 1830s, complete with a great
circular tower and typical Norman gateway. The demesne was also
landscaped at the time, with vast numbers of trees and shrubs being planted
and a number of artificial lakes constructed. It is now owned by the
Benedictine Order who run a school there. It is possible to walk through the
grounds and I recommend it, particularly in early summer when there is a
marvellous display of rhododendrons, as a pleasant preliminary to the Slieve
Felim Way.

At a Y-junction the route leaves the tarmac and goes right up a gravel
track between hedges of rhododendron. The track meanders through my
favourite kind of forestry, an informal, and not very economic, mix of
spruce, birch, rhododendron and willow, echoing with the strident song of
many wrens. A few minutes into the wood the track comes into the open

213

from where there is a broad view of the tall Galty Mountains to the south, and the Ballyhoura Hills a little to their west. Up to the left, bluffs of old red sandstone, once an ancient sea-bed, protrude from the trees. All around, and as far as the eye can see, clumps of rhododendrons richly spot the landscape with purple in early summertime.

As the track climbs through harvested forest, the many spires of Limerick city can be seen directly behind, and beyond it, the Shannon Estuary stretching westwards; in good conditions the industrial plant at Aughanish and the chimneys of Tarbert power station, 77 km (48 miles) away, can be seen from here.

The forestry road eventually levels off at the 300 m (984 foot) contour in a broad, shallow valley. When I passed here, I was entertained by the sight of a young and hoarse cuckoo attempting to make his calls from the pinnacles of spruce trees, under constant dive-bombing attacks of a squadron of small birds.

Soon the route enters the trees again, and is enclosed by a dull green wall of pine needles; from what I saw, however, it will not be long before this area is harvested. For a good distance now, if you are not walking in summertime when the margins of the track are lined with fraughan bushes and glorious spiked foxgloves, there is little to see. You may be lucky enough to come upon some of the deer that live on this hill; when I passed I only saw their prints and an occasional tuft of fur. Soon, however, the track begins to descend gently, and a brief view of the heath-mottled summit of Keeper Hill is an indication that you are making headway.

Look out on the right for a natural rock-garden that would shame even the best garden planners, with young, bonsai-like spruces growing from what looks like a carefully planned chaos of loose rocks.

It is a relief to come into the open again and see Keeper Hill dominating the scene to the north. The village of Rearcross, marked by the copper-clad church spire, can be seen a little over 1.6 km (1 mile) away to the east. The pretty church is an exotic creation, proudly claimed by the locals to be the first pre-fabricated church in Ireland, and certainly was the first building to use corrugated cast-iron sheeting in its construction. I was told that it was dismantled in its original location in Northumberland in 1804, and taken by ship to Foynes. A caravan of hay-carts manned by local people brought it to Rearcross where it was erected by local tradesmen. Such was the devotion of the people of the time.

The public road can be seen ahead, and soon the route turns abruptly off to the right, to follow a gravel pathway out of Co. Limerick and into Co. Tipperary. A timber bridge takes you across a stream and in minutes the public road is met. About 1.6 km (1 mile) away to the right now is the village of Rearcross, where Kennedy's pub can provide refreshments for tired walkers.

The Slieve Felim Way, however, turns left and after a few minutes, at

Tooreenbrien Bridge, right again through a gateway beside the gently flowing Annagh River. Here on a grassy bank by a ford is a marvellous place to have a break, and indeed cool your feet in the clearest of mountain water. Care should be taken now in watching for way-markers, as the route changes direction frequently over the next kilometre. The Way follows the track through another gateway and parallels the river for a short distance, before crossing it by a wooden bridge to follow a path which ascends along the south side of a forestry plantation. Soon the boggy path turns into the trees and in a short time reaches the end of a grassy forestry road, alive with rabbits when I passed, and turns uphill.

The route comes out of the trees into an open wilderness of well-scattered spruce trees, willows and hazels, with a rich birdlife. Mautherslieve or Mother Mountain rises to the east, while ahead, closer at every glimpse, is the heath-dappled bulk of Keeper Hill. The route drops into a valley before rising along the south flanks of wooded Knocknacappal. An ancient roadway, bounded by a moss-hung earthen ditch covered in foxgloves and backed by a curtain of birch trees, is joined, and a tiny ruined cottage is passed. With its typical open fireplace and ladder-accessed sleeping quarters in the loft, this would have been a typical dwelling of better-off rural folk of the last century; for every one of these, there would have been about thirty mud cabins, now long washed back into the earth. Just beyond the cottage, on the left, look out for a spring well beside the road with a deep basin of cool clear water. Here the people who once lived on this hillside long ago would have gathered and chatted as they collected their water.

The route zigzags up through forestry towards the top of the ridge and then turns west again, promenading along the high ground with great views to the south. As the forestry road begins to descend again, watch out for a turn-off to the right at a bend, up a track going north and finally over the ridge.

Bare Keeper Hill (695 m—2,279 feet) now dominates the scene ahead. When I passed here, bright-coloured hang-gliders were being launched off the heights of the summit, to coast back and forth like great eagles. The Slieve Felim Way has now become a vague pathway descending through young forestry; a few hundred yards below, however, a boreen heading north can be seen, and it is here that the pathway joins. The boreen follows a deep leafy valley down towards the hamlet of Toor; it can be a very damp experience in or after wet weather. The public road is met near a tiny, beautifully kept church; the Way goes to the right, but just a hundred yards to the left is a public house where refreshments may be obtained.

STAGE 2: TOOR TO SILVERMINES

DISTANCE: 12.8 KM (8 MILES). AGGREGATE CLIMB: 369 M (1,200 FEET). WALKING TIME: 4.25 HOURS.

This stage takes the route up along the flanks of dramatic-looking Keeper Hill, often a base for hang-gliding enthusiasts, and down through the Ciamaltha Woods to Glenculloo, before climbing again to a pass called Step on the Silvermines range with its glorious views to the north, and finishing at the pretty village of Silvermines. About 6.4 km (4 miles) of this stage are on tarmac, with the rest on forestry roads and paths. Silvermines has no registered accommodation, but is on the table no. 323 Roscrea–Nenagh bus route.

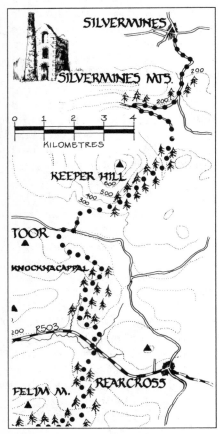

The route follows the tarmac east from Toor Church along the southern side of the deep wooded Doonane River Valley. Passing a hand-ball alley on the left the Way turns downhill and, crossing the river, ascends again towards the heather-mottled ridge of Keeper Hill. In Ballyhourigan Wood, which clothes the western slopes of the hill, General Patrick Sarsfield camped with a cavalry troop of 600 men on an August night in 1690. He was on his way to a famous victory, the destruction of the Williamite artillery and siege train at Ballyneety. Jacobite Limerick was under siege by a large Williamite army, and word was received in the city that artillery and reinforcements for the besieging forces, which would ensure a swift defeat for Limerick, were on their way from Dublin. In a daring and militarily radical manoeuvre, Sarsfield led his cavalry out of the city, by-passing and circling 60 miles around behind the besieging forces, and into the Slieve Felim Mountains to await the approach of the siege train. When it stopped for the night at Ballyneety, about fifteen miles to the south, Sarsfield's troops descended upon it, swiftly captured it and blew it sky-high, thus giving the Irish new hope and a breathing space. The siege failed, but fourteen months later, in October 1691, the Treaty of Limerick was signed, giving the city up to the Williamites. The Irish army was allowed to leave for France, where they became the forerunners of the 'Wild Geese' of the eighteenth century.

Fording a stream, the Way heads east and uphill along a track bounded by earthen ditches that were decorated in wood sorrel and violets when I passed. Behind, towards the west, the Shannon Estuary can be seen in clear weather, and to the south there is a grand prospect of the rolling Slieve Felim Hills. Soon the track enters a plantation of spruce and larch, and descends past the sad remains of a ruined stone cottage. It is just one of a number of abandoned dwellings on this hillside that housed rural families up to a couple of decades ago—a result of emigration and changing agricultural practices.

The route follows the grassy track as it fords a couple of brooks and meanders along the mountainside, and then to meet and follow a forestry road. Behind, as the road levels out, the eastern flanks of Keeper Hill can be seen rising out of a girdle of forestry. I felt slightly irritated at this stage at the seeming reluctance of the Way to turn north and cross under the hill, but soon it does eventually swing north, and the ridge of Silvermines Mountains is seen ahead.

Shortly after, the forestry road starts to ascend again, and the Way turns sharply right and descends towards the valley of the Mulkeir River by way of a steep gravel path. Watch out on the way down for a rich deposit of grey pottery clay through which the path cuts; if it is wet weather you will be aware of it because of the difficult-to-remove coat of mud it leaves on your boots.

A broad stream is crossed by stepping stones and the route joins a forestry road to continue its descent. The Silvermines ridge fills the foreground now, its western spur heather-topped, and the eastern end clothed in a patchwork of forestry seamed with fire-breaks. As the valley bottom is reached a red barn is passed on the left and the route joins a rough tarmac road which winds along between mossy walls parallel to the Mulkeir River, picturesquely overhung with willows and wildflowers. Crossing the river by way of a blue-railed bridge, the route heads steeply uphill towards the wooded southern slopes of the Silvermines Mountains.

The Slieve Felim Way comes out of the forestry again as the incline reduces and bears around towards the north. As the road climbs, there are great views behind, with Keeper Hill towering over the deep valley through which the Mulkeir meanders. After a stretch between fuchsia hedges, the road reaches a pass through the Silvermines ridge and what a wonderful arrival it is! Within a few moments, a glorious and extensive view of the Shannon basin and the rich agricultural lands to the north opens up. The town of Nenagh can be seen almostly directly north, with its church spire and tall castle. Beyond, towards the north-east, the twin cooling-towers of the power station at Ferbane can be seen 58 km (36 miles) away, while towards the north-west, beyond the swell of the Arra Mountains, stretch the waters of Lough Derg.

The route follows the road downhill as the panorama broadens to include the Slieve Bearna Mountains to the left and the Slieve Bloom Mountains 40 km (25 miles) to the north-east, and eventually the village of Silvermines, the end of the Slieve Felim Way, comes into view below.

As the road levels out between high hedges and nears the village, keep a look-out to the left for some ivy-covered, castle-like structures, built in red sandstone and brick. These are the remains of some of the old mine buildings: a footbridge crossing a wildflower-margined stream will take you to them across an area of ancient slag heaps.

Silvermines is a neat little village which was at one time on the main coach road from Limerick to Dublin. It grew up in the late sixteenth century around the extensive mines in the area, which produced a very pure lead-ore with a high content of silver. Over the years Dutch and Cornish miners were employed in the mines, bringing an influx of foreign blood to the populace of this hillside. Locals will direct you to a place behind the school where the remains of a great Cornish mine-engine still stand. The latest mining operations, which employed over 500 people, ceased in 1983; since then, Silvermines has been enjoying a quiet period in its hectic history. I liked its tree-lined main street overlooked by the church, and the public house on its east side which is a model of reticence; no familiar Guinness or Heineken plastic illuminated signs here, only a modest sign proclaiming T. O'Cairde in old Irish lettering, and an acid-etched glass panel in the door saying 'Lounge Bar' suggests the place's purpose.

Silvermines

218

13
THE WESTERN WAY

The Western Way currently amounts to some 200 km (125 miles) in length, and crosses the Counties of Galway and Mayo from the western tip of Lough Corrib in the south to the high cliffs lining the Atlantic Ocean in the north. Maum Bridge in Joyce Country is the southern terminus, and the route currently ends on the Sligo border, a few miles east of Ballina. A further stretch from Oughterard to Maum Bridge is to be approved in the future, which should make the Western Way the longest route in Ireland. Winding side-roads and forestry tracks make up most of the route, and there are two short 'mountainy' sections, the first on a pilgrim route over a pass in the Maumturks and the second being an exciting and spectacular crossing of the Sheeffry Hills. These are contrasted by the broad and sparsely inhabited upland bogs of Erris and Tirawley that both lend a sense of real wilderness to the route, and make it a really challenging trail in terms of the distances to be covered. A lack of overnight accommodation and regular public transport on some parts of the Way make it a difficult route for the average walker without access to drop-off and pick-up facilities.

The Western Way is a rich collection of great contrasts: from its impressive mountains and vast moorlands to its myriad of lakes and historical north coast, it has something for everyone. The stupendous scenery and atmosphere of the places the route passes through makes for an unforgettable experience.

How to get there
Maum Bridge is 270 km (168 miles) by road from Dublin, and is served by the table no. 419 Galway–Clifden bus and table no. 420 Galway–Cong bus.

Ballina is 246 km (153 miles) from Dublin and is well served by public transport.

Maps and Guides
The Mayo part of the route is covered in the *West of Ireland Walk Guide: Co Mayo, The Western Way*, by Joe McDermott and Robert Chapman, published by Mayo County Council. *Mountains of Connemara*, published by Folding Landscapes, covers the Co. Galway section. Discovery Series Ordnance Survey maps (1:50,000) nos 23, 24 31, 37 and 38 cover the area of the route.

Enquiries
Galway County Council Planning Department, Prospect Hill, Galway; telephone 091 63151
Mayo County Council, The Mall, Castlebar; telephone 094 24444
Bord Failte, Westport; telephone 098 25711

Maum Bridge

STAGE 1: MAUM BRIDGE TO KYLEMORE

DISTANCE: 24 KM (15 MILES). AGGREGATE CLIMB: 350 M (1,140 FEET). WALKING TIME: 7 HOURS.

This stage brings you up an ancient pilgrim path through a dramatic pass in the Maamturk Mountains, down into the scenic Inagh Valley and on to Kylemore, where the Abbey attracts tourist interest all year round. The last 4 km (2.5 miles) to Kylemore are not on the actual Western Way. 11 km (7 miles) of this stage are on tarmac side-roads, with the balance on forestry tracks, green roads and the pilgrim's path; there is also a boggy section across open moorland. Kylemore has a good quality bed-and-breakfast in addition to a hotel, both serving good evening meals, and is served by the table no. 62 Clifden–Westport bus (summer only), and the table no. 419 Clifden–Galway bus.

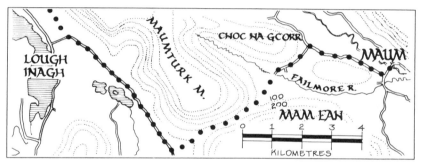

Maum Bridge is a scattered collection of houses centred on a pub and a shop. The pub is a grand early nineteenth-century building, originally built by the Scottish engineer, Alexander Nimmo, who was responsible for so many of the bridges and roads in the west, and he lived there while they were being built. The Western Way leaves Maum Bridge heading south-west, and takes the first turn right, up an unfenced road bordered with gorse and scrub. Joyce's River meanders along the valley bottom to your right, while the main feature ahead is the pointed crag of Cnoc na gCorr. Soon the road takes the Way right to the base of this hill, and the route turns a sharp left following a sign for Mam Ean.

The narrow boreen winds uphill through increasingly rugged country. The pressure on land here has always been a serious matter; to the right you can see field walls following the almost vertical hillside to the summit. Over the shoulder of a hill the bleak and lonely Failmore River Valley opens up below, while the dramatic peaks of the Maumturks fill the skyline. The Way drops steeply to cross the river which, because of the lie of the land, seems to be flowing uphill.

The Western Way now leads uphill and then away from the road to follow the pilgrim path to Mam Ean, where the shrine of St Patrick's Bed and Holy

Well attract substantial numbers of devotees. The track rises sometimes steeply along the right side of the pass, below the peak of Binn Chaonaigh, crossing numerous streams, with increasingly extensive views to the east opening up.

As the track rises the twisted metamorphic rock from which these mountains are made become stripped of their burden of peaty soil, until close to the top of the pass the Way crosses broad bare slabs of rock like gigantic crazy paving. Soon the silhouettes of crosses are seen against the sky and the route has arrived on a plateau between two great massifs, a place with a magical atmosphere. St Patrick's Well is a tiny pool surrounded by a low wall of stone, and the crevices between the stones are crammed with offerings ranging from rosary beads to ten pence pieces and even biros; the idea is to leave some personal belonging as a token of one's pilgrimage. Scattered around are a series of limestone crosses with pathways linking them, and there is a tiny chapel built into the hillside. Presiding over it all is a statue of St Patrick, represented not as a mitred bishop, but as a simple monk. Nearby a dark lake somehow adds to the remoteness and mystery of the place.

The Way descends the southern side of the pass into very different landscape than that left behind. To the south-west as far as the eye can see is a flat, heather-covered bogland, scattered with shining lakes. To the west, the 391 m (1,283 foot) Cnoc Lios Uachtar, with its green forested flanks, stands in the foreground, backed by the dramatic Twelve Bens.

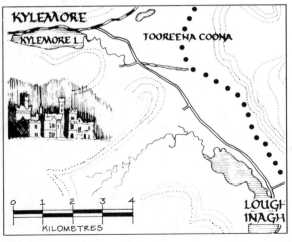

Soon a tarmac road is met and followed along the broad Inagh Valley, and every way you look is a Paul Henry composition. White-painted cottages decorate the slopes to the right, above which the western spurs of the Maumturks stand like great petrified monsters, one after another in a row, each as steep and barren as the next. To the left is scenic Lough Leitheanach, with a thickly wooded island in its centre, and as the road rises, majestic Lough Inagh comes into view at the forested foot of the Bens.

If you continue along the road when it turns left, Inagh Lodge Hotel can be reached in about 4 km (2.5 miles), but the Way continues straight across the bog on a track which is barely discernible. This was the original droving road to Leenane, and it has not been used since Nimmo built the new road in the early nineteenth century.

On the banks of the small streams that cross the track, the roots of ancient trees which spread their branches here four thousand years ago can be seen. Near a small farm the track passes a rocky knoll extending out from the base of the mountain; it is worth a visit by those interested in geology, and gives good views of the route ahead.

This track can be very boggy in places, and it can be a relief to reach the gentle wooded slopes of Tooreenacoona. Here, the Western Way enters the forest, but to get to Kylemore you do not enter the trees but follow the track to the left, which brings you past a cottage, over a bridge, and after 2 km (1.25 miles) the public road is met. Turning right, Kylemore is a little more than 2 km (1.25 miles) away.

If you are still feeling energetic after the day's walk, I recommend you follow the lough 'clothed purple and silver under windows lit by the southern sun', as St John Gogarty described it, westwards to Kylemore Abbey. This neo-gothic extravaganza was built in the 1860s by a Liverpool merchant named Mitchell Henry, the then MP for Co. Galway. In the grounds of the house he built a miniature replica of Norwich Cathedral and reclaimed acres of bogland, clothing the buildings in a rich foliage of ornamental trees, rhododendrons and fuchsia, at their best in early summer. Benedictine nuns have been in possession of the place since World War I, and it is open to visitors, with a tea-room, craft shop and pottery shop.

Killary Harbour

STAGE 2: KYLEMORE TO LEENANE

DISTANCE: 14 KM (8.7 MILES). AGGREGATE CLIMB: 140 M (455 FEET). WALKING TIME: 4 HOURS.

In spite of the extra 4 km (2.5 miles) rejoining the route from Kylemore, this is a short stage that brings you to Leenane along the western slopes of the Maumturks, from where there are dramatic views across Killary Harbour to massive Mweelrea. 0.6 km (1 mile) is on tarmac, 4.5 km (2.8 miles) on forestry roads, and the balance on the old green road to Leenane. Leenane has bed-and-breakfast accommodation and two good restaurants, in addition to its two pubs where you can get sandwiches. The village is served by the table no. 62 Westport–Clifden bus (summertime only) and the table no. 419 Galway–Clifden bus.

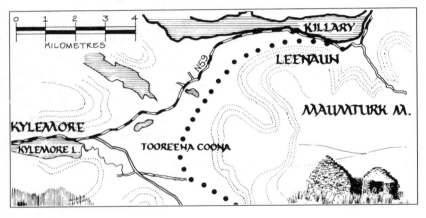

Returning to the Western Way from Kylemore, a forestry road is followed into the trees. The enclosed nature of the forest is a contrast to the openness of the previous stage, but it does not last long, and soon the route comes out of the trees onto a western spur of the Maumturks to continue along the old droving road to Leenane. In places it is so boggy and overcome by nature that it is barely identifiable as a route.

Over the tops of the trees to the left as the route rises, the first glimpses can be had of Co. Mayo, the great mountains that line the northern side of Killary Harbour. To the south-east, the bare wet rockfaces of Binn Bhan (White Peaks) reflect the sky.

As the Way proceeds, it becomes apparent that this hillside was once a busy place; all the land around, even the mountain's steep sides, are striped with the long shapes of old cultivation ridges called lazy beds. In a grove of stunted trees near a brook, the remains of a group of long-abandoned cottages can be seen. Prior to the Great Famine, the lazy beds of the Killary area supported upwards of four hundred persons per sq. mile; most of them did not survive the famine, and today the curiously patterned landscape and a few stone gables are all that remain.

Soon the dark and brooding mass that is the 814 m (2,688 foot) summit of Mweelrea, carved from Ordovician rock and rounded by glaciation, comes into view to the north. Much of the time the mountain is hidden in cloud, but on bright days with scattered clouds, a moving drapery of shadows explore its bulk and reveal the great hollow from where the Owenaglogh River drains the two lakes under its summit.

Below Mweelrea the waters of Killary Harbour soon come into sight, a 16 km (10 mile) long fiord-like inlet that geologists call a drowned river valley. It is a very deep inlet, and you will hear locally that in the old days the entire Royal Navy used to anchor in its sheltered waters.

As the valley of Glencraff opens up to the east, the Way descends to cross the Bunowen River by stepping stones, and ascends again into forestry. The public road to Glencraff is crossed, and the route climbs gently again, as the steep-sided and wooded valley of Delphi comes into sight north of Killary. The name Delphi was brought here by Howe Peter Browne, a nineteenth-century Marquess of Sligo. On a visit to his friend Lord Byron in Greece, he was most impressed by the similarity of its bare grey mountains to rugged Connemara. On his return he built a hunting and fishing lodge in the deep valley between Mweelrea and Ben Gorm, and called it Delphi Lodge in memory of his Greek sojourn. Its idyllic location has attracted many rich and famous visitors; the British royal family came here often in the nineteenth and early twentieth centuries, and the Prince of Wales visited during the historic first royal visit to Ireland in eighty years.

Far in the distance beyond the mouth of Killary a scatter of offshore islands can be seen in clear weather, dominated by the bulk of Inisturk. As the route bears around gradually to the east, the inland end of the harbour comes into view, overlooked by a great brooding mountain called Devil's Mother.

After a picturesque and thunderously cascading stream is crossed, a string of houses in the distance along the shore to the east signals the Way is approaching Leenane. The old green road descends between cyclopean boulders to meet the public road and follow it into the village. The shelter provided by the Maumturks and the warmth of the micro-climate along the edge of the harbour has allowed the people who live in Leenane to surround themselves with trees and shrubs; opposite the old Victorian Hotel, derelict when I passed, is a little park lush with magnolias, palms, azaleas and hydrangeas.

STAGE 3: LEENANE TO DRUMMIN

DISTANCE: 17 KM (11 MILES). AGGREGATE CLIMB: 200 M (650 FEET). WALKING TIME: 5 HOURS.

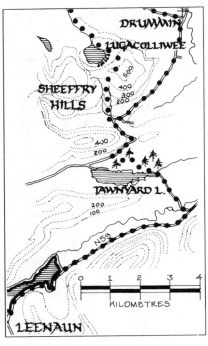

This is a fabulously scenic stage which takes the route up the Eriff River Valley, past lonely and scenic Tawnyard Lough and over the Sheeffry Hills to reach Breslin's public house in Drummin. Except for a little more than 1.6 km (1 mile) on forestry tracks and roads, this stage is all on tarmac. For the more energetic walkers, however, there is the more challenging Lugacolliwee alternative route which climbs through a dramatic mountain gap in the Sheeffry Hills and descends past Lugacolliwee Lough to loop around and return to Drummin. The Lugacolliwee route has 16 km (10 miles) on tarmac, 7.5 km (4.7 miles) on open moorland, and the balance on forestry tracks. This alternative should be avoided if visibility is, or is likely to be, poor.

The problem of lack of accommodation and public transport on the Western Way is first experienced here. The distance to Westport from Leenane is over 43 km (27 miles), and there is, at time of writing, no approved overnight accommodation available between the two places, nor any suitable public transport. There is, however, a pub and post office at Drummin, and a scattered hamlet along the route, allowing the journey to be split into two stages, leaving walkers to arrange pick-ups and drop-offs if necessary. Marion O'Malley of Liscarney can provide this (see accommodation listing at back of book). If all else fails, enquiries at either the pub (Breslin's) or the post office may put you in contact with someone in the area who will provide bed-and-breakfast.

Leave Leenane following the Westport road, passing on the right a local museum dealing with the village's past as a great wool and weaving centre. A substantial number of people were employed in the weaving trade here in years gone by, transforming local wool into homespun tweeds; today the surrounding hillsides are still scattered with sheep, and although I

226

understand Leenane still has an annual shearing festival, today the wool goes elsewhere for manufacture. The village's more recent claim to fame was its use as the location for the film, *The Field*, by John B. Keane.

Passing Leenane's graveyard, a terrace of tombstones falling towards the shore, the road climbs gently, and about 2.5 km (1.5 miles) on, after passing a bungalow with a sign proclaiming it the Rock Bar, the Killary inlet narrows and the Erriff River enters it after tumbling through the rocky and photogenic Asleagh Falls. Near here the route enters Co. Mayo, and follows the rhododendron-bounded Westport road up the Erriff Valley, enclosed on the right by the stupendous bulk of Devil's Mother Mountain, its sides striated by aeons of water draining from the plateau above. 7 km (4.5 miles) from Leenane, a valley running up into the heart of the Maumtrasna Mountains is passed, and the route turns off the main road and crosses the Erriff River.

Soon the track crosses open moorland into a coniferous plantation and the Owenduff River is crossed by way of a footbridge. A boggy track is followed past Derrinfin Lough, and 0.8 km (0.5 mile) further on, the eastern shore of picturesque Tawnyard Lough is reached, giving dramatic views into the distance along the northern slopes of Ben Gorm and Mweelrea. The continuation of the track along the lake shore looks inviting, but the route turns right and follows a stream through the forest. The ground rises, and the path climbs beside a series of waterfalls to a higher level, where it meets a forestry road. Turning left, the route soon reaches the public road, and follows it up and over a spur of the Sheeffry Hills, from the highest point of which there are fine views across the lake's silver surface below to the Devil's Mother and the Maumtrasna.

The view ahead is of the Owenmore Valley and the flatlands for miles beyond to the north-east. The road, supported by massive retaining walls, descends straight and steep along the mountain's flanks; it was designed by the Scottish engineer, Alexander Nimmo, who designed many roads, harbours and bridges in Ireland early in the nineteenth century. The road takes a sharp turn to the right when it reaches the Glenlaur River, and it is near this point that the Lugacolliwee alternative departs from the main route (see below).

The Sheeffry Bridge, a fine old humped-back structure, is crossed, and the route enters new surroundings of green fields, a contrast to the harsh moorland left behind on the higher ground. You know you have reached civilisation again when you pass the little bungalow that is Drummin post office, and a schoolhouse, founded in 1933. The Way turns left at Drummin Church, and not far from here you will find Breslin's bar and shop.

STAGE 3: THE LUGACOLLIWEE ALTERNATIVE

DISTANCE: 26 KM (17 MILES). AGGREGATE CLIMB: 580 M ((1,885 FEET). WALKING TIME: 7.5 HOURS.

Where the road takes a sharp turn to the right, above Sheeffry Bridge, the alternative route turns left to follow a rough, barely discernible track, said to be the remains of an old 'togher' or bog roadway, along the banks of the Glenlaur River. Ahead is the broad and impressive circ of the Sheeffry Mountains, the centrepiece of which, a massif that reaches 742 m (2,434 feet), is riven by a deep ravine down which tumbles the infant Glenlaur. Where a tributary joins the Glenlaur from the north, cross the river and ascend along the tributary's left bank.

Ravens patrolled the skies of this great empty moorland like vultures when I passed, empty, that is, but for scatterings of hungry-looking sheep searching out the few blades of grass remaining on its overgrazed surface. The terrain varies from dry springy grass to patches of quagmire; keeping close to the stream, which has dug itself a ravine 8 m (26 feet) deep in places, will ensure the driest ground. It is a steady climb, and frequent stops for breath can be used to take in the ever-widening vista. Across the valley, Nimmo's road cuts diagonally down the mountainside; below it, see if you can spot traces of the older road, now almost lost in bog. The long spur of the Sheeffrys, over which Nimmo's road crosses, looks like a marvellous walk in itself, from its beginnings as a hill crowned by two lakes south of the Owenmore River, up 600 m (1, 968 feet) to the narrow south-west/north-east saddle between the mountain's two summits.

Looking across at the valley below the road, one is reminded of the film *The Field* again; it is clear that cultivated land has to be wrested from the boggy desolation, and a few fields thus manufactured over decades of back-breaking labour can be seen, surrounded by strong stone walls as if to prevent them escaping again to nature. On the surfaces of these fields, and spreading out for acres onto the bracken-covered hillsides, are the traces of lazy beds.

There were no way-markers that I could find when I passed here, but with good visibility I found it easy to follow the route. As the going becomes less steep, look ahead for a ridge along the skyline. The Way continues to follow the stream up a flat valley towards the right of a little summit on the eastern end of the ridge. I found the terrain much drier along the right side of the stream and, half way up the valley when the stream disappears, I began to edge towards the right and to higher ground. The arrival at the pass, about an hour after leaving the road, is most rewarding. The Holy Mountain, Croagh Patrick, should be visible ahead in clear weather with the pilgrim's path to its summit a white streak along its eastern flanks. Behind, the mountains to the south recede in washes of blue-grey waves.

Although the route seems to skirt the 510 m (1,673 foot) summit of this spur of the Sheeffrys, it is worth taking ten minutes or so to clamber up to it for the great vistas it offers. From here the route ahead is very clear along the north bank of Lugacolliwee, and follows along the stream that drains from the lake to eventually reach the road.

The descent follows the course of a stream that flows down from the pass towards the eastern side of Lugacolliwee. The surface of the lake below mirrors the sky, contrasting with the mottled and three-dimensional characteristics of the surrounding rock and moorland. When you reach the stony lakeside, take a break, and sit for a while to absorb the surroundings. Off up to the left there are great cliffs made up of stratified layers of rock turned, in some great cataclysm, through 90 degrees. When I sat there, I was entertained by the sweet song of sleek wheat-ears perched on nearby rocks, and the antics of a pair of lemon-coloured wagtails at the water's edge.

At the far end of the lake follow the northern bank of the stream as it descends, sometimes rushing noisily over cataracts, and sometimes slowing up to drift quietly along deep, clear canal-cuttings through the peat, its waters ringed by leaping fish. A fence has to be negotiated to continue along the stream, shortly after which the road towards which you are heading should be visible ahead, to the left of a white farmhouse beside a red barn.

About a mile from the road a pair of ruined stone cottages surrounded by a few small lazy beds are passed. Hunched into hillocks to shelter from the prevailing winds, each cottage has one doorway and no windows, and it doesn't take much imagination to picture the harshness of the lives of those who lived here. A little further on I crossed the stream to the south bank, and because of the lack of way-markers, kept close to the forestry fence and headed for a place half way between two cottages. You will need to cross fences a couple of times, but you should reach a stream flowing from left to right. Turn right along it, and you will come to a roadway. The roadway is followed west and then north, to pass by small farms and in about 2.4 km (1.5 miles) the main Louisburg road is met. Breslin's pub in Drummin is a little more than 4.5 km (2.5 miles) away to the right.

STAGE 4: DRUMMIN TO WESTPORT

DISTANCE: 26 KM (16 MILES). AGGREGATE CLIMB: 270 M (877 FEET). WALKING TIME:
7.5 HOURS.

*This stage climbs north-west out of Drummin and then contours along the
southern flanks of Croagh Patrick at over 250 m (800 feet) until the broad
islanded expanse of Clew Bay is laid out below, after which the route makes
a meandering descent to Westport.*

*Westport has a wide range of overnight accommodation available, and
fine eating places, and is very well served by trains and buses. I particularly
enjoyed a visit to Matt Molloy's bar and the range of very good food in
O'Malley's restaurant across the street. Very reasonably priced and more
simple food can be had in the Central Hotel in the Octagon, as the town's
formal square is called.*

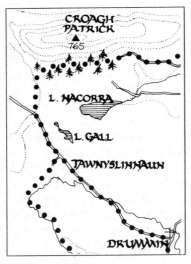

Leaving Breslin's public house, the
Sheeffry Hills fill the foreground, with a
stream cascading from the highest
summit in view. The road descends for a
while until the Owenmore River is
crossed once more, then it winds gently
upwards through sheep pastures, past
cottages surrounded by protective
rhododendrons. Before long, Croagh
Patrick, called 'The Reek' locally,
dramatically appears again over the hilly
horizon to the north, its rounded peak
topped with a tiny chapel.

The road leaves the green fields
behind and, rising and falling steeply,
enters a rugged and desolate moorland.
The craggy, serrated cliffs of the
Sheeffrys recede behind, and Croagh Patrick disappears and reappears, each
time nearer and more immense. It is a startlingly grey mountain, scree-
covered for the most part, and at this proximity the little chapel on its
764 m (2,500 foot) summit shines white when lit by the sun.

On Shrove Tuesday in the year A.D. 441 Patrick, Pope Celestine's
missionary to the pagan war-mongering Irish, climbed to the top of the
mountain, spending the forty days of Lent there in prayer and fasting.
Although not the first missionary to attempt to convert the Irish, Patrick's
campaign achieved widespread and wholesale conversions. His successful
strategy included starting from the top and getting the chieftains convinced
first, and, rather than destroying pagan totems and customs, carefully
merging them with the Christian culture. Thus sacred pagan springs

became holy wells, and ancient ritual sites, such as this mountain, sprouted little Christian chapels. During that Lent of A.D. 441 Patrick is said to have bargained with God to rid Ireland of vicious dragons and snakes. The mountain has since been a popular place of devout pilgrimage, particularly on the last Sunday of July, when thousands of fasting pilgrims climb the reek, some in bare feet, to hear Mass on the summit.

As the road tops the 220 m (700 foot) contour a great vista opens up, with the ridge of Croagh Patrick leading the eye northwards over the twin bumps of Ben Goram, to the Corraun Peninsula and Achill Island beyond. Here the route turns off the road and heads across trackless hillocks of boggy moorland towards the reek. A few hundred metres from the road, part of Lough Nacorra can be seen to the right beyond a dense forestry plantation, and shortly after, the beautiful meandering chain of Loughs Beg, Oughter and Gall appear, seemingly stepping downhill towards the east. Shaggy mountain sheep were scattered across the landscape when I passed here, and hooded crows, that rather handsome member of the crow family with the light grey body, seemed to be everywhere. I was to see this bird so frequently along the Western Way I felt it could become the mascot of the route.

When I walked here, there were few way-markers to guide me, and I found that the route indicated on both the Ordnance Map and the 1993 edition of the *Walk Guide West of Ireland* disagreed with the posts I did find. The easiest way to stay on the route is to head across a boggy valley to the left side corner of the forestry ahead and follow a broken-down boundary fence up the heather-covered hill ahead. At the top of the hill there is a wonderful vista all round in clear weather. To the west the island of Inisturk rises from the waters of the Atlantic Ocean, while to the south-west the 814 m (2,670 foot) summit of Mweelrea rises beyond the Sheeffrys. Beyond the east spur of Croagh Patrick the far side of Clew Bay can be seen, with the Nephins forming the horizon.

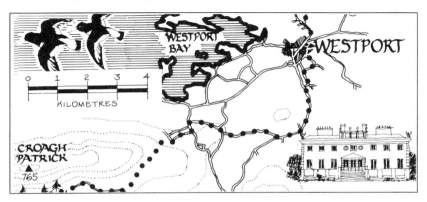

The route drops down along the fence across ground that is very boggy in places, to reach a thick forestry plantation on the southern slopes of the reek and, turning east, follows a forestry road through it. Emerging into the open again, the end of the Teevenacroaghy public road is met and followed along the flanks of Croagh Patrick, with the pilgrim's path a white streak reaching to the summit. After 2.5 km (1.5 miles) the route turns left off the tarmac onto a green road parallel to the pilgrim's path above. As the reek begins to drop below the horizon behind, the Way passes the remains of a ruined settlement, the stone gables of eight or nine roofless cottages, some with the vestiges of their window-frames still remaining. What must have been the residences of quite well-off farming folk, today only shelter the ragged black-faced sheep of the mountain; it is a sight that is to be seen at many points along the Western Way, a relic of the Great Famine of the nineteenth century as much as a reminder of the flight from the land in more recent times.

Gently on uphill the green road rises, growing ever greener as it goes, until it tops the spur extending eastwards from Croagh Patrick, and a breathtaking panorama of Clew Bay unfolds ahead. A myriad of islets, inundated moraines left by the receding glaciers of the Ice Age, cluster the inland end of the bay, and on the far side, the soft rounded shapes of the Nephins form a backdrop to the coastline. In clear weather the great bulk of Nephin Peak, reaching 806 m (2,646 feet) can be seen at the eastern end of the chain. Below, the grey slated roofs of Westport town can be seen nestling at the south-east corner of the bay.

The Western Way now follows the green road downhill beside a tumbling stream. Soon a tarmac public road is met, and instead of heading straight into Westport, the Way, having given you a glimpse of the town to whet your appetite, dallies tantalisingly along by-roads to the south. The ruins of a five-storeyed mill is passed on the left, while to the right above the road can be seen Clonagh Lodge, a residence which seems to have grown from a fortified building. Eric Cross, the author who became famous after his book, *The Tailor and Ansty*, was banned in the 1940s, lived here at one time. The tailor and Ansty were a couple who lived near Gougane Barra in Co. Cork, and around whose fireside people gathered every night to chat. Eric Cross wandered by chance into this forum, and was so taken by the conversation ranging from orgies at wakes to the value of newspapers, and from 'Healy's Comet' to poteen, that he recorded the whole ambience of the situation. The book appeared in 1942 to enthusiastic reviews, but like so much of the finest in Irish literature, it was banned as indecent.

Passing to the south of Killeencoff Hill, the route turns north and winds its way into Westport, hidden until the last minute in a hollow surrounded by trees.

Westport is well worth enjoying for a few days. It is a pleasant town of Victorian shop-fronts and Late Georgian houses, informal enough to disguise that it has been laid out to a carefully designed late eighteenth-century plan, the main features of which are the mall with its tree-lined ornamental river, and the Octagon, where three streets meet and the buildings are gathered around a central monument in a continental manner. Westport House, built in the early eighteenth century to designs by the German architect Richard Cassels, and its gardens are open to the public.

Croagh Patrick

STAGE 5: WESTPORT TO NEWPORT

DISTANCE: 14 KM (8.5 MILES). AGGREGATE CLIMB: 140 M (460 FEET). WALKING TIME: 4 HOURS.

This is an easy, but not particularly interesting stage, almost all on tarmac side-roads, meandering through drumlin country. It can, however, be increased to 23 km (14 miles) if you are prepared to carry on and stay overnight at the youth hostel at Treanlaur, thus decreasing the following Stage 6 from 35 km (21 miles) to 27 km (16 miles). Newport has bed-and-breakfast accommodation, a fast-food takeaway, and pubs serving simple food. For a gourmet meal, Newport House, off the main street, is recommended. Newport is served by the table no. 66 Westport–Belfast Expressway bus, and the table no. 440 Dooagh–Ballina bus.

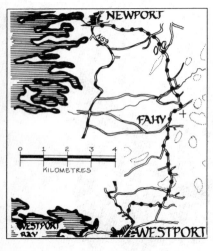

The route leaves Westport following the Newport road, and opposite the Teagasc Centre, turns right onto a minor road. A monument to Michael Davitt commemorating a National Land League meeting which he addressed at this place in 1879 is passed on the left, and after 0.4 km (0.25 mile) the tarmac road comes to an end near a rusty grey barn, and the route continues uphill along an overgrown grassy path. After a short distance, the path becomes a boreen, and then a tarmac road promenading eastwards overlooking Westport's industrial suburbs and the main Castlebar road. In the distance, Croagh Patrick still dominates the horizon to the south.

Turning north the Way follows a busy minor road up and down lush green drumlins towards the Nephin Mountains on the northern horizon. Fahy village with its church and tiny one-classroom schoolhouse is passed before the route descends to cross Brockagh Bridge, near which are the remains of a castle.

Each time a drumlin is topped the Nephins look distinctly closer, while over to the right the 430 m (1,410 foot) high hill of Croaghmoyle comes into sight, as the route passes between a cluster of small lakes. In nearby Cortoon is a cottage where the grandfather of Princess Grace of Monaco was born; at the time of writing local people plan to restore the cottage as a memorial to the princess. When the road turns west, the church tower at Newport can be seen ahead, and passing a unique luxury handball alley with a viewing terrace, the main road is met and the route enters the village of Newport.

Newport, once called Newport Pratt, and before that Burrishule, developed where the Newport River drains into Clew Bay from Beltra Lough, a famous salmon lake. It was once the main port of Mayo, and the limestone plaques with incised street names allude to the place's former importance. The substantial river walls and quays today only serve pleasure boats, and the town depends, apart from the farming community, on angling and tourism. The massive railway viaduct (the rail route is now defunct) and the towering church lead one to expect a bigger place than it turns out to be. Look out for the shop that advertises on a canopy 'Fancy Goods, Minerals, Sweets, Undertakers'!

Newport

STAGE 6: NEWPORT TO BELLACORICK

DISTANCE: 35 KM (21 MILES). AGGREGATE CLIMB: 250 M (820 FEET). WALKING TIME: 10 HOURS.

This is a wonderful day's walking, in summertime, taking you past scenic Lough Feeagh, up through a forested pass in the Nephins and down through a wilderness landscape to cross Ireland's most extensive bogland. It is, however, another stage with a serious lack of accommodation possibilities. Bellacorick has a pub, a shop, a public telephone, but no overnight accommodation, so walkers have to arrange a pick-up there, or walk to Bangor, 12.8 km (8 miles) off the route to the west, which has accommodation. The stage can be reduced to 27 km (16 miles) if an overnight is taken at Treanlaur Youth Hostel, or a drop-off is arranged there.

Bellacorick is served by the table no. 446 bus which provides a limited service between Ballina and Blacksod.

The Bangor Trail, another walking route, coincides with the Western Way from Newport until it turns west beyond Srahmore Lodge; it is marked with green numbered arrows.

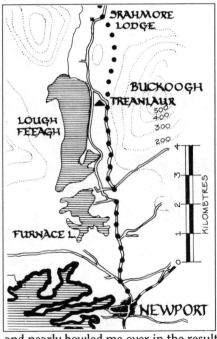

The Western Way takes the Mulranny road north out of Newport, and turns off onto a side-road going 1 km (0.6 mile) out of town. To the left the sharp pinnacle of Ben Gorm rises, while straight ahead is the broad bulk of Buckoogh Mountain. The route passes Furnace Lough with its picturesque islands on the left, and as scrubland takes the place of better farming land and roadside hedges are left behind, the Way leaves the road briefly to follow an old stony boreen overhung with thorn bushes. When I walked here and picked my way around long troughs for sheep feed, the local flock of scraggy, hungry mountainy sheep thought I was their meal ticket and nearly bowled me over in the resultant charge! Reaching tarmac again, the route continues to climb gently up the lower slopes of Buckoogh, with ever-expanding views to the west.

The narrow road now becomes a wonderful promenade along the western side of Buckoogh with great views all the way. I was lucky enough to have a bright sunny morning when I passed here, the air loud with lark-song. When long Lough Feeagh comes into view at the foot of a broad valley descending between Ben Gorm and the Nephins, the picture is complete; you might as well be walking along the lid of a chocolate box! See if you can spot the promontory fort on a narrow peninsula extending into the lough; probably Iron Age in origin, the remains of the defensive rampart of stones can still be made out.

Before the northern end of the lough is reached, the route leaves the road again and follows a boreen up and along the east side of Shramore Hill. Continuing along the road and turning left at the lough shore will bring you to Treanlaur Youth Hostel in about fifteen minutes. The boreen takes you gently uphill to where not a single road or house can be seen; Croagh Patrick still looms in the distance behind, and there is wilderness all around. Soon even the boreen itself seems to vanish, leaving you to spot and follow faint traces of it ahead until you round the west side of a hillock, and tarmac can be seen ahead. The road is rejoined beneath a great dome of rhododendrons, and followed past Srahmore Lodge, a most unexpected sort of building, a stone-built delight with a round tower attached. A narrow avenue of rhododendrons is followed until, just after crossing a bridge over the Srahmore River, the route turns left into the Letterkeen forestry plantation, one of the largest coniferous plantations in Ireland, heading towards a conical crag.

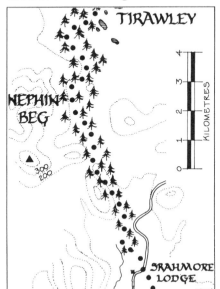

About 1 km (0.6 mile) into the forestry, the Bangor Trail, which has coincided with the Western Way since Newport, departs to the west, and the Western Way meets and follows the Altaconey River for a while. At one particular bend in the river there is a beautiful set of small waterfalls like a glistening crystal staircase. Soon after the river is crossed the forestry road climbs steadily to run along the heathery mountain flanks.

As the route passes by the towering and tempting Nephin Beg, you are coming close to the 140 m (459 foot) contour, the highest part of this stage. When I walked here, the still air of the enclosed forestry road began to be disturbed by a welcome breeze, and I knew I was close to seeing the promised land! Sure enough, after a long bend around to the left, a junction is passed and if the visibility is good, you will see a tiny segment of the great Erris Bog ahead framed by hills, from which rise a series of white column-like structures. These are the windmills of the Bellacorrick windmill farm, and after the trek you have behind you, a very welcome sight!

Further downhill the great cooling-tower of the turf-burning station at Bellacorrick also comes into view far ahead, and the forestry road passes through the more open surroundings of younger trees. The vastness of the Erris and Tirawley bogs begin to become clear here on the northern slopes of the Nephin range. It is a great wilderness only retained in the west by the northern portals of Nephin Beg, in the east by the lone grey-streaked massif of Nephin, and seems to stretch into infinity in the hazy horizon of the north. But for the power station below, and one visible cluster of buildings at Eskeragh, this could be a wilderness anywhere in the world. To the north-east the faint outline of the Ox Mountains, where the Western Way ends, were visible when I passed.

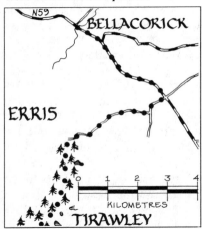

The forestry road levels out in a thickly forested area scattered with nearly fifty small lakes and ponds, only a few of which can be seen between the trees. These secluded and sheltered waters are breeding-grounds for many wildfowl, including the shy teal, Ireland's smallest duck. In places here the forestry road is cut into the bog, exposing the make-up of the peat layer on the original soil, sometimes showing the roots of ancient trees beneath the peat.

The last stretch in the forest becomes a little monotonous, and it is a relief to reach a gate and exit from the trees, although the route tantalisingly takes you at first away from the power station into open bogland. Eventually, however, tarmac is reached, and then the main Bangor to Crossmolina road, and the route turns left for the last 4 km (2.5 miles) to Bellacorrick.

To the right is the strange sight in this place of the Bellacorrick windmill farm, a scattering across the bog of tall, slender, white aerofoils slowly rotating. It is an experimental station which, if successful, will take over from the turf-burning station when its plant becomes obsolete, as many have been in recent times. There is something very beautiful about these moving aerodynamic forms in this landscape. The bridge at Bellacorrick was designed by an engineer called Bald and built in 1820, and whether by design or not, it has a fascinating and unique quality. If you get a large rounded cobble of over 5 lb weight, and run across the bridge sliding the stone on the parapet, you will make a piece of ghostly xylophonic music.

STAGE 7: BELLACORICK TO BALLYCASTLE

DISTANCE: 33 KM (21 MILES). AGGREGATE CLIMB: 230 M (755 FEET). WALKING TIME: 9 HOURS.

This stage takes you through the vast Sheskin forests, and around the Maumkeogh Hills to reach the Atlantic coast. Sheskin is the largest and most sparsely peopled townland in Ireland; it has never had a population of more than one hundred people, and the remoteness of the place is tangible. It is another long stage with little opportunity to reduce the distance; there are prolonged enclosed sections through forestry with little outlook, and it can be a relief to leave the trees behind at Glenora and see the Atlantic Ocean again.

Ballycastle has some bed-and-breakfast accommodation, and I was told there was a good restaurant nearby, although I did not find it. Ballycastle is served by the table no. 445 Ballycastle–Ballina bus.

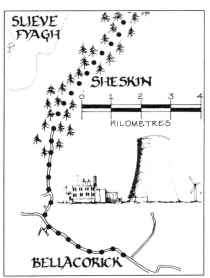

Leaving Bellacorick and its musical bridge behind, follow the road towards Bangor, following the scenic Owenmore River. Past the church at the little hamlet of Ballymonnelly the route turns north along a tarmac track. Soon the track becomes a gravel one, as it passes out over a vast extent of bog, layer upon layer of dark brown in a rich variety of shades. In the far distance when I passed I could see and hear great cumbersome-looking machines quartering this prairie to harvest peat for burning in the power station. 2.5 km (1.6 miles) from the main road, a broad open forestry road through the Sheskin forestry plantation is entered, a vast area of coniferous forest extending towards the north Mayo coast. In the distance ahead the long and low ridge of Benmore and Maumkeogh can be seen; along the flanks of the latter the Western Way will climb before descending to Ballycastle.

The increase of rhododendrons along the trackside, and the gradual change of the forestry on both sides to a more informal mixture of conifers and other species are indications that the route is nearing Sheskin Lodge. A river is crossed and passing through an area of forestry, where skeletons of

239

dead pines and monkey-puzzle trees tower high above the newer conifers, the crumbling gateway to the lodge is reached. A visit to this fast-deteriorating building is worth a little detour.

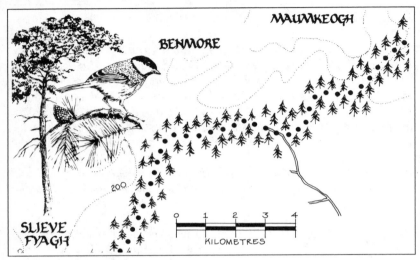

It's a place of dying, lichen-covered trees and undergrowth, filled with birdsong. The lodge, when I passed, was in the last stages of deterioration, an example of nature's invasive powers at work. A window frame lay on the rotting wooden floor, pushed in by a blindly seeking rhododendron branch. A robin's nest occupied the shelf of a wardrobe where a last forlorn clothes-hanger still hung. An ash tree which had lodged in a gutter had eventually spread roots down into the building, gradually stripping off the roof for the weather to finish the job of demolition.

The lodge was originally built and its demesne planted in the early nineteenth century when this country was open, heather-covered bogland. The Jameson family, famous for their whiskey, used the place as a hunting lodge up to World War II, and the writer, T. H. White, wrote part of *The Godstone and the Blackamor* when he stayed here during the war.

Back on the route, the forestry road follows a 2.7 km (1.5 mile) long straight towards the north-east. There is not a lot to see, but the road surface is firm and a good pace can be set. After turning left at a fork, the road begins a slow steady climb up the next low tree-covered ridge. There is little to relieve the monotony other than the occasional sheep and ubiquitous chaffinch, a bird I came to like and appreciate very much on this stage.

Even the transition to a boggy fire-break is, for a short time anyway, welcome, but it is a relief to eventually come out of the trees again, into a gap between tracts of forestry near the Altderg River. After a short stretch in the open, a disused farmhouse is passed, shortly after which the route leaves the comparative comfort of the road again and crosses a fence into forestry once more. A broad, and in places very boggy, fire-break is followed in a north-east direction, passing Altderg Lough on the left, hidden behind a thick screen of trees. The fire-break becomes a wide, grassy, heathery expanse between thick forestry, with no defined path, where care has to be taken not to twist an ankle. When the occasional opening occurs, you get a view of . . . more trees! There is a gentle but steady climb all the time, and the terrain is tiring, so it is with relief that a forestry road is met in less than an hour.

When the road comes out into the open, you get a chance to glimpse far below Altderg Lough, and almost in line beyond it, Ballincorick power station and Nephin. Otherwise there is little to see as the route climbs to the 230 m (755 foot) contour and swings around the southern slopes of Maumkeogh, except for the chaffinches and great-tits which seem always to keep one company in forestry. This sense of remoteness, of being apart from the world, becomes more tangible as this stage progresses. I walked here on my own, and found a sense of isolation that I have not experienced anywhere else in Ireland; sudden movements like the occasional stray sheep darting suddenly away from the edge of the track were unusually startling and set the heart racing.

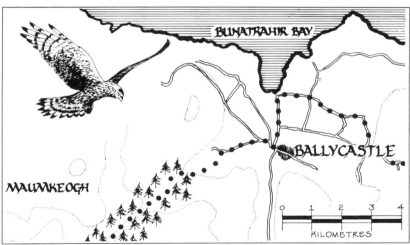

Not long after the road begins to descend, a broad expanse of open moorland appearing in the distance between the trees announces that the route will soon leave the forestry, and at Glenora the road enters a long and shallow valley extending to the north-east, patrolled when I passed by hovering kestrels. The monotony of yet another long straight section of forestry road is dispelled by the first glimpse of the Atlantic Ocean at surf-ringed Buntrahir Bay. Soon the town of Ballycastle, a cluster of grey-slated roofs, appears to the right ahead, and by then the coast is in sight again, with Downpatrick Head and its neighbouring sea-stack, Dún Briste, easily identifiable.

The tarmac is reached and the trees finally left behind at Sralagagh East, and the road promenades towards Ballycastle; just short of the town the route turns left, but this stage ends at the village.

Apart from the beauty of its scenery, the main tourist attraction in this area is a place known as the Ceide Fields, on the clifftops a few kilometres to the west of Ballycastle. As the blanket bog was removed over the years for fuel, collapsed stone walls were revealed underneath where the peat ended, about a metre and a half below the surface. It was not until recent times that the significance of these walls was fully realised. If the bog took more than four thousand years to develop, then the walls beneath the bog must have been built by people who farmed here nearly five thousand years ago. A detailed examination of the site was carried out over a number of years, during which time many acres of field systems were found, indicating a large settled population existed here in the Neolithic period. A dramatic pyramidic Interpretative Centre has been built on the clifftops telling the story of those early settlers, and it is worth a visit if time allows.

Sheskin Lodge

STAGE 8: BALLYCASTLE TO KILLALA

DISTANCE: 23 KM (14 MILES). AGGREGATE CLIMB: 160 M (525 FEET). WALKING TIME:
6.25 HOURS.

*This stage is a complete contrast to the last two stages, in that they passed
through a practically uninhabited wilderness, and now the signs of man's
occupation of the land, both today and for centuries past, are all around. If
you are interested in history particularly, you may take a long time to
cover this stage, there is so much to see. The stage is entirely on tarmac.*

*Killala has plenty of bed-and-breakfast accommodation available, and
while some of them will serve an evening meal, I found that Seán and May
Golden's pub in the town serves exceptionally good food. There is also a
takeaway.*

*Killala avails of a limited service provided by the table no. 445 Ballina–
Ballycastle bus.*

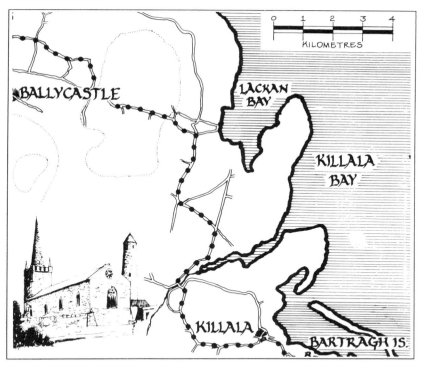

The Western Way heads north towards Bunatrahir Bay along a side-road,
and soon arrives at the beach. I am sure it is a great place in summertime;
when I passed a little earlier in the year it was occupied by a great flock of
oyster-catchers, which took off in an amazing rhythmic striped formation as
I stepped on the sand. Across the bay can be seen the former coastguard

station, and judging by its brightly painted walls and windows, it is enjoying a new lease of life.

As the road turns inland and ascends, the spectacular sea-stack called Dún Briste (the Broken Fort) can be seen off to the left. Up to six hundred years ago this stack was connected to the mainland by a narrow neck of land, and was in use as a defensible promontory fort in the early Christian period. Records tell that there were still people living on it up to 1393 when the connecting isthmus collapsed during a great storm.

It is a pleasant road to walk, with plenty of views. What is remarkable is the number of disused and ruined houses by the roadside, some abandoned during the Great Famine when the population of Ballycastle fell from 798 to 372 persons, but more were left behind during periods of high emigration in recent years. The ruins of one of the many little churches which served the old population is passed further on; today its grounds are still used to bury the remaining inhabitants. It is still a tradition here that when someone dies, the menfolk of the family and friends dig the grave on the day of the funeral. When the route turns left at a T-junction another feature of this landscape can be seen in a field on the right. A nondescript cluster of stones marks a 'cillín', a burial place for infants who have died without baptism.

As the hilltop is reached there are great views all round, as the road descends towards the great Killala Bay. It was here in 1798 that one of the many attempts by the French to invade England by the back door was actually successful in landing troops in substantial numbers. Commanded by General Joseph Humbert, a 31-year-old war veteran, 1,100 troops came ashore and were joined by a host of Irish peasants, and they proceeded to take the British by surprise, capturing Killala and Ballina within three days. Castlebar was next taken from a superior force who retreated in confusion, a rout that became known amongst the Irish as 'The Races of Castlebar'. Humbert set up a Provisional Government of Connaught at Castlebar, and moved on eastwards. There were no more victories for the French, however, because the expected rising of the people was not as had been hoped for, and Humbert became overstretched. At Ballinamuck in Co. Leitrim, the British under Cornwallis surrounded the French, and after a short battle, Humbert surrendered. The British took a month to recapture the territory held by the rebels, resulting in great loss of life on the rebel side.

Another ruined church is passed on the way downhill, and if you look up on your left you will see a strange spire-like structure on the hilltop, a local folly called 'The Gazebo'. Turning right at a T-junction, at a place called Garryfrancach, a monument to the first French soldier killed on Irish soil during the 1798 Invasion is passed. The road descends to Carrowmore, passing Maugham's pub, opposite yet another ruined church, this one a rather fine Neo-Gothic building, built as late as 1843.

Turning east again, the road passes by megalithic tombs and an ogham stone, and at a T-junction where the Way turns right, the ruins of Rathfran Friary, a Dominican foundation established in 1274 and worth a visit, can be seen to the south-east, near the banks of the Cloonaghmore River. It is overlooked by the ruin of a fine and elegant eighteenth-century house, Summerhill, said to have been abandoned because it was haunted.

Continuing on the Way, Rathfran Dolmen, a fine Neolithic court tomb, is passed on the left, before the road reaches and crosses Palmerstown Bridge over the Cloonaghmore River. The route turns south-east now and loops around to reach the town of Killala.

Killala is a tight-knit little town of winding streets, retaining much of the character it must have had in 1798 when, for a brief few weeks, it enjoyed 'liberation'. Sections of limestone pavements and cobbled gutters can still be seen underfoot, while the scale and feel of the streets made it an ideal and realistic location for the filming of the TV movie, *The Year of the French*. The town's buildings are mainly eighteenth and nineteenth century, and rising from their midst is an eleventh-century round tower, the sole survivor of monastic Killala, and the seventeenth-century cathedral, which has a souterrain in its graveyard.

Old Churchyard at Ballintemple

STAGE 9: KILLALA TO BALLINA

DISTANCE: 15 KM (9 MILES). WALKING TIME: 3.75 HOURS.

This is a short stage running south, entirely on tarmac, along the Moy Estuary to the busy town of Ballina. Again there are plenty of sites to interest the antiquarian, and indeed those who are interested in wildlife have plenty to watch out for; I saw stoats and a mink in addition to a wide range of birds when I passed. Ballina has plenty of accommodation and excellent eating places. Murphy Brothers' beautifully restored pub overlooking the Moy is worth a visit; pub food is served in the spacious and atmospheric bar, while upstairs there is a full restaurant. Ballina is well served by public transport, bus and rail.

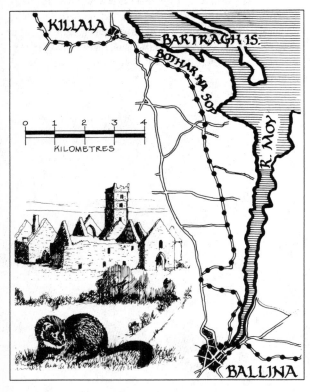

The Western Way leaves Killala following the main road to Ballina, and passing the An Oige Youth Hostel, which occupies Killala House, once owned by the Gores and where William Butler Yeats stayed frequently. The route turns onto the old Ballina road, signposted 'Moyne Abbey'; to the right is a bridge that used to serve the old railway. This is the route travelled by the French army in 1798, and was known as Bothar na Sop, or Road of Straw, because of the straw beacons lit by the local people to welcome and guide the French.

The road climbs gently with broad views across to Bertagh Island, a sand spit lying across the bay. Moyne Abbey is a couple of fields away from the route and worth a visit because of its unusually good state of preservation. A Franciscan foundation dating from 1460, it was burned by the English in

1590, and the last friars had left by 1618. The damage to the building seems only to have affected the timber parts, and over four hundred years later it is amazing how little the stonework, which includes the upper floors, has deteriorated. It does not take much imagination to visualise how the place was during its heyday.

As the route reaches the high point of the hill beyond Moyne Abbey there are wonderful views to the north over Killala Bay. An amazingly straight road rises and falls ahead for nearly 4 km (2.5 miles), lined with lush, wildflower-rich hedgerows providing cover for a host of birds. A side-road to the left will take you in less than 1.5 km (1 mile) to Rosserk Friary, another fifteenth-century monastery. It had been established about twenty years before Moyne Friary was built, but the friars at Rosserk had a disagreement with their superiors and refused to vacate the monastery, so to maintain their presence in the area the Franciscans had to build another friary at Moyne! The stone mason who worked at Rosserk had a good sense of humour; see can you spot his carving of a tiny angel in flight, holding up one corner of the high tower.

From the high points of this road the Ox Mountains, where the Western Way comes to an end, can be seem forming the horizon beyond the Moy. The route continues through rich rolling countryside, but as it bears right and winds on, take care at sharp corners of oncoming traffic.

The route joins the main road briefly before returning to an ash tree-lined side-road, and soon the demesne walls of Belleek Manor, built in 1831 at a cost of £10,000, are passed. Soon the spire of Ballina Cathedral comes into sight ahead, and passing out through the gates of Belleek Manor demesne, which is strange, because you don't realise you have been in the demesne, the route enters Ballina, the largest town in Mayo. It is a prosperous and bustling town that was founded in 1729, and must have shown great promise in the early nineteenth century when two bridges, quite close to each other, were built over the Moy. Long before this, however, Bronze Age people had a settlement by the river here, leaving after them a megalithic monument which can be seen near the railway station. The Augustinians founded a monastery here in the early fifteenth century; its remains can be seen near the town's cathedral, erected in 1892. Ballina was the birthplace of Mary Robinson, 7th President of Ireland and the first woman to hold the office.

STAGE 10: BALLINA TO THE SLIGO BORDER

DISTANCE: 22 KM (13 MILES). AGGREGATE CLIMB: 220 M (722 FEET). WALKING TIME: 6.5 HOURS.

This is a stage that is probably meant for the purists who insist on finishing the route to the very end, although it is not very practical, as there is no accommodation available at the Sligo border, nor a bus connection which will take walkers back to Ballina.

The Way follows winding countryside roads to climb towards the foothills of the Ox Mountains, and finish at a pass appropriately named The Gap. The route, with the exception of less than 7 km (4 miles) on mountain tracks and bogroads, is mainly on quiet tarmac side-roads. 1 km (0.6 mile) beyond the finish is the hamlet of Largan, which has a pub and a post office.

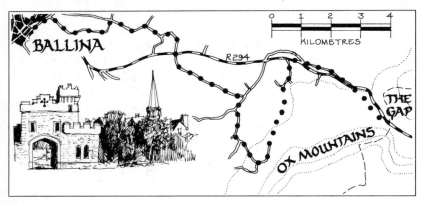

The route follows the N59 out of the town, and crossing the Brusna River where it enters the Moy, turns uphill along it. It is a pleasant suburban riverside walk for nearly 1 km (0.6 mile), passing picturesque cascades frequented by dippers, the little white-fronted bird that dives for his food, and is so-called because of his constant and amusing dipping as he stands on a rock.

Leaving the river the Ox Mountains, a long and low range of hills, the highest of which is 417 m (1,368 feet), come into view ahead. The route twists and winds eastwards through pleasant rural surroundings. Crossing the main road, look out on the right for an unusual roadside shrine, something more likely to be seen in Crete.

The route begins to climb eventually up the lower flanks of the Ox Mountains, and as the tarmac is left behind, the road becomes a gravel track. As the craggy, heather-covered 120 m (394 foot) contour is reached, the track swings around towards the north, and promenades along at that height, with wonderful views out over east Mayo where a chain of smaller lakes lead the eye towards the broad reaches of Lough Conn, beyond which the bulk of Nephin rises. Soon forestry blocks the view, and the track takes on a tarmac surface as it descends into farmland again.

Turning east for the last time, the side-road crosses the main Sligo road and runs parallel and above it, climbing gently all the time. As Knocknasliggaun and Benalta, the south and north portals of The Gap come into view ahead, the route crosses the road again, and follows a bog road, probably the original road across the mountains, through a heather-covered landscape to rejoin the main road at the Sligo border.

Mweelrea and Killary Harbour

14
THE WICKLOW WAY

The Wicklow Way was Ireland's first way-marked trail and is the most-used walking route in the country. The trail extends 132 km (82 miles) from the suburbs of Dublin across the Dublin and Wicklow Mountains to finish in east Co. Carlow. The Dublin and Wicklow range forms part of the most extensive surface granite fields in the British Isles and the largest mountainous area in Ireland. The Great Pleistocene Ice Age sculpted the rounded shapes the mountains have today, ornamenting them with the lakes and rivers that give them an exceptionally picturesque quality.

The Wicklow Way is richly varied, with the more dramatic and scenic stretches at the northern end, through what seems to be very remote territory, although the Way is never more than a couple of kilometres from a public road. Due to being Ireland's first way-marked trail and its proximity to Dublin, the route is probably the most popular of Ireland's Ways, but this has led to considerable erosion problems in places, in addition to difficulties with rights of way. Consequently there have been nearly a dozen alterations in sections of the route in recent years, and there will be more to come.

How to get there
Marlay Park, where the Wicklow Way starts, is in the southern suburbs of

Dublin, about 13 km (8 miles) from the city centre, and is well served by buses.

Maps and guides

The route is covered by the Ordnance Survey 1:127,000 (0.5 inch to 1 mile) map nos 16 and 19, and the Discovery Series map nos 50, 56 and 62 (1:50,000). The 1:63,000 (1 inch to 1 mile) Wicklow district map covers the route to south of Glenmalure. The route is described in *The Complete Wicklow Way* by J. B. Malone, the late founder of the Wicklow Way, and in *East West Mapping's Wicklow Way Map Guide*.

Enquiries

Wicklow County Council, County Buildings, Wicklow; telephone 0404 67324

Footbridge at Laragh

STAGE 1: MARLAY TO KNOCKREE

DISTANCE: 21 KM (13 MILES). AGGREGATE CLIMB: 600 M (1,968 FEET). WALKING
TIME: 7 HOURS.

*The route of this stage brings you, in a surprisingly short time, up out of
Dublin's suburbs into the foothills of the Dublin Mountains. The
magnificent views back over the city and the bay are soon left behind as the
Way takes you across two mountain ridges to reach Knockree, a wooded
hill straddling Glencree Valley. The youth hostel is nearby; if you want a
higher standard of accommodation and meals you will need to walk a
further 4 km (2.5 miles) to Enniskerry, where you will find a range of
hotels, guesthouses and restaurants. Terrain on this stage consists mainly
of good forestry roads, with 5.5 km (3.5 miles) on tarmac and the rest on
mountain tracks. There is no regular bus serving Knockree.*

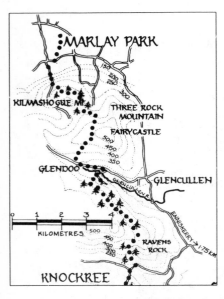

The Wicklow Way starts from
Marlay Park in the south Dublin
suburb of Rathfarnham, one of a
number of demesnes in the Dublin
area that the Parks Department has
acquired and developed in recent
years, providing exceptional
outdoor amenities for the citizens
of the city and county. The
demesne was first laid out and
landscaped in the late eighteenth
century by a Dublin Huguenot
merchant and banker named La
Touche, who had more than three
hundred varieties of trees and
shrubs planted and the Little
Dargle River harnessed into a series
of lakes and cascades. Some of the
trees planted then can still be seen,
in addition to the many planted by the Parks Department, which has also
developed a nine-hole golf course, tennis courts, playing-fields, and a great
adventure playground.

The Way leaves the park and follows the public road up towards
Kilmashogue Mountain, whose rounded bulk is visible from the start.
Nearby is St Columba's College, a boarding-school once considered the Eton
of Ireland. Fast-flowing mountain streams and their tributaries are
abundant in these foothills, and led to the establishment of many pre-Steam
Age industries such as paper-making, cloth-making, and cotton and silk
processing.

The Way soon leaves the public road and passes through Kilmashogue Wood, from where the first good view of the city and its southern suburbs can be seen. Near the entrance to the wood the remains of two prehistoric tombs discovered here in 1950 can be found. One was built by the Neolithic peoples who farmed the fertile Dublin plain four thousand years ago, and the other, sheltering decorated pottery filled with cremated bones, was constructed by Bronze Age farmers one-and-a-half millenniums later. The Bronze Age people appear to have vandalised the older tomb for material to build their own!

The Way swings round the north and east sides of Kilmashogue and leaves the trees to exit onto open moorland and follow an ancient stone wall, thickly clothed in cushions of fraughan, heather and gorse, out across heather-covered mountain. Red grouse are common here, and if you don't get a glimpse of the bird whirring away seeking cover, you may hear its hag-like cackling call.

Behind as you rise, the city of Dublin and Dublin Bay are laid out below, and the eye can wander up along the east coast from the promontory of Howth to Skerries, with Lambay Island standing offshore; and in clear weather the humped Mourne Mountains line the horizon beyond. Kilmashogue and other foothills of the Dublin range—Mount Pelier and Killinarden Hill—stretch westwards now, and as more altitude is gained the ridge of Tibradden Mountain can be seen to the right. Beyond, the flowing outline of Glendoo Mountain, its surface scarred by generations of peat-cutting, leads the eye deep into the Dublin and Wicklow range, signposted by the television mast on the summit of Kippure.

Before the Way drops into the valley of Glendoo, the conical quartzite peak of the Sugar Loaf comes into view to the south-east. A short distance uphill to the left and out of sight is a Bronze Age cairn called the Fairy Castle. Glendoo is said to be named after a tenth-century local chieftain called Niall Ghleann Dubh (Niall of the Black Glen) who was killed in a battle with the Danes of Dublin and is said to have been buried under another cairn on nearby Tibradden Mountain.

Meeting the public road in the valley, the Way follows it for a while before dropping to cross the Glencullen River and ascend through the old-world hamlet of Boranaraltry. Forestry is entered again as the route climbs the flanks of Glencullen Mountain to cross the county border into Wicklow near a promontory called Ravens' Rock.

Over the trees looking south the summits of Maulin (570 m—1,870 feet) and Djouce Mountain (727 m—2,385 feet) fill the horizon now before the Wicklow Way drops through Curtlestown Wood to meet the public road in the valley of Glencree. At this point the village of Enniskerry is about 4 km (2.5 miles) to the left. The Way continues round the western flanks of Knockree, a rounded hill rising from the valley floor. This area was a royal park in the thirteenth century, stocked with red deer from the royal forest at Chester. A thick oakwood clothed the valley and mountainsides at that time, and a palisaded embankment was constructed to contain the deer for the hunting pleasure of the Anglo-Norman kings.

This stage ends where you meet the public road along the south side of the hill. The youth hostel at Knockree is 500 m (0.3 mile) to the left.

Stag

STAGE 2: KNOCKREE TO ROUNDWOOD

DISTANCE: 22 KM (13.5 MILES). AGGREGATE CLIMB: 550 M (1,800 FEET). WALKING TIME: 7 HOURS.

This stage of the route is a magnificent one, climbing the side of the Powerscourt deer park and crossing the dramatic open moorland of Djouce Mountain, bringing the Way to an incomparable viewpoint over Luggala Lake before dropping to Roundwood. This stage includes nearly 11.5 km (7 miles) of forestry roads and the first lengthy stretch, 4.75 km (3 miles), over exposed and open mountainside.

There are a number of guesthouses in the Roundwood area, and a hotel that boasts a good restaurant. Bar food is also available. Roundwood is not on a Bus Éireann route but is served by a private firm, St Kevin's Bus Service.

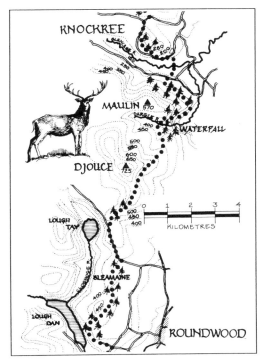

The Way enters the forest west of Knockree Hostel, where a rich mixture of deciduous and coniferous trees abound, and descends to reach the Glencree River. The fast-flowing waters are followed as the river meanders eastwards, and after nearly 1 km (0.5 mile) a timber footbridge is crossed to the south bank.

The route goes uphill to reach the public road and after a few minutes turns into Crone Wood, most of this end of which has been harvested. The bare mica schist of O'Toole's Rock above gleams wet from the film of water that seems permanently to pour down it. The route winds up through the harvested forest, passing on the way the old demesne wall of the Powerscourt estate, which once extended to 105 sq. km (41 sq. miles) of woods, glens, mountainside and farmland in this area. The history of the estate reads like a miniature history of Ireland. In ancient times it belonged to the tribes of the territory of Cuala, then it came into the Norman de la Poer family through one of Strongbow's followers. It was taken back by the local O'Toole clan in 1535, and retaken by the English later and given by King Henry VIII to the Talbots. The Wicklow clan Kavanagh took it back for the Irish in 1556, but lost it to Sir Richard Wingfield, who later became Viscount Powerscourt and in whose family it remained until 1961.

Shortly after a dramatic view of the conical Great Sugar Loaf is seen through a gap in the trees, the route suddenly and spectacularly moves out of the forest onto a clifftop promontory overlooking Powerscourt deer park. After the previous thirty minutes enclosed in thick dark-green coniferous woodland, this really is a pleasant surprise; to the west the River Dargle flows roaring over a precipice and drops 150 m (492 feet) almost sheer to the flat valley floor below, where it quietly and picturesquely meanders away past the ruins of an old church and a banqueting hall to join the Irish Sea at Bray.

The far side of the valley is clothed in modern forestry, while the slopes below the Wicklow Way are covered with the oaks, holly and birch that are probably the descendants of the great wildwood that covered all this area up to the fifteenth century. To the south-west the dome of Djouce Mountain, referred to in Wright's *Guide to Wicklow* (1822) as 'this stupendous mass of matter', dominates the scene, while the Great Sugar Loaf, looking a lot higher than its 504 m (1,654 feet), points to the sky.

The Way follows the pathway as it circles the steep sides of the glen towards the waterfall, before reaching which it turns into the dark of the close-planted trees. Heading uphill, it comes after a few minutes suddenly out of the wood into the wide open mountainscape of Glensoulan, with Djouce and rounded War Hill on its south side and Tonduff beyond Maulin on its north, another delightful surprise 'arrival'. There is a magnificent solitude about this great mountain amphitheatre, particularly in winter snow, when even the silence can be sensed.

The Way now drops to cross the Dargle River before rising and, leaving the trees behind, heading south out across the eastern flanks of Djouce Mountain. At the path's nearest point to the summit of Djouce, a well-beaten track leads off to the right up to it, now 0.5 km (0.25 mile) away and well worth the visit. From the summit, where a couple of ragged crags of mica schist burst through the peat, there are breathtaking views all round.

Continuing along the Way, the path winds upwards through the heather to White Hill, which at 633 m (2,077 feet) is the highest the Way will get until it reaches Mullacor, just south of Glendalough. From White Hill (probably named from the outcrops of gleaming quartz that speckle its slopes) the views of the mountains to the south and west are almost as good as those from Djouce. One of the most recognisable peaks towards the south-west is Turlough Hill, which has a power station reservoir on its summit, seen as a perfectly flat plateau from which a little tower rises. To its right a little further south is another smaller-looking plateau-topped summit; this is Lugnaquillia, Wicklow's highest peak at 926 m (3,038 feet).

The Way now descends and follows a broad flat ridge, often very boggy, going south-westwards. As the southern end of the ridge is reached, the third truly dramatic surprise vista of this section suddenly presents itself. In a short distance the ground falls away, exposing a deep fertile valley, at each end of which is a lake, joined by the meandering Cloghoge River. Lough Dan at the southern end is only barely visible, but the oval Luggala Lake lies almost in plain view directly below, under the towering crags of Luggala; and, as the Victorians would say, 'The prospect is exceedingly fine!'

The route now descends steeply towards the valley, passing an upstanding erratic boulder, beside which is an appropriately sited granite memorial to J. B. Malone, who planned and laid out the Wicklow Way. The public road is reached and followed downhill until the Way turns right onto a broad forestry road. It is useful to note that this part of the route has been revised since the printing of the original 1981 edition of the Wicklow Way Ordnance Survey map, which shows the route continuing on the public road to south of Lough Dan.

The forestry road is followed as it winds southwards, with views first to the south-east of the Vartry Reservoir, which serves Dublin city, and then to the south-west towards the pointed summit of Scarr Mountain, with Tonelagee, Wicklow's third-highest mountain, in the background. After a while enclosed by trees, an opening gives a great view of dark Lough Dan below, shortly before the Way leaves the forest to reach the public road, passing Forest Way Lodge which provides bed-and-breakfast accommodation. Turning right, at the next crossroads the Wicklow Way continues straight, but the suggested end of this stage, Roundwood village, is about 1.5 km (1 mile) to the left.

Roundwood boasts of being the highest village in Ireland, and the Ordnance Survey maps note that the top of its main street is 238 m (781 feet) above sea level. In the old days there was a fair held here eight times a year, where cattle and frieze (a kind of coarse woven cloth) were sold. Wright's 1822 guide tells us that Roundwood 'affords tolerable accommodation to a party of walkers but the premises are not sufficiently extensive for parties attended by servants and travelling equipages'.

Red Grouse

STAGE 3: ROUNDWOOD TO LARAGH

DISTANCE: 19 KM (11.75 MILES). AGGREGATE CLIMB: 550 M (1,800 FEET). WALKING
TIME: 6.25 HOURS.

*This stage follows for a short while an ancient pilgrims' road to
Glendalough, and then escapes out onto erratic-strewn Paddock Hill before
dropping to the village of Laragh. The stage includes 14.5 km (9 miles) on
tarred roads and the rest on forest tracks and open hillside.*

*Laragh has a number of bed-and-breakfast houses, a couple of shops, a
pub and a restaurant, and is served by St Kevin's Bus Service. There are two
hostels and a hotel in nearby Glendalough.*

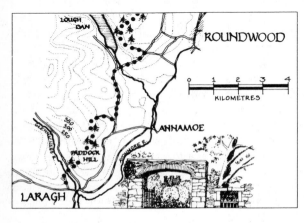

Rejoining the
Wicklow Way at the
crossroads, turn
south and downhill
through a remain-
ing fragment of
oakwood to Old-
bridge. The oaks
here are not the
great trees of the
demesnes but
smaller, wilder
mountainy trees,
covered with lichen
and mosses, their canopy sheltering a carpet of fraughans, through which
herds of deer often browse.

The Avonmore River is crossed by a concrete bridge built in 1934, one of
the many that have spanned this stream over the centuries. The first,
probably wooden, was erected to allow pilgrims, monks and journeymen
travelling between the busy monasteries of Tallaght, Clondalkin and
Glendalough to cross the river in safety. This is an ancient road, and you will
be excused if you sense that you are not alone as you pass here: you walk
with the shades of many a monk and pack-horse man!

Oldbridge Cross is reached a little further on, where a turn right will
bring you after 3 km (1.75 miles) down to the shores of Lough Dan. The
Wicklow Way carries on straight, past the back gates of Glendalough House,
one-time home of Robert Barton. A progressive landlord, Barton resigned
his commission in the British Army in 1916 in the wake of the Rising to join
the IRA, and became Sinn Féin MP for West Wicklow in 1918. One of the
signatories of the Anglo-Irish Treaty in 1921, he was sickened by the ensuing
political upheaval and civil war and, after a period as an abstentionist
member of the Free State Dáil, he turned his back on politics in 1927 and

returned to farm his lands here until his death in 1975.

The Way now ascends the road beside the Glendalough House demesne wall, dropping briefly to cross a stream before rising again and turning right off the road onto a gravelly boreen heading west. Leaving the public road, a field called the Wart Stone Field is passed on the left, where there can be found a granite slab with a basin hollowed out in it. These stones are called balláns or 'bullauns' and are frequently found near old monastic buildings and Early Christian sites. Historians are unsure of the use they were put to, but one explanation that seems reasonable is that they were small querns for the grinding of grain for altar bread.

The end of this boreen is called the Brusher Gate, and it is said to be one of the places where food and supplies were left for the rebel Michael Dwyer and his band, who ran rings round the English authorities for some years after the rebellion of 1798.

The Way now rises onto the flat top of Paddock Hill, while the great fingers of Brockagh, Camaderry and Derrybawn Mountains come into view to the south-east, enclosing the deep valleys of the Wicklow Gap and Glendalough. The village of Laragh, the destination of this stage, can be seen 1.5 km (1 mile) away.

The Way drops through forest to reach the public road. This is the Military Road, constructed by the English authorities after the 1798 Rebellion to link a number of barracks dotted through Co. Wicklow in a final attempt to rid the mountains of rebels. Since Norman times the wilderness of Wicklow had hidden and protected the Irish from the military might of the Crown, giving them a safe haven from which to stage frequent raids on the 'civilised' Pale. Attempts to follow the rebels into the mountains usually ended in disaster for the English, for the Irish were very successful early practitioners of guerrilla warfare. The Military Road, with its garrisoned barracks, put an end to that state of affairs.

Turning left, follow the road for about three hundred metres before the Way turns right into the trees onto an old Mass path and crosses the Glenmacnass River by a picturesque wooden bridge. The Mass path leads within a few minutes to the village of Laragh. A barracks was built here in 1801 where the Military Road crosses the Glenmacnass River, and within fifty years a thriving village had grown up around it, with a watermill, a church and a pub. Its proximity to Glendalough, one of the biggest tourist attractions on the east coast, guarantees that it continues to thrive.

Glendalough, where St Kevin founded a monastic settlement in the sixth century, is about 1.5 km (1 mile) to the west. The dramatically enclosed valley has the remains of numerous religious buildings erected between then and the twelfth century scattered around its two picturesque lakes: a history park in the most magnificent of settings.

STAGE 4: LARAGH TO GLENMALURE

DISTANCE: 16 KM (10 MILES). AGGREGATE CLIMB: 500 M (1,640 FEET). WALKING
TIME: 5.5 HOURS.

*During this stage the Wicklow Way passes through its most remote
mountainous terrain as it rises above Glendalough to Mullacor, at 657 m
(2,155 feet) the highest point of the Way, and drops into the deep glacial
valley of Glenmalure to reach Drumgoff Cross. Over 14 km (8.75 miles) of
this stage is on forestry roads and mountain tracks, with the balance on
tarred roads. Although it is not taxing in good weather, inexperienced
walkers would be well advised not to attempt this stage in bad or doubtful
conditions.*

*Accommodation in Glenmalure is limited to bed-and-breakfast in the
old Glenmalure Inn, or the youth hostel, a tiny, picturesque house
dramatically sited at the remote end of the valley nearly 6 km (3.75 miles)
from Drumgoff Cross. The nearest bus connection to Glenmalure is at the
village of Rathdrum, more than 8 km (5 miles) to the east, where the table
no. 133 bus serving Dublin, Wicklow and Arklow can be accessed.*

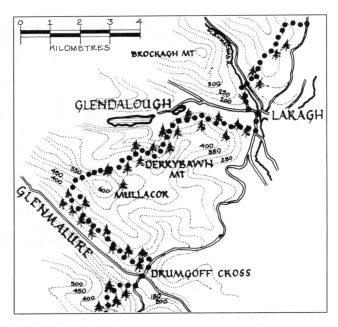

The Wicklow Way leaves Laragh heading towards Rathdrum, and after a few
minutes turns right following signs for a Craft Centre and Hostel, and
crosses a humped-back bridge over the Glendassan River.

The route passes through the Craft Centre, winds around into the wood,
and after about ten minutes passes a sign for the ruins of St Saviour's Priory,

a couple of minutes away to the right, and worth a visit. Founded for the Augustinians about 1162, it is a Romanesque building with much richly carved stonework, including some finely incised nineteenth-century graffiti. The Way descends to the Glendassan River and soon a round tower appears ahead, below the bulbous eastern spur of Camaderry Mountain. Footbridges cross the river to connect with Glendalough's Visitors' Centre, the tower, and the many historic monastic buildings that surround it. The monastic 'city' of Glendalough grew up around a religious settlement founded in the sixth century, and became a popular place of Christian pilgrimage. It was plundered and burned many times, by the inhabitants of Dublin as well as the Vikings, but its stone buildings have survived remarkably well. The most dramatic of the buildings is the 31 m (103 foot) round tower, described by an early visitor as 'well calculated to inspire the imagination with religious dread and horror'.

The path now bears around towards a dramatic steep-sided glacial valley as the smaller of the two Glendalough lakes, Loch na Peiste (Lake of the Beast) is passed on the right. After passing a Tourist Information Centre, the Upper Lake appears ahead; the Way turns left to climb past Poll an Easa waterfall, which over the centuries has scooped deep pools out of the mica schist bedrock as it thunders down into the valley. The Way goes left when a forestry road is met, and keeps left to cross the river again and climb through forestry up the western flanks of Derrybawn Mountain.

Soon Brockagh Mountain comes into view again to the north, with the village of Laragh nestling at its southern foot. In the background the ragged outline of Scarr Mountain can be easily identified.

There is a strong feeling of remoteness here as the Way begins to ascend through harvested forest towards Mullacor, taking steep short-cuts between hairpinning forestry roads. As height is gained, the views become more magnificent. Camaderry fills the foreground; the absolutely flat-topped mountain to the north-west is Turlough Hill, with its power station reservoir on top, first seen from White Hill north of Luggala Lake. Another unmistakable shape is that of the Great Sugar Loaf on the horizon to the north.

The route eventually leaves the trees behind and crosses a heather-covered saddle north-west of Mullacor. If the weather is good it is worth taking the short climb to the top, one of the few summits in these mountains not marked with a cairn of some sort. You know you are there, however, as soon as you can see the horizon through all points of the compass. And what a view it is! On all sides, rounded worn granite and schist mountains are laid out, 'ag bagairt a gceann ar dhroim a chéile'. Just south of west, an undistinguished-looking plateau blocks the view beyond; this is Lugnaquillia, Wicklow's highest mountain.

The Wicklow Way descends into Ballinafunshoge Wood to meet a forestry road, and turn left to descend gradually into the valley of Glenmalure. If you are heading for Glenmalure youth hostel for the night, aim for the north-west corner of the forest as you cross the saddle, then descend very steeply keeping the forest on your left to reach the public road after less than 1.5 km (1 mile). The hostel is less than 3.25 km (2 miles) down the road to your right.

Glenmalure was for centuries an ultimate refuge for Irishmen in rebellion or on the run from the Crown, since the chieftain Fiach Mac Hugh O'Byrne confirmed its sanctuary status in 1580 by defeating here a powerful English Army sent by Queen Elizabeth to put an end to his rule. Eight hundred militia were said to have been killed in the battle, which ended with the young Walter Raleigh and the poet Edmund Spenser among others fleeing in disarray over Table Mountain to the west.

The Wicklow Way meanders down the northern side of Glenmalure to reach the Military Road; turn right, and after a short distance Drumgoff Crossroads is met. The old Glenmalure Inn is 50 m (164 feet) to the left, and Glenmalure youth hostel is a little over 5.5 km (3.5 miles) up the road to the right.

The Glenmalure Inn has been looking after travellers who venture this deep into Wicklow for about two hundred years. Anne Plumptre, however, who passed here in 1815, was not impressed when kept waiting for two hours for a chicken lunch! But things apparently improved: the place is praised in Wright's *Guide to Wicklow* (1822) as 'a most comfortable inn, kept by an English settler'.

Drumgoff Barracks

STAGE 5: GLENMALURE TO BALLYGOBBAN HILL

(Overnighting at Aghavannagh or Aughrim)

DISTANCE: (A) TO BALLYGOBBAN FOREST ENTRANCE, 12 KM (7.5 MILES); (B) TO AUGHRIM, 20 KM (12.5 MILES); (C) TO AGHAVANNAGH, 14.5 KM (9 MILES). AGGREGATE CLIMB: 425 M (1,400 FEET). WALKING TIME: (A) 4.25 HOURS; (B) 6.25 HOURS; (C) 4.75 HOURS.

During this stage the surroundings of the Wicklow Way change character from high, dramatic mountains to lower tree-clad hills rising from a carpet of fertile farmland. Most of the route to Ballygobban Forest entrance is over forestry roads, with the spurs to Aghavannagh and Aughrim on tarred roads.

Accommodation is very limited in this area: the choice is between the youth hostel at Aghavannagh—a converted early nineteenth-century barracks—and bed-and-breakfast at Aughrim. Neither Aughrim nor Aghavannagh are served by bus.

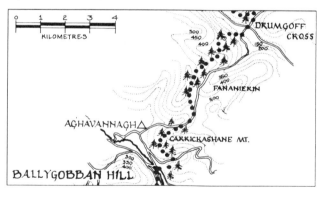

Leaving the crossroads and heading south, the steep-sided valley of Glenmalure opens up towards the west. It is a typical example of a U-shaped glacial valley, carved out of the granite by a great thousand-metre ice sheet that millenniums ago moved slowly but inexorably south-eastwards. As the Ice Age began to come to an end, a river flowed under the glacier, depositing vast quantities of ground rock in the form of the gravel that now makes up the valley floor. A quarry, opened to retrieve this valuable gravel, is threatening what is left of Drumgoff Barracks, built here on the Military Road about 1800.

After a couple of minutes the Way turns off the tarmac onto a forestry road that zigzags up the south side of the valley, recently shorn of the coniferous wood that clothed it for the last forty years. Thirty-five minutes

263

after leaving the public road the Way crosses a forestry bridge over the Cloghernagh stream, and soon after, leaves the road to head up a ride line through a harvested area. Cloghernagh East rises to the right, while the long ridge of Fananierin forms the horizon to the left, Croghan Moira at its southern end.

Soon a forestry road is reached again, and the Way continues up the treed northern slopes of Slievemaan before dropping towards the south-east to reach the public road. The road is followed southwards until, minutes after entering a dense coniferous wood, the Way turns left onto a forestry road. This road brings the Way up the north-western flanks of Carrickashane Mountain, with great views to the right of the valley of the Ow River and across many hectares of coniferous forestry to Lugnaquillia and its foothills. The Ow rises below the cliffs to the north of the summit of Lugnaquillia and flows, via Aughrim and the Avoca River, into the Irish Sea at Arklow.

The route winds round the western flanks of the hill and drops again; ahead now are two hills, the far one, Shielstown Hill, forested to the summit, and the nearer one, Ballygobban Hill, a patchwork of trees and harvested areas. In the distance to the right of Ballygobban Hill an unusual profile can be seen: this is Eagle Hill in Co. Carlow, and near it, if the weather is clear, the village of Hacketstown is visible.

The Way descends now towards the south-east, and Croghan Moira comes into view again before the route meets and follows a public road briefly before descending into the Ow Valley to reach Ironbridge, a picturesque narrow bridge over the Ow River. If you are taking a break at Aghavannagh, do not cross the bridge but keep on straight and westwards to reach the youth hostel after nearly 2.5 km (1.5 miles). The road ascends from the bridge a short distance up the northern slopes of Ballygobban Hill and reaches a junction, the end of this stage. To the left now, about 8 km (5 miles) away, is the village of Aughrim.

Monument at Garryhoe

STAGE 6: BALLYGOBBAN HILL TO TINAHELY

DISTANCE: 22 KM (13.5 MILES). AGGREGATE CLIMB: 275 M (900 FEET). WALKING TIME: 6.25 HOURS.

This stage begins with some long stretches on enclosed forestry roads with little outlook, but makes up for it in the last few kilometres, when it promenades along a grand green road round Coolafunshoge Mountain.

There are a number of guesthouses in the Tinahely area; Murphy's in the village square provides accommodation, some rooms with bathrooms en suite, and generous country meals at any time of the day. Tinahely is served by the table no. 132 Dublin–Carnew bus and the table no. 391 Dublin–Wexford bus (limited service).

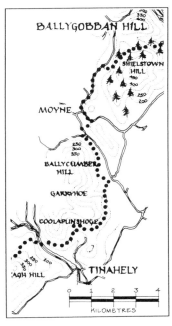

Turning left at the junction above Ironbridge, the Way passes through a section of Ballygobban Forest and, after a short stretch on the public road again, re-enters forestry after the tiny Ballyteigue Bridge. The Way now steadily climbs the northern flanks of Shielstown Hill; soon the summit of Lugnaquillia can be seen rising beyond the precipitous cliffs of the South Prison, above a band of coniferous woodland. Behind, the conical summit of Croghan Moira can be seen over the treed east shoulder of Ballinagappoge Mountain.

As the route levels off there is a series of welcome clearances to the right, allowing fine views of the lowlands of west Wicklow and east Carlow, the border of which is now about 6 km (3.75 miles) away. The south-west bastion of the main Wicklow Mountains, Keadeen, can be seen towards the north-west.

Local people still talk of a disaster that occurred on the far side of Shielstown Hill in the nineteenth century. After a heavy snowfall, young people having a snowball fight started an avalanche that thundered down the hillside and swept away a cottage and its occupants.

The route now zigzags downhill to the public road and follows it towards the south-west. A little more than 2 km (1.2 miles) further on a turn to the right is passed which leads to the hamlet of Moyne. The place is well worth visiting for its old-world atmosphere; apart from the telephone kiosk on the corner it is almost untouched by the years. A very early national school building with the date 1822 inscribed over its door is still in good condition, as are the other houses and cottages, probably of earlier date, and the fine little church.

Continuing along the road, the Way soon turns right and descends a grassy boreen to reach a place called Sandy Ford, where a narrow bridge takes the road over a river. Rounding the east side of Ballycumber Hill, thick forestry rises above on the right, and after a while Croghan Kinsella comes into view on the horizon ahead.

The route passes the old Ballycumber school before descending very abruptly into the valley; and as the road bears round left to cross a bridge the Way leaves it, going right to ford the stream. An overgrown grassy boreen, decorated with bluebells and a few spotted orchids when I passed, takes the route steeply uphill and out onto the open, bracken-covered hillside.

Looking back now, see the conical peak of Croghan Moira on the skyline, and beyond the western end of the Ballycumber Valley the steep flanks of Lugnaquillia rise. Dappled Croghan Kinsella with its ragged peak is now the dominant feature on the eastern horizon. This is Wicklow's gold-rush mountain, the scene of frantic prospecting for a brief period in 1799 after a large nugget of gold was found in one of its many streams. A more recent mining operation at the northern end of the mountain, this time for copper, also had a short life, and closed in 1970, when world prices dropped.

The Way continues southwards along the eastern slopes of Garryhoe Hill, passing an eroded ring-fort. Called Raheen, it consists of a substantial earthen platform built into the hillside, with a circular earthen bank of 15 m (50 feet) diameter. Probably once the main farmstead this side of the hill, it could date from as far back as Early Christian times, and would originally have contained timber-framed thatched dwellings surrounded by a thick, impenetrable whitethorn hedge.

Soon a new landscape comes into view to the south, backed by the rolling blue forms of the Blackstairs Mountains and Mount Leinster with its television mast. As the eastern slopes of Muskeagh Hill appear ahead, a stone cross mounted on the wall and surrounded by iron railings is passed, erected in memory of a doctor who died in an accident here many years ago, before the Way loops around through a small wood to meet Coolafunshoge Lane. This was probably once a droving road, but is now narrowed by gorse and bracken and carpeted with grass kept tight by grazing rabbits. It provides an excellent promenade around the hillside, with great views out across the lush Wicklow landscape to the east and south and down to the grey-roofed cluster of buildings that is Tinahely.

Dropping down the southern side of Coolafunshoge Hill, the Way winds down to cross the Derry River by a rickety wooden bridge. The main Tinahely–Hacketstown road is met on the far side. To the left now, just over

1.5 km (1 mile) off the Wicklow Way, is Tinahely and the end of this stage. Tinahely is a Late Georgian village nestling in the valley of the Derry River. It was devastated in the 1798 Rebellion and almost completely rebuilt by the second Earl Fitzwilliam, who had succeeded to vast estates in Co. Wicklow in 1782 and was for a few months Lord Lieutenant of Ireland. A previous Lord Lieutenant, Thomas Wentworth, Earl of Strafford, was also a previous owner of these rich lands, and close to the town are the remains of his vast unfinished mansion, now buried for safety and called by the local people 'Black Tom's Cellars'.

Raheen

STAGE 7: TINAHELY TO SHILLELAGH

DISTANCE: 16.5 KM (10.25 MILES). AGGREGATE CLIMB: 225 M (738 FEET). WALKING TIME: 4.75 HOURS.

Except for a short stretch on an overgrown boreen, all of this stage is on tarred side-roads. The hills of Co. Wicklow are becoming fewer and lower as the Way goes further south, and habitations and settlements are becoming more frequent, so there are opportunities to enjoy typical south Wicklow villages such as Mullinacuff and Shillelagh.

Shillelagh has a hotel and some guesthouse accommodation. The village is served by the table no. 391 Dublin–Wexford bus (limited service), which also connects with Tinahely.

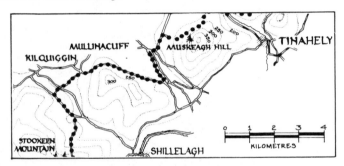

After crossing the wooden bridge over the Derry River, the Way reaches the Tinahely–Hacketstown road and heads briefly eastwards towards Tinahely before turning right up a narrow side-road. After nearly 0.75 km (0.5 mile) the route turns left onto an overgrown boreen that wanders with a few short interruptions up the north-west flanks of Muskeagh Hill. The antiquity of the boreen is evidenced by the substantial stone walls that at times bound it.

The route rises and falls as it meanders along the hillside, with wide views opening up to the north-west to Seskin with its twin summits nearby, and Eagle hill, with the 'bite' out of it, rising from the plain south of Hacketstown.

Soon after dropping into a group of trees and passing a barn on the right, the boreen meets a slab of coniferous forestry covering half the hillside, and becomes a forestry track that descends to the public road. To the south now is the rolling ridge of Cronelea Hill, with a distinct cairn on its western summit.

The Way turns left and follows the road southwards to reach the little village of Mullinacuff. More of a hamlet than a village, Mullinacuff consists of a couple of stone-built cottages, a post office, and a gem of a Neo-Gothic pinnacled church with latticed windows.

Turning left and passing the post office (which differs little from the other cottages) and telephone kiosk, the Way follows the road southwards and then westwards round the flanks of Cronelea. Soon the road descends, with the church and graveyard at Kilquiggin in view ahead; not long afterwards the modern church is passed. In the second field east of the graveyard can be found a large stone with a socket in it that used to house a high cross, probably destroyed by Cromwellian soldiers in the seventeenth century, all that remains here now of a much older religious establishment.

The route now comes to the main Shillelagh road; about 4.75 km (3 miles) to the right can be found Rathgall, a stone-walled circular hill-fort enclosing an area of 7.2 ha (18 acres). It and a smaller example at Baltinglass are the only forts of their kind in the east of Ireland; excavations at Rathgall —which means the Fort of the Foreigner—revealed traces of occupation and metal-working dating back to about 700 B.C.

Crossing the main road, the Way follows a side-road towards the south-east; look out for a cottage on the right with a plaque on its gable commemorating a famous local Boley tug-of-war team of 1933.

About 3.25 km (2 miles) from Kilquiggan the road starts to go steeply downhill to rejoin the Shillelagh road, but before reaching the junction with the main road, the Wicklow Way turns south. To reach Shillelagh and the end of this stage, carry on down to the main road and turn right; Shillelagh is just over 2 km (1.25 miles) away.

Great oakwoods once blanketed this whole region, the oaks from which were well known all over Ireland and Britain from early times for their strength and resistance to rot. The Norman King William Rufus requested oaks from here for the construction of Westminster Hall, London, in the eleventh century, and in subsequent centuries many went towards the construction of the ships of the English navy. Shillelagh alone was reported in 1608 to have enough wood for the king's ships for twenty years. The woods here eventually suffered the same fate as all the other native woodland in Ireland, being gradually eroded for building, construction of ships, production of charcoal for iron-smelting, and of course being cleared to destroy cover for the rebel Irish.

The village of Shillelagh is distributed around what may have been a bleaching-green in the old days, through which the Derry River, crossed previously by a wooden bridge west of Tinahely, flows. The stone-built estate-houses, the church on the hill and the clock tower with its almost eastern flavour are rather fine and worth noting.

STAGE 8: SHILLELAGH TO CLONEGALL

DISTANCE: 19 KM (12 MILES). AGGREGATE CLIMB: 275 M (900 FEET). WALKING TIME: 5.5 HOURS.

This final stage winds round the last hills of south Wicklow to reach the village of Clonegall, a few kilometres into Co. Carlow. About 6.5 km (4 miles) is on forestry roads and the rest on tarred public roads, with the last 4.75 km (3 miles) on a main road into Clonegall. As the southern borders of Co. Wicklow are approached there are glimpses of the next range of mountains to the south, the Blackstairs.

Accommodation is scarce in the Clonegall area but the Osbourne family of Park Lodge Farm will be happy to pick you up and drop you to a convenient bus the following morning if you make arrangements in advance.

Clonegall has no regular bus service; the nearest town served by bus is Bunclody, 6.5 km (4 miles) to the south, where the table no. 5 Waterford–Dublin bus may be accessed.

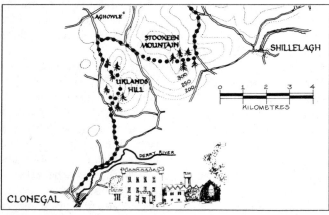

Returning westwards out of Shillelagh to rejoin the Wicklow Way, take the first left turn after turning left off the main road. The Way now climbs one of the steepest road stretches of the whole route; for about 0.75 km (0.5 miles) the road aims for the sky like a launch ramp, coming close to a gradient of 1 in 7 near the top.

Soon the road descends again, and the Way turns right onto a forestry road. A great view of the countryside to the south, screened up to now by the forested hill, can be seen. The prominent hill in the near distance is the 325 m (1,066 foot) Gibbet Hill in Co. Wexford, the border of which is now less than 6.5 km (4 miles) away.

The Way meanders through the forestry until the curtain of trees clears to display the Blackstairs Mountains, with the main peak, Mount Leinster, easily identified by the television mast on the summit. Shortly afterwards, the route leaves the forestry to follow a green road crossing the open hillside.

This route is the remains of an old droving road that was used to herd sheep to the market at Shillelagh. The hillside here, with its great expanse of south-facing pasture, has a considerable population of sheep in late spring. The ewes and new-born lambs are constantly stalked by hooded crows and ravens, which regulate the hatching of their young to coincide with lambing.

The drovers' road descends the hillside, with good views to the south and west. The hills of Moylisha and Urlands rise from the valley to the left, and the fertile farmlands of Co. Carlow can be seen stretching off to the west to the valley of the Barrow River and the hills beyond. Meeting a public road, the Way continues downhill for 5 km (3 miles), when it turns to the left onto a side-road.

At this point, if you have the energy, it is worth making a detour totalling 4.75 km (3 miles) to see the early twelfth-century Damhliag Achadh Abhall (Aghowle Church) with its 3.4 m (11 foot) high cross, site of a monastery founded by the celebrated St Finnian of Clonard. Standing high on a mound of very ancient and probably pagan origin, the roofless ruin with its trabeate doorway and tiny Romanesque windows was in use up to the early eighteenth century. It is said that St Finnian lived here in the valley until he moved to Clonard, near Kinnegad in Co. Westmeath, and established there a major monastic settlement.

Continuing on the Way and following the road as it winds round the northern slopes of Moylisha Hill, one can just make out the grey stone gables of Aghowle Church in the midst of the many-shaded patchwork of fields down in the valley. The sheep pastures on the side of Moylisha Hill are billiard-table smooth in springtime, in beautiful, delicate shades of new-growth green. The Way follows the road as it winds round to the western side of the hill and then heads south.

Beyond Moylisha Hill is forested Urlands Hill, and after a row of cypresses on the left of the road the Way turns left onto a forestry road. As the road rises, the Blackstairs come into view again to the south-west. Soon the route winds steadily up round the northern side of Urlands Hill, with views out to the left of Stookeen Mountain and, in the distance to its left, the steel slopes of Keadeen Mountain, western outlier of the Wicklow range.

The route now turns south, and before long the attractive stone-built Urlands House can be seen below. This is an early nineteenth-century farmhouse, with extensive outbuildings, one of which has a belfry for calling the labourers of another age in from the fields for their midday meal. Clumps of wild strawberries are common in the violet-sprinkled grass along the road margins here in early summer, when the trees below resound with the squawking of pheasants and the rasp of blue jays.

As the route drops downhill through a mossy-floored woodland, where wood anemones and bluebells are profuse in early summer, Urlands House is passed before the public road is reached. The tarmac is now followed down into the valley of the Derry River, where the route enters the county of Carlow. A few hundred metres to the east, also following the river, is the Co. Wexford boundary. Soon after the twin church towers of Clonegall come into sight to the right ahead, the village and the end of the Wicklow Way are reached.

Clonegal is an exceptionally fine village, full of old buildings of great character, sited on the Derry River. A plaque mounted on a bridge at the south end of the village commemorates the men of Clonegall who died in the Rebellion of 1798. On the Wexford side of the bridge is the much smaller hamlet with the romantic-sounding name of the Watch House.

There are two pubs in Clonegall, which are used to walkers and cyclists arriving with prodigious appetites and thirsts. One of them, Osbourne's, is a real old-world place with a pot-bellied stove and a counter made from coffin wood, dating back to the days when selling drink and groceries and undertaking were all carried on from the same shop.

Behind the main street and open to the public on Sundays is Huntington Castle, built in 1625 by the Esmonde family. Originally with four corner turrets and its own chapel attached, the building has been extended quaintly and many times over the centuries. The formal gardens are not extensive but are beautifully laid out with specimen trees and sculptures.

The Blackstairs from Urlands Hill

APPENDIX

BED-AND-BREAKFAST ACCOMMODATION ALONG THE ROUTES

On the basis of my own personal experience, or as specifically indicated by the proprietors, walkers are welcomed at the following bed-and-breakfast establishments. Where the accommodation is more than 3 km (2 miles) from the route, the distance is noted after the telephone number; in most of these cases proprietors offer to pick up and drop off walkers if arranged in advance. Evening meals and/or packed lunches, if required, should generally be requested in advance.

The list given here is by no means comprehensive, and the fact that some of the routes have few entries is more to do with the general scarcity of registered accommodation and less an indication that walkers are not welcome!

KEY TO ABBREVIATIONS:
Evening Meal   EM
Packed Lunches   PL
Pick-Up and Drop-Off   PU

THE ARAN WAYS

Inis Mór
Mrs Enda Gill, 'Ard Einne Guesthouse', Inis Mór, Aran Islands,
Co. Galway.
Tel. (099) 61126, Fax (099) 61388. EM PL
Treasa Joyce, Kilmurvey House, Kilronan, Inis Mór, Aran Islands,
Co. Galway.
Tel. (099) 61218, Fax (099) 61397. EM PL
Veronica McDonagh, Bayview House, Kilronan, Inis Mór, Aran Islands,
Co. Galway.
Tel. (099) 61260, Fax (099) 61260. EM PL
Mrs B. Conneely, Beach View House, Oat Quarter, Inis Mór, Aran Islands,
Co. Galway.
Tel. (099) 61141. EM PL

Inis Meáin
Angela Faherty, 'Craigmor', Inis Meáin, Aran Islands, Co. Galway.
Tel. (099) 73012. EM PL

Inis Oírr
Brid Poll, 'Radharc An Chlair', Castle Village, Inis Oírr, Aran Islands,
Co. Galway.
Tel. (099) 75019, Fax (099) 75019. EM PL

Appendix

BALLYHOURA WAY

Ursula Farrell, Cooleen House, Ardane, Glen of Aherlow, Co. Tipperary.
Tel. (062) 54392. 8 km PU EM PL

THE BARROW WAY

Lorum Old Rectory, Kilgraney, Bagenalstown, Co. Carlow.
Tel. (0503) 75282. 6.4 km PU EM PL
Pat and Noeleen Dunne, Green Lane House, Dublin Road, Carlow.
Tel. (0503) 42670. PL
Bryan Leech/Martin Marley, Kilgraney Country House, Bagenalstown,
Co. Carlow.
Tel. (0503) 75283, Fax (0503) 75283. 6.4 km PU EM PL
The McCabe Family, Brandon View House, Ballyogan,
Graiguenamanagh, Co. Kilkenny.
Tel. (0503) 24191, Fax (0503) 24451. EM PL

THE BEARA WAY

Bridget O'Shea, 'Magannagan Farm', Derryconnery, Glengarriff, Beara,
Co. Cork.
Tel. (027) 63361. EM PL
Jane O'Sullivan, Beachmount, Trafrask East, Adrigole, Beara, Co. Cork.
Tel. (027) 60075. EM PL
Mrs Margaret O'Sullivan, 'Ocean View House', Faha East, Adrigole,
Beara, Co. Cork.
Tel. (027) 60069. EM PL
Craigies Hotel, Cametringane House, Castletownbere, Co. Cork.
Tel. (027) 70379. EM PL
Mr & Mrs B. Harrington, Castletown House, Bank Place,
Castletownbere, Co. Cork.
Tel. (027) 70252. EM (Restaurant on premises) PL
Noralene McGurn, 'Sea Breeze', Derrymihan, Castletownbere, Co. Cork.
Tel. (027) 70508. PL
Mrs Mary O'Sullivan, Sea View Guest House, Allihies, Beara, Co. Cork.
Tel. (027) 73004. PL
Ms Mary P. O'Shea, The Lake House, Tuosist, Kenmare, Co. Kerry.
Tel. (064) 84205. 4 km PU EM PL
Geraldine Topham, Greenane Heights, Greenane, Ring of Kerry Road,
Kenmare, Co. Kerry.
Tel. (064) 41760. PL
Patrick Foley, Henry Street, Kenmare, Co. Kerry.
Tel. (064) 41361, Fax (064) 4l799. EM PL

Dympna O'Sullivan, 'Fern Height', Castletownberehaven Road, Lohart, Kenmare, Co. Kerry.
Tel (064) 84248. EM PL
Mike and Anne Murphy, Laburnum House, Sneem Road, Kenmare, Co. Kerry.
Tel. (064) 41034. EM PL

THE BURREN WAY

Christine and James Keane, Merrijig Farmhouse, Lismactigue, Ballyvaghan, Co. Clare.
Tel. (065) 77020. EM PL
Maeve Fitzgerald, 'Churchfield', Doolin, Co. Clare.
Tel. (065) 74209, Fax (065) 74622. PL
Marian and Martin McDonagh, Glasha Meadows, Doolin, Co. Clare.
Tel. (065) 74443. EM PL
The Petty Family, Sunville, off the Doolin Road, Lisdoonvarna, Co. Clare.
Tel. (065) 74065, Fax (065) 74065. 5 km PU EM PL
Mrs Christine O'Neill, O'Neill's Town Home, Lisdoonvarna, Co. Clare.
Tel. (065) 74208, Fax (065) 74435. 4.8 km PU EM PL

THE DINGLE WAY

Tim and Mary Walshe, 'The Willows', 5 Clonmore Terrace, Tralee, Co. Kerry.
Tel. (066) 23779. PL
Eileen Phelan, 'Kilkerry', 12 Castle Demesne, Tralee, Co. Kerry.
Tel. (066) 22823. PL
Mrs Colette Quinn, 'Villa de Lourdes', Brewery Road, Oakview, Tralee, Co. Kerry.
Tel. (066) 26278. PL
Damien MacAodha, 'Driseog', Ath A' Chaisle Thuaidh, Caislean Ghriaire, Tralee, Co. Kerry.
Tel. (066) 39451. EM PL
Margaret Ryle, 'Crana Li', Curragraigue, Blennerville, Tralee, Co. Kerry.
Tel. (066) 24467. EM PL
Dora McCarthy, Caherbla House, Inch, Anascaul, Co. Kerry.
Tel. (066) 58120. EM PL
Mrs Eileen Kennedy, 'Waterside', Inch, Anascaul, Co. Kerry.
Tel. (066) 58129. 3 km PU EM PL
Bill and Vivian O'Shea, Alpine House, Mail Road, Dingle, Co. Kerry.
Tel. (066) 51250, Fax (066) 51966. PL

Appendix

Mrs Padraig O'Neill, Kruger's Guesthouse, Ballyferriter, Dingle,
Co. Kerry.
Tel. (066) 56127. EM PL

Michael and Josephine Walsh, 'The Townhouse', Main Street, Dingle,
Co. Kerry.
Tel. (066) 51147 or (066) 52044. EM PL

Michael and Becky O'Connor, The Old Stone House, Cliddaun, Dingle,
Co. Kerry.
Tel. (066) 59882. PL

Mrs. A. Neligan, Duinin House, Conor Pass Road, Dingle, Co. Kerry.
Tel. (066) 51335. PL

Mary Carroll, 'Ceann Tra Heights', Ventry, Dingle, Co. Kerry.
Tel. (066) 59866. EM PL

Noirin Garvey-Rohan, Baile Moir, Ventry, Dingle, Co. Kerry.
Tel. (066) 59820. PL

Jacqueline O'Shea, 'Torann na dTonn', Ventry, Dingle, Co. Kerry.
Tel. (066) 59952. PL (Restaurant nearby)

Garvey's Farmhouse, Kilvicadownig, Ventry, Tralee, Co. Kerry.
Tel. (066) 59914. EM PL

Brid and Ted Moriarty, Moriarty's Farmhouse, Rahanane West, Ventry,
Tralee, Co. Kerry.
Tel. (066) 59037. EM PL

Alice Hannafin, An Speice, Ballyferriter West, Co. Kerry.
Tel. (066) 56254. PL

Martin Hurley, 'An Dooneen', Kilcooley, Ballydavid, Dingle, Co. Kerry.
Tel. (066) 55112. EM PL

Mrs M. D. Nic Gearailt, Bothar Bui, Baile na Ngall, Ballydavid, Co. Kerry.
Tel. (066) 55142. EM PL

Sile and Vincent O'Gormain, Caife Na Mara, Glaise Bheag, Ballydavid,
Dingle, Co. Kerry.
Tel. (066) 55162. EM PL

Kitty Brosnan, 'Abhainn Mhor', Cloghane, Co. Kerry.
Tel. (066) 38211. EM PL

Veronica Maunsell, Loch An Duin, Ballyhoneen, Conor Pass Road,
Cloghane, Co. Kerry.
Tel. (066) 38163. 4 km PU EM PL

Fiona Knott, 'Tigh Nuadha', Knocknagower, Cloghane, Tralee, Co. Kerry.
Tel. (066) 38221. EM PL

Mrs Paula Walsh, 'Sea-Mount House', Cappatigue, Conor Pass Road,
Castlegregory, Co. Kerry.
Tel. (066) 39229. EM PL

Agnes Reidy, 'Goulane House', Stradbally, Castlegregory, Co. Kerry.
Tel. (066) 39174. EM PL

THE GRAND CANAL WAY

Catherine Byrne, Auburn Lodge, Colonel Perry Street, Edenderry,
Co. Offaly.
Tel. (0405) 31319. EM PL
Mrs Mary Margaret Smyth, Beechlawn Farmhouse, Clyduff, Daingean,
Co. Offaly.
Tel. (0506) 53099. EM PL
Larry and Agnes Mealiffe, Ballinamona Farmhouse, Durrow, Tullamore,
Co. Offaly.
Tel. (0506) 51162. 4.8 km PU EM PL
Bernadette Keyes, 'Canal View', Killina, Rahan, Co. Offaly.
Tel. (0506) 55868. EM PL
Carmel Mitchell, Daragh, Ballyclare, Ferbane, Co. Offaly.
Tel. (0902) 54196. PL PU
Mrs Kitty Galvin, Cnoc Ban, Gallen, Ferbane, Co. Offaly.
Tel. (0902) 54175. EM PL
Claire Moore, Highfield Farmhouse, Rosfaraghan, Ferbane, Co. Offaly.
Tel. (0902) 54387. 4.8 km PU EM PL
Nancy O'Hara, The Old Rectory Country Guesthouse, Deerpark,
Shannon Harbour, Co. Offaly.
Tel. (0902) 57293. EM PL
Bridie Mahon, Ashling, Cuba Avenue, Banagher, Co. Offaly.
Tel. (0509) 51228. 4.8 km PU EM PL
Vera Carty, Ashbrook Farmhouse, Shannonbridge, Co. Offaly.
Tel. (0905) 74166. 16 km PU EM PL

THE KERRY WAY

Mrs Margaret Lanigan, Caragh House, Scrahan Court, Ross Road,
Killarney, Co. Kerry.
Tel. (064) 34637. PL
Noreen Sheahan, Countess House, Countess Road, Killarney, Co. Kerry.
Tel. (064) 34247. PL
Lily Cronin, 'Crab Tree Cottage', Mangerton Road, Muckross, Killarney,
Co. Kerry.
Tel. (064) 33119. EM PL
Mary J. O'Neill, Saratoga House, Muckross Road, Killarney, Co. Kerry.
Tel. (064) 31970, Fax (064) 35689. PL
P. & C. Courtney, Courtmurph House, Muckross Road, Killarney,
Co. Kerry.
Tel. (064) 34586. PL

Appendix

Mrs Noreen O'Sullivan, Lios Na Manach Farm House, off Mill Road, Muckross, Killarney, Co. Kerry.
Tel. (064) 31283. 3 km PU EM PL

Kathleen O'Brien, Avalon House, Gortroe, Killarney, Co. Kerry.
Tel. (064) 33156. EM PL

Breen Village House, The Village, Glenbeigh, Co. Kerry.
Tel. (066) 68128, Fax (066) 68486. EM PL

Owen and Mary Landers, Fransal House, Foilmore, Cahirsiveen, Co. Kerry.
Tel. (066) 72997. EM PL

Joan O'Shea, Pine Crest, Cappaghs, Cahirsiveen, Co. Kerry.
Tel. (066) 72482. EM PL

Christina O'Neill, 'Iveragh Heights', Carhan Road, Cahersiveen, Co. Kerry.
Tel. (066) 72545. EM PL

Eileen O'Donoghue, Harbour View Farmhouse, Farraniaragh, Caherdaniel, Killarney, Co. Kerry.
Tel. (066) 75292. 3.2 km PU EM PL

Angela O'Sullivan, O'Sullivan's Country Home, Caherdaniel, Co. Kerry.
Tel. (066) 75124. EM PL

Klondyke House, Waterville, Co. Kerry.
Tel. (066) 74666. 7.25 km PU PL

Eileen McGillicuddy, Birchgrove House, Castlecove, Co. Kerry.
Tel. (066) 75106. EM PL

Margaret and Noel Harrington, Bank House, North Square, Sneem, Co. Kerry.
Tel. (064) 45226. PL

Mary Teahan, Derry East Farmhouse, Sneem, Co. Kerry.
Tel. (064) 45193. EM PL

Mrs Maura Hussey, Avonlea House, Sneem, Co. Kerry.
Tel. (064) 45221. PL

Evelyn Breen, Coral Beach Farmhouse, Kelly's Cross, Sneem, Co. Kerry.
Tel. (064) 45339. EM PL

Mrs Helen Foley, 'Hillside Haven', Tahilla, Sneem, Co. Kerry.
Tel. (064) 82065. EM PL

James and Deirdre Waterhouse, Tahilla Cove Country House, Tahilla, Nr. Sneem, Co. Kerry.
Tel. (064) 45204, Fax (064) 45104. EM PL

Mike and Ann Murphy, Laburnum House, Sneem Road, Kenmare, Co. Kerry.
Tel. (064) 41034. EM PL

Geraldine Topham, Greenane Heights, Greenane, Ring of Kerry Road, Kenmare, Co. Kerry.
Tel. (064) 41760. PL

Dympna O'Sullivan, 'Fern Height', Castletownberehaven Road, Lohart,
Kenmare, Co. Kerry.
Tel. (064) 84248. EM PL
Patrick Foley, Henry Street, Kenmare, Co. Kerry.
Tel. (064) 41361, Fax (064) 41799. EM PL
Mrs M. O'Mahony, 'The Arches', Blackwater Bridge, Kenmare,
Co. Kerry.
Tel. (064) 82030. EM PL

THE LEITRIM WAY

Mrs Mairin Heron, 'Fraoch Ban', Corlough, Drumshanbo, Co. Leitrim.
Tel. (078) 41260. EM PL
Mary McPartland, 'Laurel Lodge', Clooneen, Manorhamilton, Co. Leitrim.
Tel. (072) 55018. PL

THE MUNSTER WAY

Hanora's Cottage, Nire Valley, Ballymacarbry, Co. Waterford.
Tel. (052) 36134, Fax (052) 36540. 6.4 km PU EM PL
Martin and Una Moore, Bennetts Church Old School House,
Ballymacarbry, Nire Valley, Co. Waterford.
Tel. (052) 36217 or (088) 571203. 5.6 km PU EM PL
Mrs and Mr Gleeson, 'Nagles', Kilsheelan, Clonmel, Co. Tipperary.
Tel. (052) 33496. EM PL
Jo and Lynda Buckley, Lady's Abbey, Ardfinnan, Clonmel, Co. Tipperary.
Tel. (052) 66209. 7 km PU EM PL
Laurence and Catherine McCarra, Rivervalley Guesthouse, Newcastle,
Clonmel, Co. Tipperary.
Tel. (052) 36105 or (088) 502738. EM PL
Liam and Helen McGrath, Newcastle Village, Clonmel, Co. Tipperary.
Tel. (052) 36359. Self-catering

THE SLIEVE BLOOM WAY

Mrs Mary Lalor, High Pine Farm, Annaghmore, Kinnity, Co. Offaly.
Tel. (0509) 37029. 4.8 km PU EM PL
Frank and Rosemarie Kennan, Roundwood House, Mountrath,
Co. Laois.
Tel. (0502) 32120. 8 km PU EM PL
Bertha Shaw, Clonkelly House, Rosenallis, Portlaoise, Co. Laois.
Tel. (0502) 28517. EM PL

Appendix

THE SLIEVE FELIM WAY

Mary Walsh-Seaver, 'Rinnaknock', Glenstal, Murroe, Co. Limerick.
  Tel. (061) 386189. EM PL
Marie Tuohy, 'Newport House', John's Avenue, Cork Road, Newport,
  Co. Tipperary.
  Tel. (061) 378623. 7 km PU EM PL

THE WESTERN WAY

Little Killary Adventure Centre, Salruck, Renvyle, Co. Galway.
  Tel. (095) 43411, Fax (095) 43591. 8 km PU EM PL
Mrs and Mr O'Neill, Glen Valley House, Glencraff, Leenaun, Connemara,
  Co. Galway.
  Tel. (095) 42269. EM PL
Mary King, Killary House, Leenaun, Co. Galway.
  Tel. (095) 42254. PL (Restaurants nearby)
Jamie Young, Killary Lodge, Derrynasliggaun, Leenane, Co. Galway.
  Tel. (095) 42276, Fax (095) 42314. EM PL
Marian O'Malley, Moher House, Liscarney, Westport, Co. Mayo.
  Tel. (098) 21360. EM PL
Noreen Reddington, 'Brooklodge', Deerpark East, Newport Road,
  Westport, Co. Mayo.
  Tel. (098) 26654. PL
Paul and Elizabeth Bree, 'Sunnyside', Deerpark East, Westport,
  Co. Mayo.
  Tel. (098) 26883. PL
Mrs Evelyn Cosgrove, Hillcrest House, Main Street, Bangor Erris,
  County Mayo.
  Tel. (097) 83494. 12.8 km PU EM PL

THE WICKLOW WAY

May Clarke, Cregg House, Glencree Road, Enniskerry, Co. Wicklow.
  Tel. (01) 2863557. PL
Mary Byrne, 'Doire Coille House', Cunnentragh, near Glendalough,
  Co. Wicklow.
  Tel. (0404) 45131. PL
Lawless's Hotel, Aughrim, Co. Wicklow.
  Tel. (0402) 36146. 8 km PU EM PL
Bridie Osborne, Park Lodge, Clonegall, Shillelagh, Co. Wicklow.
  Tel. (055) 29140. EM PL